Islam In The Heartland Of America

Imam Omar Hazim
Edited by Khalil Green

Copyright © 2024 **Imam Omar Hazim**

All rights reserved. No part of this publication may be reproduced, distributed, or transmitted in any form or by any means, including photocopying, recording, or other electronic or mechanical methods, without the prior written permission of the publisher, except in the case of brief quotations embodied in critical reviews and certain other noncommercial uses permitted by copyright law. For permission requests, write to the publisher, addressed "Attention: Book Rights and Permission," at the address below.

Published in the United States of America

ISBN 979-8-89395-709-9 (SC)
ISBN 979-8-89395-708-2 (Ebook)

Library of Congress Control Number: 2024921817

Imam Omar Hazim
222 West 6th Street
Suite 400, San Pedro, CA, 90731
www.stellarliterary.com

Order Information and Rights Permission:

Quantity sales. Special discounts might be available on quantity purchases by corporations, associations, and others. For details, contact the publisher at the address above.

For Book Rights Adaptation and other Rights Permission. Call us at toll-free 1-888-945-8513 or send us an email at admin@stellarliterary.com.

بِسْمِ ٱللَّهِ ٱلرَّحْمَٰنِ ٱلرَّحِيمِ

With God's Name, the Merciful Benefactor, the Merciful Redeemer

In memory of Aliya Sumayyah Hazim,
my beloved wife of forty-seven years.
She returned to Allah on September 13, 2010.
May Allah grant her an everlasting place in paradise. Ameen.

بِسْمِ ٱللَّهِ ٱلرَّحْمَٰنِ ٱلرَّحِيمِ

CONTENTS

FOREWORD 9
ACKNOWLEDGMENTS 13
INTRODUCTION 15
AN INTRODUCTION TO THE QUR'AN 19
JIHAD: A SPIRITUAL STRUGGLE 23

CHAPTER 1 HISTORY AND BIOGRAPHY 25
History of the Islamic Center of Topeka 26
Biography of Imam Omar Jaleel Hazim 28

CHAPTER 2 FAITH AND PRACTICE 30
Al-Fatiha 31
The Opening Chapter of the Holy Qur'an 31
Three Faiths, One God 35
Faith and Human Behavior 38
Patience and Conviction 41
Developing Spirituality: Sunday Class at Islamic Center of Topeka 44
Religion Should Cultivate Moral Qualities 48
The Muslim Women Eloquently Recite the Holy Qur'an in Topeka 50
Holy Qur'an Daily Reading 53

CHAPTER 3 MOTHERHOOD IN ISLAM 55
Honoring Parents 57
Honoring Motherhood 59
The Butcher's Mother 63
Love and Respect for Motherhood 65

CHAPTER 4 KHUTBAH 68
Imam Warith Deen Mohammed Day in Topeka, Kansas 69
The Swallows Come Back to Capistrano 72

The Family Tree 76
Keys to a Good Life: Salat (Prayer) 79
ALLAH's Plan 83
The Diversity that Allah Has Created 85
The Spiritual and Moral Health of the Heart 92
Darkness of Arrogance and the Light of Reasoning 99
Created in Pairs 102
Restraining Anger 108
Seizing Opportunities 112
Transforming Spiritual Growth into What Is Practical 116
The Cycle of Good Deeds 119
The Future is Bright for Muslims in America 122
The Caretaker of Allah's Earth 124
The Parable of a Good Word 127
The Verse of Light 130
Social Connections 133
Chapter (Surah) Najm—The Star—
    Chapter 53 in the Holy Qur'an 137
Stages of Human Development: Part I 140
Stages of Human Development: Part II 142
Dressing for the Battlefield 145
Excerpts from the Sermon "Identity" 149
Appreciating the Holy Qur'an 151
Striving for Excellence 153
Cultivating The Garden Of Our Souls 156
Moving Forward in the Direction of Rasullulah
    (Prophet Muhammad [PBUH]) 160
Protecting Our Life through Protecting Our Behavior 164
Moral Accountability in Islam 166
The Jinn 169
Trials and Temptations 172
Purity in Islam (Taharah) 176
The Uniqueness of Our Dependency upon Each Other 178
Patriotism 180

CHAPTER 5 ARTICLES IN THE TOPEKA CAPITAL-JOURNAL 184

Islamic Leader Calls on Local Muslims to Devote
Their Lives to Their Faith. 185
"Building Bridges of Understanding." 187
A Spiritual Journey: Millions of Muslims Take Part in Hajj 191

Muslims Cringe at Terror Tie 194

Chapter 6 RAMADAN AND EID 197
Injustice Anywhere is a Threat to Justice Everywhere 198
Eid-ul-Adha 2005 202
Eid Prayer 2001 206
Historical Events of Ramadan 211

CHAPTER 7 PUBLIC RELATIONS 215
Ramadan: Time of Repentance, Gratitude 218
Condemnation of the Bombing in London 220
Observation: Islamic Center Is Open to Public 222
Id Ul-Fitr: Feast after the Fast 224
Out of Topeka Masjid Comes One Calling to Faith:
    The Contribution of Islam to a Pluralistic Society 226
Prayer for the United States of America 229
Unity through Diversity 231
Kansas Governor Kathleen Sebelius and
    Mayor James McClinton of Topeka Attend Eid Celebration 233
Invocation to the Kansas House of Representatives (April 28, 2004) . 236
Prayer for the Second-District Convention:
    Barack Obama for President 237
Invocation for City Council 239
Appreciating Allah's (SWT) Generosity 241
Zulfiqar Malik and Phil Anderson
    Receive the Community Service Award 243
Islamic Faith Blamed Unfairly 245
The Islamic Center of Topeka: An Important Contributor
    to Interfaith of Topeka and Religious Understanding
    in the Community 247
Baha'i Community 251
Welcome to the Muslim Journal 256
About the Editor of the *Muslim Journal* 259

CONCLUSION 261
A Walk through Jerusalem: A Trifaith Historical Event 262
Concluding Prayer 267
Glossary 269
References 275

FOREWORD

بِسْمِ ٱللّٰهِ ٱلرَّحْمٰنِ ٱلرَّحِيمِ

With Allah's name, the merciful Benefactor, the merciful redeemer.

**From william Franklin to Imam omar hazim:
An Islamic American story**

William Franklin grew up in Kansas City in the 1940s and 1950s, a time when American apartheid was vigorously enforced, when blacks were excluded from white neighborhoods, schools, theaters, and churches. William remembered his parents warning him not to wander off to the south side of the Twenty-seventh Street where the whites lived and where black boys could be arrested for trespassing. "Resentment, not really," said William, "for that was the way of life back then."

Back then, however, William did see the ugliness of racism. At fifteen, he was arrested when a white policeman was killed in the city and the authorities rounded up more than a hundred black men. William, like most other detainees, was innocent and let go. At seventeen, while using a restroom in Mississippi, William remembered how a man banged at the restroom door and yelled, "This restroom is for whites only. It's not for -_____!" The blank was filled with the N-word, a word of racial contempt and hatred, commonly used to address a black man, any black man. Back then, almost every black person had to endure such microaggressions nearly every day.

Growing up in Kansas City, William would go to "their" church with his brothers and sisters. In the church, everyone was black except for the image of Jesus. William noted the blond hair, blue eyes, and the white skin of Jesus, a figure he worshipped as Allah (SWT) but a figure that looked, said William, awfully similar to slave owners who forcibly abducted men, women, and children from Africa, shipped them to America, depriving the imported cargo of its cultural and religious heritage, denuding the newcomers of their language, personal histories, even African names. A gradual realization that American Christianity has been tainted with racism sowed the seeds of William's transformation.

At eighteen, William dropped his last name, Franklin, an English name that he thought represented not him but some past white master. Discarding such last names was common when men joined the Nation of Islam. This black organization was launched by a mysterious foreigner called Fard Muhammad. After espousing that black is divine and leaving the Nation in the hands of Elijah Muhammad, Fard disappeared. The Nation began to believe that he was Allah (SWT). As a ritual of worship, Fard's picture was hung in every member's house, including William's.

The Nation gave William a new way of thinking. William now started to believe, as did most members of the Nation, that blacks were noble and divine, whereas whites were wicked and evil. Fard had turned American racism on its head. For the next thirteen years, William performed various ministerial activities and later met Elijah on a monthly basis as one of his ministers. Black pride liberated William's mind and freed his soul. Lurking behind this uplifting experience, however, was a disturbing irony. Fard, the Nation's Allah (SWT), was not a black man. Fard's white complexion most apparent in the picture that hung in William's house belied the belief that white is evil. The change was therefore inevitable.

In 1975, under the leadership of W. Deen Mohammed, the Nation began to move toward traditional Islam. So did William. He first changed his name to Imam Omar Hazim. A couple of years later, Omar went to Hajj and, for the first time in his life, saw a sea of Muslims of all colors, races, and ethnicities. Black eyes glimpsed divinity in brown and blue eyes. And blue eyes were lowered with as much humility as were brown and black eyes. And at the conclusion of Hajj, all men shaved their heads whether the color of their hair was black or blond. Through this experience of universal brotherhood, Omar could no longer accept that any race is inferior or superior.

On embracing traditional Islam, Omar removed Fard's picture from the wall. Allah (SWT) is not man, nor is He black or white. "There is nothing that resembles Allah (SWT)." This powerful message of the Holy Qur'an transformed Omar's mind and soul, which had been marred twice by racism, first white then black. Discarding all race-based views of Allah (SWT) and religion, Omar now devoted himself to learning more about Islam.

But his learning of Islam was not abstract. Omar has been a professional mason all his life. He first built Nation's temples. Omar now employs his masonry skills to construct mosques. He built a mosque in Kansas City, the Inshirah Masjid, not far from the south side of Twenty-seventh street. He has also built the Islamic Center of Topeka, where he is now the imam.

Imam Omar Hazim's khutbas (sermons) often emphasize the Islamic ethics of patience and tolerance. Prophet Muhammad (PBUH) faced all forms of adversity, false accusations, and threats to his life. But during this ordeal, the imam reminds the audience, the Prophet remained an inexhaustible source of tolerance, patience, and kindness. Imam Hazim's personal life experiences, now spanned over sixty-seven years, have taught him the wisdom of staying in the course with patience while life reveals its mysteries. And as a Muslim, he firmly believes that Allah (SWT) is with those who practice perseverance and patience (Holy Qur'an 2:153).

Unfortunately, says Imam Hazim, Muslim countries fail to practice patience and tolerance. In Pakistan, he points out that the bloody feud between Shias and Sunnis is mind boggling. In Afghanistan, Iraq, Bangladesh, and Sudan, Muslims are killing Muslims. The subjugation of women, including honor killings, has no place under the liberating principles of the Holy Qur'an and the Sunna. These and other stories, even when exaggerated in the Western press, undermine Islam's teachings of compassionate equality, human dignity, and authentic tolerance.

True to his words, Imam Omar Hazim leads the Islamic Center of Topeka with an open and generous heart. Over the years, many Americans have accepted Islam at the mosque. Even newborns, including my own two sons, listen to the imam as he chants the first *adhan* (call to prayer) in their ears. In a spirit of mutual respect, American Jews, Christians, Hindus,

Buddhists, all are invited to attend khutbahs, prayers, and *iftar* dinners during the month of Ramadan. Reciting chapters (surah) of the Holy Qur'an with accruing facility, the chapter (surah) that tells the stories of Ibrahim, Moses, and Jesus, the chapter (surah) that recognizes the dignity of all colors and languages, and the chapter (surah) that forbids compulsion in religion, Imam Omar Hazim leads prayers attended by blacks and whites, men and women, Arabs and non-Arabs, Sunnis and Shias.

Dr. Khan is a professor of law at Washburn University in Topeka, Kansas.

Professor Ali Khan

بِسْمِ ٱللَّهِ ٱلرَّحْمَٰنِ ٱلرَّحِيمِ

ACKNOWLEDGMENTS

With Allah's name, the Merciful Benefactor, the Merciful Redeemer, may the prayers and peace be upon Allah's (God) generous and kind messenger Muhammad (peace be upon him). I wish to greet you all with the greetings of Islam, the greeting of peace, *as-salaam alaikum*.

I thank Allah (SWT) for the thoughts, the inspiration, and the desire I have to share this work with the general public. The intent is to help clarify some of the misunderstandings in the air about the religion of al-Islam. I thank Allah for the leadership I have associated myself with and became a student of in 1975; that is, the leadership of Imam W. Deen Mohammed. May Allah the exalted and most high grant him the highest places in paradise.

I give acknowledgment to my wonderful wife, Aliya, my best friend and best supporter for over forty-seven years at the time of this writing. She has encouraged me, and her help has been tremendous. She has worked with me on the book over the last several years, the typing, communicating, and brainstorming.

I thank Brother Khalil Green, who is a writer and has become the editor of this body of work. He is also an assistant imam at the Islamic Center of Topeka. His work has been essential for this book to be completed and published at this time. A *khutbah* (sermon) of his is featured in this book also. Thanks to the imams who came to Topeka and gave khutbahs featured in this work; they are Imam Muhammad Shabbazz, Imam Rudolph Muhammad, Imam Hanif Khalil, Imam Bilal Muhammad, and Imam Sulaiman Z. Salaam Jr, Zaid Hayyeh, and Imam Samuel Ansari.

Very special thanks to one of the founders of this community whose two sermons (khutbahs) are also in this book, Dr. Ashraf Sufi. I thank Professor Ali Khan, professor of law at Washburn University and a member of our community. He has been very helpful and inspirational to me over the years. His words are used in the preface of this book, and one of his sermons (khutbahs) is in this book. I thank Dr. Syed Akhtar for submitting his article titled "Introduction to the Qur'an" in this work.

With deep love, honor, and respect to my mother, Lee Edna Rollins, who allowed me to use a current picture of her as featured in the section of this book about motherhood.

I end these acknowledgments with a *dua* (short prayer):

O, Allah, our Lord, Creator of the heavens and earth and everything contained therein, let this work be a tool to help open the minds and hearts of the people so that they may see and understand the beauty and wisdom in the religion of al-Islam, and reward all those who participated in this work. We pray for Allah's forgiveness if any mistakes are made in this book.

Ameen.

Imam Omar Jaleel Hazim

INTRODUCTION

The purpose of this book is to inform and educate the general public of how Islam is taught in a mosque in the heartland of America. It includes some Friday khutbah (sermons) by Imam Omar Hazim and several other imams (spiritual leaders). Some of these sermons are excerpts published online. The hope is to clarify some of the misconceptions and distortions about the religion of Islam. In addition to the sermons, there will be articles from other publications, excerpts of sermons, and photos. Included also is information about the diversity among the Muslim population in the heartland of America. This book is very timely as Islam has been reported as being the fastest growing religion in the world.

For anyone who ever thought about or wondered what is taught in the Friday services at a mosque, for them, this book is a must read.

The preface was written by Professor Ali Khan, who is a professor of law at Washburn University. In his preface, he focuses on the major driving force behind the success of the Islamic Center, Imam Omar Hazim. Professor Ali Khan takes us on a journey through the childhood and early years of Imam Omar Hazim as he grew up in a segregated Kansas City. Imam Omar Hazim spent his early years as a member of the Nation of Islam under the leadership of the Honorable Elijah Muhammad until his introduction to and acceptance of traditional Islam, under the leadership of Imam W. Deen Mohammed. Imam Omar Hazim remains the first and continues to be the only imam that the Islamic Center of Topeka has ever had since it was established as a nonprofit organization in 1987.

Helping with the editing of this work is Khalil Green, who has obtained a degree in religious studies and philosophy from Washburn University. He has served as a state chaplain for the State of Kansas, becoming the first full-time-staffed Muslim chaplain for the state in a prison environment.

He continues to serve his community by writing articles online and editing this book.

In the body of this book, there are several sections detailing the accomplishments and relationships that the center has with the public. The Islamic Center of Topeka has appeared in many articles written by Phil Anderson and others of the *Topeka Capital-Journal*. Phil's writings represent a deep respect that the city of Topeka has for the Islamic community at large. During past Islamic gatherings, Mayor Joan Wagnon, Governor John Carlin, Senator Sam Brownback, Congresswoman Nancy Boyda, and Mayor James McClinton have visited the Islamic Center and celebrated special occasions with the local Muslims. Governor Kathleen Sebelius and Mayor James McClinton shared special eid celebrations with our Islamic community and received a copy of the Holy Qur'an. Imam Omar Hazim has the distinction of being the first Muslim imam to give the opening prayer for the Kansas senate and the city council of Topeka.

Also visiting the Islamic Center in 2001 was none other than Imam W. Deen Mohammed (may Allah be pleased with him and accept him into the highest places of paradise). Mayor Joan Wagnon presented him with the key to the city.

This book represents a thought-provoking account and a comprehensive look at Islam as it is experienced and shared in the heartland of America.

We often hear in the media how Islam is a thorn in Western society, how the woes of this century began on the shoulders of the Islamic faith. I think this book holds the key to refreshing the perception of Islam through a portrait or snapshot of Islam in the Midwest, the very heart of America.

The great state of Kansas feeds so many of the people here in America through its wheat and beef. Now America will be fed accurate information about the religion of Islam as it is practiced in the heartland of America.

Imam Omar Hazim, who has stood as the leader of the Topeka community, has earned the respect and the good graces of politicians, fellow imams, rabbis, reverends, and other religious leaders. He has visited Mecca twice, once with Imam Warith Deen Mohammed and a large American delegation in 1977 and again with his wife of over forty-seven years, Aliya, in 1998.

This book is an anthology of articles and events that have taken place in Topeka since the inception of the Islamic Center. This work, however, is not all inclusive for the simple fact that instead of a book, volumes would be necessary to include all the contributions to Topeka that the Islamic Center of Topeka has performed.

The Islamic Center of Topeka has produced the first Islamic advisor to the state, Imam Omar Hazim. It has also produced its first full-time Muslim chaplain in a state-prison setting, Khalil Green.

The membership of the Islamic Center of Topeka comprises Muslims from all over the world. Members of the community are from Tunisia, Arabia, Bangladesh, Pakistan, Senegal, Egypt, and areas of Europe. American Muslim members of the Islamic Center come from African American and Caucasian racial stocks.

One in four people in the world call themselves Muslim and state that their religion is Islam. Islam is the name of the religion and means peace through submitting to Allah. A Muslim is one who submits his or her will to Allah. Thus, through Islam and its practices of prayer, worship, charity, fasting, and pilgrimage does Allah grant peace to the adherent. This peace is a spiritual peace. Thus do the struggles of this world continue.

In this work, two forms for the name of the Divine are used: Allah (SWT) and Allah. Allah is simply the Arabic form for the Divine. In the Middle East, people of all religions and creeds use this name if they speak Arabic. It does not matter if they are Muslim, Jew, or Christian. This is much like the use of the word *God* in American society.

The word *Allah* is often used by Muslims who follow the leadership of Imam W. Deen Mohammed. Imam Mohammed introduced this usage as a way of distinguishing God from any opposite. If you write the word *God* backward, you will have *dog*. However, *Allah* has no opposite.

This work also contains the Arabic equivalent for every verse that is quoted. The Arabic of the Holy Qur'an has had many translators. They don't always use the same words, but for the most part, the various translations have synonymous meanings. However, the true Holy Qur'an is the Arabic as such it is the same in every Holy Qur'an.

At the end of the word for Allah (Allah), *SWT* is placed. It is an expression of praise to Allah. In the same way is PBUH (peace be upon him) placed behind Prophet Muhammad's (PBUH) name.

I think you will find this book enjoyable and educational. May Allah guide you during your reading of this work.

بِسْمِ ٱللَّهِ ٱلرَّحْمَٰنِ ٱلرَّحِيمِ

In the name of God, the Beneficent, the merciful

An Introduction to the Qur'an

Dr. Syed Akhtar

What Is the Qur'an?

The Qur'an is the divine scripture, the word of God, revealed to Muhammad (peace be upon him), the Prophet of God. It was revealed, starting in the year AD 610. The revelations came gradually over twenty-three years. The Archangel Gabriel brought the revelations initially in the city of Mecca and subsequently in the city of Medina.

language of the Qur'an

The language of the Qur'an is Arabic, which is the language of the people of that region. The Qur'an has been translated into one of the most known languages of the world. The divine message is prose but of a poetic nature. The recitation in a rhythmic manner is powerful and moving to the listener, even one who is not familiar with the language.

The Arrangement of the subject matter in the Qur'an

The text is arranged into 114 chapters. Long chapters are in the beginning and smaller chapters are toward the end. The subject matter is not organized chapterwise; instead, the subjects are scattered all over the book. This makes the Qur'an unique, unlike any other book. Muhammad Pickthall, one of the translators of the Qur'an, says, "The very sound of which makes men move to tears and ecstasy." A. J. Arberry wrote, "It is neither prose nor poetry, but a unique fusion of both."

The Qur'an and the previous scriptures

The Qur'an acknowledges the previous scriptures of God revealed to the prophets of the old: the Psalms of David, the Torah revealed to Prophet Moses, and the Bible (the New Testament) revealed to Prophet Jesus.

The Qur'an and other prophets

The Qur'an acknowledges all the prophets, named and unnamed, who were sent to humankind by God Almighty and who are mentioned in the Old Testament and the New Testament. Some of the prophets mentioned in the Qur'an include Adam, Job, Elisha, David, Abraham, Moses, Aaron, Jesus, Amran, Elias, Isaac, Lot, Mary (mother of Jesus), Ishmael, Zachariah, Noah, Solomon, Ezra, Saul, John the Baptist, Jonah, Jacob, and Joseph (peace be upon them all).

The preservation of the Qur'an

The revelations, as they were brought to Muhammad (P) by Archangel Gabriel, were memorized by his disciples. Thus, the original text was preserved in the memory of his followers meticulously, word for word. Today, tens of thousands of believers have memorized the whole Qur'an, word for word. This unique method of preserving the scripture is unparalleled in modern history. Thus, the Qur'an is the only scripture that claims to be the original word of God (in Arabic), unaltered by passage of time or by human interference.

Proofs of the divine origin of the Qur'an

The literary excellence, the eloquence, and the poetic nature of its verses were unmatched by the greatest scholars of the time:

- The wisdom, guidance, and knowledge contained therein are beyond the scope of the most learned human beings.
- Many of the prophecies in the Qur'an have already been fulfilled.
- The scientific statements in the Qur'an about physics, biology, anatomy, human and animal reproduction, astronomy, etc., have borne out to be true after several hundred years. In fact, they proved to be amazingly accurate.

- Despite the revelations spanning over twenty-three years, there is no contradiction or inconsistency in the statements. This is not possible in any book written by a human.

Western scholars' Views on the Qur'an

A work, which calls forth so powerful and seemingly incompatible emotions even in the distant reader—distant as to time and still more so as mental development. A work, which not only conquers the repugnance, which the reader may feel as he begins its perusal, but also changes adverse feeling into astonishment and admiration. Such a work must be a wonderful production of the "human mind" indeed and a problem of the highest interest to every thoughtful observer of the destinies of mankind. (Dr. Steingass in T. P. Hughes's *Dictionary of Islam*, p.526)

The hypothesis advanced by those who see Muhammad (P) as the author of the Qur'an is untenable. How a man, from being "illiterate" (untutored), could become the most important author, in terms of literary merit in the whole of Arabia? How could he then pronounce truths of a scientific nature that no other human being could possibly have developed at that time, and all this without once making the slightest error in his pronouncement on the subject? (Maurice Buccaille in *The Bible, the Qur'an, and Science*, p.125)

God challenged the skeptics and doubters. There were many who disbelieved in the Qur'an as a divine word. They accused the Prophet of making false claims. In response, God revealed following verses:

> And if ye are in doubt concerning that we reveal unto our servant (Muhammad [P]) then produce a Chapter of the like thereof. (Chapter 2, verse 23)

> And before this was the book of Moses, as a guide and a mercy. And this Book confirms (it) in Arabic, to admonish the unjust, and as glad tidings for the righteous. (Chapter 46, verse 12)

The Qur'an confirms that the earlier prophets, including Moses and Jesus, were true messengers of God. The previous scriptures, the Torah and the Bible, in their original forms were the true messages from God.

The true purpose of the Qur'an is to restore and safeguard the message of God in its totality. Why was another scripture needed? The Qur'an is a summation of all the previous scriptures, as they originally existed. It points out inaccuracies that have crept into the older scriptures. It contains the law, the code of ethics, guidance, and in conjunction with the teachings of Prophet Muhammad (P), it has guidance for the believer in every aspect of life. Even the minutest details are addressed for day-to-day conduct of religion, business, social interactions, etc. The Qur'an is a message to all humanity.

The Qur'an addresses not just Muslims. It is a book for followers of Judaism and Christianity, and in fact, it is for all humanity. Some of the verses in the Qur'an directly address the entire humanity.

The verses of the Qur'an that point to the inclusive nature of the message are as follows:

> Say: we believe in God and that which is revealed unto us, and that which was revealed unto Abraham and Ishmael and Isaac and Jacob and the tribes, and that which Moses and Jesus received, and which the prophets received from their Lord. We make no distinction between any of them, and unto Him we have surrendered. (The Qur'an, chapter 2, verse 136)

> Say: O' people of the Book, (Jews and Christians) Come to common terms as between you and us: That we worship none but God; that we associate no partners with Him; that we erect not from among ourselves, lords and patrons other than God. (The Qur'an, chapter 3, verse 64)

بِسْمِ ٱللَّهِ ٱلرَّحْمَٰنِ ٱلرَّحِيمِ

With God's Name, the Merciful Benefactor, the Merciful Redeemer

Jihad: A Spiritual Struggle

Imam Omar Hazim

Special to the *Topeka Capital-Journal*

Jihad is a greatly misunderstood word. It is derived from the Arabic root word *juhd*, which means the exertion of one's power or abilities to please the Creator. The word *jihad* itself means to struggle or to strive, and it applies to any effort of good exerted by anyone, Muslim or non-Muslim. When we are faced with two competing interests, it becomes a jihad to choose the best or right one.

There are many components to jihad. The preaching of God's Word throughout the world to mankind and helping to improve the quality of life to all is jihad. Traveling to a distant land for higher education and knowledge in the name of God is a jihad. Going on a *hajj* or pilgrimage and practicing the other pillars of Islam are components of jihad.

Some Muslims and non-Muslims have generally translated *jihad* as "holy war." This is a great misconception popularized by a lack of knowledge or incorrect information. According to Islamic teachings, it is unholy to instigate or start war. However, some wars are inevitable and justifiable.

The word *jihad* is not synonymous with external war or holy war. The Holy Qur'an was revealed in Arabic. If holy was in it, it would read close to this "harbun muqaddashah." This phrase "holy war" is not found in the Qur'an, nor is it found in the authentic Hadiths (sayings of the Prophet, PBUH).

Many Islamic historians believe the use of the word *jihad* as a holy war came about due to the influence of Western propaganda. This could be a reflection of the Crusades of over one thousand years ago.

Islam, like Christianity, permits fighting in self-defense and on the part of those who have been expelled forcibly from their homes. Islam has strict rules of combat, which include prohibition against harming civilians and against destroying crops, trees, and livestock.

The Qur'an mentions jihad or strive in many places. Two of these verses are:

وَجَٰهِدُوا۟ فِى ٱللَّهِ حَقَّ جِهَادِهِۦ ۚ هُوَ ٱجْتَبَىٰكُمْ وَمَا جَعَلَ عَلَيْكُمْ فِى ٱلدِّينِ مِنْ حَرَجٍ ۚ مِّلَّةَ أَبِيكُمْ إِبْرَٰهِيمَ ۚ هُوَ سَمَّىٰكُمُ ٱلْمُسْلِمِينَ مِن قَبْلُ وَفِى هَٰذَا لِيَكُونَ ٱلرَّسُولُ شَهِيدًا عَلَيْكُمْ وَتَكُونُوا۟ شُهَدَآءَ عَلَى ٱلنَّاسِ ۚ فَأَقِيمُوا۟ ٱلصَّلَوٰةَ وَءَاتُوا۟ ٱلزَّكَوٰةَ وَٱعْتَصِمُوا۟ بِٱللَّهِ هُوَ مَوْلَىٰكُمْ ۖ فَنِعْمَ ٱلْمَوْلَىٰ وَنِعْمَ ٱلنَّصِيرُ (٧٨)

"And strive (jihad) for God with the endeavor which is right. God has chosen you and has not laid on you in the religion any hardship." (Qur'an 22:78)

وَمَن جَٰهَدَ فَإِنَّمَا يُجَٰهِدُ لِنَفْسِهِۦٓ ۚ إِنَّ ٱللَّهَ لَغَنِىٌّ عَنِ ٱلْعَٰلَمِينَ (٦)

"And whosoever strives (jihada) strives for their own souls, for God is free of all needs from His creation." (Qur'an 29:6)

Jihad is striving in the way of righteousness and improving one's self, family, and society. Jihad is for repelling evil, and it is therefore a defensive act and not an offensive act. Jihad does not include striving for individual or national power, dominance, glory, wealth, prestige, or pride. The prophet (PBUH) said, "The strength is not in the one who is able to subdue the other, but the strength is in the one who uses self restraint." He also said, "The greater jihad is the struggling against one's own weaknesses for its betterment," which continues throughout life.

O, Allah, help humanity strive for peace and understanding in this world. Amen.

Chapter 1

History and Biography

History of the Islamic Center of Topeka

Topeka is the capital city of Kansas and has a population of approximately 170,750 people. There are 150 churches of various denominations, one Jewish synagogue, and one Masjid at this time. Topeka is also known for the 1954 Supreme Court landmark decision *Brown v. Board of Education*, which allowed schools to be physically integrated by all races.

In the early 1970s, a few Muslims families lived in Topeka: Fidel Abdelalim and family, Imam Yahya Furqan and family, Atif Abdel Khaliq and family, and a few others. They helped to promote Islam under the leadership of Minister Nathaniel Muhammad, son of Elijah Muhammad. They helped to open up Islamic temples on Huntoon Street and California Avenue. Other Muslims came to Topeka from Kansas City, Missouri, including myself and family, to help in this cause. May Allah reward them for their work and sacrifices.

In the early 1987, four Muslim families and a couple of single brothers got together and met in various places, clubhouses, community centers, and individuals' homes to have Sunday classes for children to learn the Holy Qur'an, adults to read and discuss the Holy Qur'an and offer salat-ul-zuhr together. As the spirit increased in us to share al-Islam with others, we began to look for a permanent place to worship. In 1991, we started to have Jumah in various places around the city. These sincere and devoted few founders of the Islamic Center of Topeka are Brother Dr. Syed Akhtar, Sister Malik Akhtar, Brother Dr. Ashraf Sufi, Dr. Qaiser Sufi, Brother Harris Mustafa, Sister Nilofer Mustafa, Brother Dawar Saeed, Brother Luqman Shabazz, Sister Aliya Hazim, and Brother Omar Hazim. All the above founders have served in some positions, either as teacher, president, secretary, treasurer, or board member. May Allah (SWT) reward them for their sincere efforts.

In 1992, the Islamic Center was incorporated as a nonprofit tax-exempt religious organization. In the same year (1992), an unused, dilapidated one-story structure was located at 1115-17 SE Twenty-seventh Street. The fund-raising was started, and within sixty days, Allah (SWT) blessed us to raise about $60,000, al-hum-du-Lillah. Our imam, who owns a small construction business, undertook the project to renovate this building into a Masjid. The Islamic Center opened for worship about six weeks after its purchase. By Allah's blessings and guidance, we saw a consistent growth in numbers in our Islamic community and in our spirituality. Two years later, in 1994, a few brothers visited our Friday prayer service from another country, stated that they were inspired by the work they observed, and asked what they could do to help. We met with them in the office, and they left a donation of $5,000 cash and said for us to look for some more money soon. Three weeks later, we received a check made out to the Islamic Center of Topeka for $100,000, praise be to Allah (SWT). These brothers were not known in this community before that time and have not been seen in this community since that time. Allah put his goodness in the hearts of men and women. With this money, we bought the house next door to the Masjid for $25,000 and built a parking lot, added a new entranceway, and built a new prayer hall (Masala area). Our imam was given the contract, after receiving competitive bids from three other local builders. His bid was $25,000 lower than the other bids. In 1994, as we continued to grow in numbers, Allah blessed us with the help of some of our founding members to raise more money to buy a triplex across from the Masjid; this rental property helps with the Masjid expenses and is rented out to Muslims in our community. In 1995, our imam was asked to open the state senate meeting with prayer. Our community has grown to have about 150 believers in the city; eighty to one hundred come out to Jumah on Fridays. We have weekly Arabic classes, children's educational classes, and adult Holy Qur'anic classes and discussions. We have representatives on the board of directors of Interfaith of Topeka and the Center for Peace and Justice. We provide service to the Kansas Department of Corrections and the many correctional facilities in the state of Kansas. We offer dawah activities, visiting schools, churches, youth centers, civic clubs, and other places we are invited to explain Islam.

We thank Allah (SWT) for granting us this Masjid. We thank him for the diversity, peace, and unity we have. We ask Allah (SWT) to bless and protect this Masjid and those who enter it for his sake. Ameen.

Imam Omar Hazim

بِسْمِ ٱللَّهِ ٱلرَّحْمَٰنِ ٱلرَّحِيمِ

With Allah's name, the merciful Benefactor, the merciful redeemer

Biography of Imam Omar Jaleel Hazim

Imam Omar Hazim is the imam of the Islamic Center of Topeka. He is the Islamic advisor to the Kansas Department of Corrections and has served in this position since 1990.

Hazim accepted Islam in 1962 under the leadership of the Honorable Elijah Muhammad. He served as a minister under Elijah Muhammad's son, Minister Nathaniel Muhammad. Afterward, he served directly for Elijah Muhammad as a minister. He has also been a student of Imam W. Deen Mohammed since 1975.

Imam Hazim is a builder by trade and has helped to establish many mosques and Islamic Centers in the Kansas City and Topeka area over the past forty-seven years. He is also one of the founders of the Islamic Center of Topeka.

He is a member of the Midland Islamic Council and a member of the Islamic Society of North America.

He was the first Muslim to give the invocation to the Kansas House of Representatives and Senate.

Hazim served on the board of directors for Interfaith of Topeka Inc. for seven years. He has also been associated with Interfaith for more than twenty years.

Hazim wrote an article that appeared in the *Muslim Journal,* which is an international publication, on January 20, 1995, entitled "Contributions of Islam to a Pluralistic Community." Over the years, he has written many articles for the *Topeka Capital-Journal*. His articles focused on Islam and current issues affecting the world.

To increase understanding and awareness, Hazim has addressed issues on death, sickness, suffering, social justice, the status of women in Islam, jihad, human and civil rights, and the Islamic view on life after death at Stormont-Vail Hospital, the Menninger Foundation, St. Francis Hospital, Washburn University, various churches, schools, civic clubs, etc., in Topeka since 1975.

Imam Hazim has been married to Aliya Hazim since 1963; she is his best friend and supporter. They have eight children who all graduated from Topeka West High School and went on to college. Hazim has been a Topeka resident since 1975.

Omar and Aliya were recognized as ambassadors for peace in December 2003 by the Interreligious and International Federation for World Peace.

Chapter 2

Faith and Practice

بِسْمِ ٱللَّهِ ٱلرَّحْمَٰنِ ٱلرَّحِيمِ

وَٱسْتَعِينُوا بِٱلصَّبْرِ وَٱلصَّلَوٰةِ وَإِنَّهَا لَكَبِيرَةٌ إِلَّا عَلَى ٱلْخَٰشِعِينَ

"Seek (Allah's) help with patient perseverance and prayer: It is indeed hard, except to those who bring a lowly spirit." (Chapter [surah] 2:45)

بِسْمِ ٱللَّهِ ٱلرَّحْمَٰنِ ٱلرَّحِيمِ

With Allah's name, the merciful Benefactor, the merciful redeemer

May the prayers and the peace be upon Allah's noble and kind messenger, Muhammad.

Al-Fatiha

Imam Omar Hazim

The Opening Chapter of the Holy Qur'an

بِسْمِ ٱللَّهِ ٱلرَّحْمَٰنِ ٱلرَّحِيمِ (١)
ٱلْحَمْدُ لِلَّهِ رَبِّ ٱلْعَٰلَمِينَ (٢) ٱلرَّحْمَٰنِ ٱلرَّحِيمِ (٣) مَٰلِكِ يَوْمِ ٱلدِّينِ (٤) إِيَّاكَ نَعْبُدُ وَإِيَّاكَ نَسْتَعِينُ (٥) ٱهْدِنَا ٱلصِّرَٰطَ ٱلْمُسْتَقِيمَ (٦) صِرَٰطَ ٱلَّذِينَ أَنْعَمْتَ عَلَيْهِمْ غَيْرِ ٱلْمَغْضُوبِ عَلَيْهِمْ وَلَا ٱلضَّآلِّينَ (٧)

"In the name of Allah, Most Gracious, Most Merciful.
Praise be to Allah, the Cherisher and Sustainer of the worlds;
Most Gracious, Most Merciful;
Master of the Day of Judgment.
Thee do we worship, and Thine aid we seek.
Show us the straightway,

The way of those on whom Thou hast bestowed Thy Grace, those whose (portion) is not wrath, and who go not astray." Al-Fatiha, the opening chapter and seven often-repeated verses of the Holy Qur'an, is the chapter with which prayers are begun. The opening chapter of the Holy Qur'an is also known as the mother of the book (Umm Al-Kitab). It is also called the praised (Al-Hamd) and the prayer (As-Salah), the Prophet said. When Allah's (SWT) servant says "All praise is due to Allah," he is praising the Lord of all existence. It is called as-salah because reciting it is a condition for performing prayers correctly. Change to English first.

According to the well-respected Hadith (stories about the prophet) writer Abu Hurairah, the Prophet called al-Fatiha the greatest chapter (surah) in the Holy Qur'an.

Prophet Muhammad (PBUH) stated that "I will teach you the greatest chapter, [surah] in the Holy Qur'an before you leave the masjid." As they, Prophet Muhammad (PBUH) and some companions, walked to the door, one asked, "What is the chapter that you promised to teach us?" "By Him in whose hand is my soul, Allah has never revealed in the Torah, the Injil, the Zabur, or the Furqan a chapter [surah] like it. It is the seven repeated verses that I was given," replied the Prophet.

It is called Surat Al-Du'a, the chapter of supplication, because the entire chapter is a supplication or a prayer to the great creator of the heavens and earth.

Below are some names given to this chapter:

Mother of the book, basis of the book, the foundation, the treasure, the whole, the healer and the healing, the praise, the thanksgiving, the essence of the book.

With Allah's name, the Merciful Benefactor, the Merciful Redeemer (Bismillah ar rahman nir rahim) is also the beginning supplication of every one of the other 113 chapters of the Holy Qur'an, except for the ninth. A Muslim should commence every important affair with *bismillah*; this is the right attitude of the human mind toward God. It is a prayer for the guidance of every Muslim. The first three verses speak of the four chief divine attributes. During the latter part of the prayer, we express our desire to walk in righteousness without stumbling on either side; we take the middle course.

The name *Allah* is found in the Holy Qur'an about 2,800 times; the attribute *Rabb* (Lord) is found about 960 times in the Holy Qur'an. *Rabb* signifies the fostering of a thing in such a manner as to make it attain one condition after another until it reaches its goal of completion. In the use of the word *Rabb*, we acknowledge that everything created by God bears the imprint of divine creation, and continues to move in the characteristic of developing from lower to higher stages. Rabb (Lord) brings forth maturity and evolution from the earliest state to the highest state. He sees to the necessary provisions for all life in its journey. This word *Rabb* also points to the law of evolution in physical and spiritual worlds.

The creative force of Allah (Allah) is not a blind force but one possessing wisdom and acting with a purpose. The attribute or word *Rahman* signifies that love is so predominant in the divine nature that He, Allah, bestows his favors and shows His mercy even though man has done nothing to deserve them. The granting of the means of subsistence for the development of the physical life and the divine revelation for man's spiritual growth are due to God's divine love.

Ar-Rahman, the Prophet said, is the attribute of the beneficent God whose love and mercy are manifested in the creation of this world, and al-Rahim is the attribute of the merciful God whose love and mercy are manifested in the state that comes after. Rahman can only be applied to Allah. As such, Allah (SWT) is the mercy that goes before the need even arises; the grace which is ever watchful. The point of al-Fatiha is to seek guidance to excellence and the right way. Allah has given us this prayer and constructed it in a way that we implore guidance from Him not in a proud way but in a humble way. This imploring comes from our inner soul. We are saying, "O, Allah, please guide us for we may be wandering in error and may not be able to find our way to the right path without your help and mercy."

Imam W. Deen Mohammed (may Allah accept him in the highest places of paradise) encouraged the imams and others who associated with his leadership to become students of the Holy Qur'an.

We should seek the guidance of the Holy Qur'an like the day seeks to catch up with the night and like the night seeks to overtake the day. Seeking knowledge, wisdom, and understanding is an obligation of our religion al-Islam. The Prophet said, "It is a duty on every man, woman and child to seek knowledge from the cradle to the grave."

May Allah increase us with His guidance and knowledge. Ameen.

بِسْمِ ٱللَّهِ ٱلرَّحْمَٰنِ ٱلرَّحِيمِ

with Allah's name, the merciful Benefactor, the merciful redeemer

Three Faiths, One God

Submitted by Imam Omar Hazim

Islamic Center of Topeka

إِنَّ ٱلَّذِينَ ءَامَنُوا۟ وَٱلَّذِينَ هَادُوا۟ وَٱلنَّصَٰرَىٰ وَٱلصَّٰبِـِٔينَ مَنْ ءَامَنَ بِٱللَّهِ وَٱلْيَوْمِ ٱلْءَاخِرِ وَعَمِلَ صَٰلِحًا فَلَهُمْ أَجْرُهُمْ عِندَ رَبِّهِمْ وَلَا خَوْفٌ عَلَيْهِمْ وَلَا هُمْ يَحْزَنُونَ (٦٢)

"Those who believe in the Holy Qur'an, and those who follow the Jewish scriptures And the Christians and the Sabians, Any who believe in Allah [SWT] and the Last Day, and work righteousness, Shall have their reward With their Lord: on them Shall be no fear, nor shall they grieve." (The Holy Qur'an, 2:62)

Judaism, Christianity, and Islam have many aspects in common and share many beliefs.

All true believers in these great religions believe that the One God has created the entire universe. They believe that besides Jesus, Moses, and Muhammad, peace be upon them, that the Almighty God sent many other prophets to humanity. They believe in the resurrection, heaven and hell, angels, and in good moral values.

Chapter 3:84 of the Holy Qur'an states,

> We believe in Allah, and in what has been revealed to us and what was revealed to Abraham, Isma'il, Isaac, Jacob, and the Tribes, and in (the Books) given to Moses, Jesus, and the prophets, from their Lord: We make no distinction between one and another among them, and to Allah do we bow our will (in Islam).

In Islam, the first and most fundamental teaching of Prophet Muhammad (PBUH) and the Holy Qur'an, is the belief in the oneness of Allah (SWT). This is the bedrock and foundation of Islam. All the religions revealed to the prophets have the same essence, the belief and the oneness of God, the oneness of our universe, and the oneness of humanity.

Anyone who studies religious literature on a wide scale will find that the broad principles of the faith of our father Abraham (PBUH) was to believe in one God, to establish a community life of peace with love, good works, religious tolerance, and respect for diversity.

Our own existence is the proof of the existence of Allah (Allah). Nothing comes into being just by itself; it absolutely must have a maker. Look at the clock; we see it is made of wood, metal, glass, etc. We will see its form is square, round, etc. Its purpose is to tell time. We may not see the designer of the clock, but do we therefore deny the existence of the clockmaker? We see the vast, enormous sky, with its sun, moon, and stars. The sun rises and sets, the moon comes out and disappears from view, day gives way to night and night turns into day, the month and seasons change in absolute order. All these things we see and know even if we cannot see with our physical eye the creator. Can we deny the existence of the One God who created these events? Our eyes see, our ears hear, our hands feel and we walk with our feet, our minds have the power to comprehend, and our hearts feel love, joy, sorrow, compassion, and grief. The true believers in God, be they Christians, Jews, or Muslims, do not deny the fact that the One God who brought humanity into existence is the same God that gave us these wonderful gifts.

Prophet Muhammad (PBUH) said that "love is a condition of faith and also a condition of getting into paradise; never will you enter paradise until you have faith, and never will you have faith until you practice loving one another."

Left to right: Rabbi Debbie Stiel of Temple Beth Shalom, Imam Omar Hazim of the Islamic Center of Topeka, and Reverend Steve Lipscomb of Grace Cathedral.

بِسْمِ ٱللَّهِ ٱلرَّحْمَٰنِ ٱلرَّحِيمِ

With Allah's name, the merciful Benefactor, the merciful redeemer

May the prayers and the peace be upon Allah's noble and kind messenger, Muhammad.

Faith and Human Behavior

Imam Omar Hazim

One of the most serious ills of the modern day is the partial or total loss of faith in Allah (SWT). Much of the modern materialistic world, grown out of scientific and technical advancement, finds no place or need for Allah (SWT) because they think that the universe is ran by a self-regulating system, and that Allah (SWT) has no function in the lives of humanity.

However, Allah (SWT) says in Holy Qur'an 22:74 and 39:67

مَا قَدَرُوا ٱللَّهَ حَقَّ قَدْرِهِ ۗ إِنَّ ٱللَّهَ لَقَوِىٌّ عَزِيزٌ (٧٤)

"No just estimate have they made of Allah (SWT) for Allah (SWT) is He who is powerful and able to carry out His will."

As such, all that has ever been said or written about Allah (SWT) falls short of his true nature.

The Holy Qur'an states in chapter (surah) 33:41-42 that

يَٰٓأَيُّهَا ٱلَّذِينَ ءَامَنُوا ٱذْكُرُوا ٱللَّهَ ذِكْرًا كَثِيرًا (٤١) وَسَبِّحُوهُ بُكْرَةً وَأَصِيلًا (٤٢)

"O you who have faith, celebrate the praises of Allah and do this often, and glorify Him morning and evening".

Al-Iman—faith—has been mentioned in Holy Qur'an over 841 times. In English, al-Iman has no one single word to explain it. Faith, belief, credence, fidelity to one's promises, allegiance of duty to one's self or family or to Allah (SWT); it also means loyalty. This word encompasses a whole series of branches, a series of documents, and a series of facts. The Prophet said al-Iman has over seventy branches.

There is no Allah but Allah, and the lowest of faith is the removal of harmful things from the road. The seventysome branches of al-Iman are mentioned by the Prophet so that the meaning becomes elaborate.

Some elements of Iman are:

- Believing in the Unseen
- Allah
- Angels of Allah
- Prophets and Messengers of Allah
- Books of Allah
- Predestination
- Day of Judgment
- Life after Death

This type of belief or faith is the strongest motivation to do righteous deeds. The consciousness of Allah (SWT) and the above mentioned, once instilled in our minds, show themselves in our behavior and actions. It helps us to strive to do right and avoid the wrong.

In chapter (surah) 13:28, the Holy Qur'an states,

ٱلَّذِينَ ءَامَنُوا۟ وَتَطْمَئِنُّ قُلُوبُهُم بِذِكْرِ ٱللَّهِ أَلَا بِذِكْرِ ٱللَّهِ تَطْمَئِنُّ ٱلْقُلُوبُ (٢٨)

"Those who believe, and whose hearts find satisfaction in the remembrance of Allah: for without doubt in the remembrance of Allah do hearts find satisfaction."

Believing in Ourselves

Many people or most people die with their songs still in their hearts. This means they never achieve their dreams or their goals, often because they have never cultivated or developed the faith or the belief in their selves.

The emotions of faith are one of the most powerful of all the major positive emotions. When faith blends with deep thought, the subconscious mind picks up the vibration and translates it into a spiritual value. Your belief or faith is the element that determines the action of your subconscious mind. Faith is a state of mind that can be developed greatly; it can make a person achieve what they thought could only be accomplished in dreams.

Faith is the mystical power that gives men and women the ability to master powerful difficulties. It is critical for us to encourage the positive emotions as dominating forces of our mind and discourage and eliminate the negative emotions. Faith in one's self gives life, power, and actions to the impulse of thought. Faith is the only known antidote to failure; try and try again.

Our subconscious mind works with what material we feed it, translated into reality and thoughts driven by fear, courage, and faith. Children who are morally and spiritually conscious develop a sense of their own self-worth. A person with healthy self-esteem is more capable of making decisions. Helping their children develop a healthy self-esteem is one of the most important things that a parent can do for them.

Unknown Poet

> If you think you are beaten, you are
> If you think you dare not, you don't
> If you like to win, but you think you can't it is almost certain you won't.
> If you think you'll lose, you're lost, for out in the world we find success begins with a fellow's will, it is all in the state of mind
> If you think you are out classed, you are, you've got to think high to rise.

Life's battles don't always go to the stronger or faster man, but sooner or later, the man who wins is the man who thinks he can.

May Allah increase us in our faith in Him, and faith in our own self.

Ameen.

$$\text{بِسْمِ اللهِ الرَّحْمَٰنِ الرَّحِيمِ}$$

With Allah's name, the merciful Benefactor, the merciful redeemer.

May the prayers and the peace be upon Allah's noble and kind messenger, Muhammad.

Patience and Conviction

Imam Omar Hazim

The Holy Qur'an states in chapter 103 that

$$\text{وَالْعَصْرِ (١) إِنَّ الْإِنْسَانَ لَفِي خُسْرٍ (٢) إِلَّا الَّذِينَ آمَنُوا وَعَمِلُوا الصَّالِحَاتِ وَتَوَاصَوْا بِالْحَقِّ وَتَوَاصَوْا بِالصَّبْرِ (٣)}$$

"By the token of time, through the ages, verily man is in loss except those who have faith, and do righteous deeds, and join together in the mutual teaching of truth and of patience."

Allah (SWT) has mentioned patience and perseverance in the Holy Qur'an in many places. In chapter 16:127, the Holy Qur'an states, "And be patient for your patience is but by Allah." Also, chapter 52:48 states, "Now await in patience by the command of your Lord." Patience is made a condition of success and prosperity.

The Holy Qur'an states in chapter 3:200 that,

$$\text{يَا أَيُّهَا الَّذِينَ آمَنُوا اصْبِرُوا وَصَابِرُوا وَرَابِطُوا وَاتَّقُوا اللَّهَ لَعَلَّكُمْ تُفْلِحُونَ (٢٠٠)}$$

"O You who believe! Persevere in patience and constancy; vie in such perseverance, strengthen each other, and fear Allah that you may prosper."

Patience means to keep your feelings and passions under control, avoid rashness, bewilderment, despair, greediness, keep cool and calm, make considered decisions, remain firm and steadfast in the face of dangers and difficulties.

Patience and faith are prerequisites for leadership in religion. Holy Qur'an 32:24:

$$وَجَعَلْنَا مِنْهُمْ أَئِمَّةً يَهْدُونَ بِأَمْرِنَا لَمَّا صَبَرُوا ۖ وَكَانُوا بِآيَاتِنَا يُوقِنُونَ (٢٤)$$

"And we appointed, from among them, leaders, giving guidance under our commands, so long as they persevered with patience and continued to have faith in our signs."

Patience is the way to earn the companionship of Allah (SWT). Holy Qur'an 8:46 states, "And be patient and persevere, for Allah is with those who patiently persevere."

People who have patience are the true winners in this world and the next because they have the companionship of Allah.

Holy Qur'an 2:155-156 states,

$$وَلَنَبْلُوَنَّكُم بِشَيْءٍ مِّنَ ٱلْخَوْفِ وَٱلْجُوعِ وَنَقْصٍ مِّنَ ٱلْأَمْوَالِ وَٱلْأَنفُسِ وَٱلثَّمَرَاتِ ۗ وَبَشِّرِ ٱلصَّابِرِينَ (١٥٥) ٱلَّذِينَ إِذَا أَصَابَتْهُم مُّصِيبَةٌ قَالُوا إِنَّا لِلَّهِ وَإِنَّا إِلَيْهِ رَاجِعُونَ (١٥٦)$$

"Be sure we shall test you with something of fear and hunger, some loss in goods or lives or the fruits (Of your toil), but give Glad tidings to those who patiently persevere, who say, when afflicted with calamity: "To God we belong, and to Him is our return."

The Prophet Muhammad's life and the other Messengers of God are signs for human beings who find themselves in the most unfavorable circumstances or hardships. They are signs that say you must keep to patience, you must keep your human excellence, and you must persevere in the original pattern that God has created you in.

Patience is a quality of endurance without complaint, to continue in spite of counterinfluence, opposition, obstacle, or discouragement. Perseverance is a statement of integrity that transcends the concept of patience. It includes patience, but only in its most basic form. Perseverance is a special type of patience that denotes the additional idea of endurance. Perseverance is the art of continuing an assignment even without seeing the results of that assignment being manifested.

We have to be willing to live and even die for an effort without seeing that effort's end, but being convinced that the good effort is not in vain. Faith is conviction of the heart, the only antidote to failure. Perseverance includes the dedication necessary to upkeep a situation until it can be responsibly passed on to future generations, even without obtaining the gold ourselves.

In the story of Prophet Moses and Khidr (a servant of Allah), Moses and Khidr are badly treated by a community they visited, even being denied room and board. Khidr repaired the wall that was falling in the town. However, the values under the falling wall were for the next generation. This shows the importance of making preparations for the future generation.

For humans, patience is like a light; it lights the way when difficulties and hardships confront us. When the darkness of adversities and suffering become long in our lives, it is patience that saves us from disappointment, depression, and frustration. Patience lets us proceed with courage in the face of afflictions and temptations on the road that God has chosen for us.

Remember and reflect on the story of Prophet Job (PBUH) in the Holy Qur'an and in the Bible, where he lost everything, but through patience and perseverance, he recovered everything he lost. That story is very important for the benefit our lives!

May Allah accept our prayers and help us to cultivate more patience in our lives.

بِسْمِ اللهِ الرَّحْمَٰنِ الرَّحِيمِ

With Allah's name, the merciful Benefactor, the merciful redeemer

May the prayers and the peace be upon Allah's noble and kind messenger, Muhammad.

Developing Spirituality:
Sunday Class at Islamic Center of Topeka

Sister Aliya Hazim

In understanding the development of our spirituality, we need to have a firm grasp of a few terms.

Spirit is a force within a human being thought to give the body life, energy, and power. *Soul* is the presence of God in human life.

Spirituality is here defined as a concern with matters of the spirit, however that may be defined, but it is also a wide term with many available readings. It may include belief in supernatural powers, as in religion, but the emphasis is on personal experience. It may be an expression for life perceived as higher, more complex, or more integrated with one's worldview, as contrasted with the merely sensual. It is an essential part of an individual's holistic health and well-being.

Other key concepts are

- Meaning—significance of life, making sense of situations deriving purpose
- Values—beliefs, standards, and ethics that are cherished
- Transcendence—experience, awareness, and appreciation to life beyond self
- Connecting—increased awareness of a connection with self, others, God, and nature

- Becoming—an unfolding of life that demands reflection and experiences, includes a sense of who one is and how one knows

Most unhappiness that people experience can be attributed to our preoccupation with materialism. We are trained to work toward accumulating "things," and our lives revolve around the competition involved in pursuing this futile quest. We must work in order to provide ourselves with the necessities of life, which requires us to participate in the physical aspects of materialism, but as individuals, we are under no obligations to participate in the spiritual aspects conditioned into us by society.

There are two aspects to the way we perceive the world:

- Physical—things and concepts we can see and verify logically.
- Spiritual—concepts of the mind which are abstract, without tangible substance. The two concepts are usually categorized as either fact or belief.

In the broad scope of spiritual life, we see faith not as something you have but as something you are in a relationship with. It involves an awareness of and an attunement to God's presence in our everyday life.

Those who do wish for the (things of) hereafter and strive therefore with all due striving and have faith—they are the ones whose striving is acceptable (to Allah).

Chapter (surah) 2:201 states

وَمِنْهُم مَّن يَقُولُ رَبَّنَا ءَاتِنَا فِى ٱلدُّنْيَا حَسَنَةً وَفِى ٱلْءَاخِرَةِ حَسَنَةً وَقِنَا عَذَابَ ٱلنَّارِ (٢٠١)

"And there are men who say: "Our Lord! Give us good in this world and good in the Hereafter, and defend us from the torment of the Fire!"

Chapter (surah) 58:22 states

لَا تَجِدُ قَوْمًا يُؤْمِنُونَ بِٱللَّهِ وَٱلْيَوْمِ ٱلْءَاخِرِ يُوَآدُّونَ مَنْ حَآدَّ ٱللَّهَ وَرَسُولَهُۥ وَلَوْ كَانُوٓا۟ ءَابَآءَهُمْ أَوْ أَبْنَآءَهُمْ أَوْ إِخْوَٰنَهُمْ أَوْ عَشِيرَتَهُمْ ۚ أُو۟لَٰٓئِكَ كَتَبَ فِى قُلُوبِهِمُ ٱلْإِيمَٰنَ وَأَيَّدَهُم بِرُوحٍ مِّنْهُ ۖ وَيُدْخِلُهُمْ جَنَّٰتٍ تَجْرِى مِن تَحْتِهَا ٱلْأَنْهَٰرُ خَٰلِدِينَ فِيهَا ۚ رَضِىَ ٱللَّهُ عَنْهُمْ وَرَضُوا۟ عَنْهُ ۚ أُو۟لَٰٓئِكَ حِزْبُ ٱللَّهِ ۚ أَلَآ إِنَّ حِزْبَ ٱللَّهِ هُمُ ٱلْمُفْلِحُونَ (٢٢)

"Thou wilt not find any people who believe in Allah and the Last Day, loving those who resist Allah and His Messenger, even though they were their fathers or their sons, or their brothers, or their kindred. For such He has written Faith in their hearts, and strengthened them with a spirit from Himself. And He will admit them to Gardens beneath which Rivers flow, to dwell therein (for ever). Allah will be well pleased with them, and they with Him. They are the Party of Allah. Truly it is the Party of Allah that will achieve Felicity."

Abu Hurairah narrated the following Hadith:

> Prophet Mohammed (PBUH) said, "Riches do not mean having a great amount of property, but riches are self contentment."

Spiritual Bankruptcy

Prophet Mohammed once asked, "Do you know what it means for a member of my community to be bankrupt?" His companions replied, "The bankrupt among us is someone who has neither money nor goods." But the blessed Prophet said, "In my community, the bankrupt is one who presents himself on the day of resurrection with his prayers, his fasting and his alms due, but who also presents himself as one who has reviled somebody, accused somebody falsely, misappropriated somebody's goods, shed somebody's blood and ruined somebody. He will be made to sit while compensation for all this is paid out of his good deeds, if his good deeds should be exhausted before the accounts are settled, sins will be subtracted from those he has harmed and will be added to his. Then he will be cast in the fire."

The symptoms of spiritual sicknesses are vanity, pride, hypocrisy, anger, envy, and the lust for wealth and status. These are illnesses no doctor can cure.

Belief requires prayer as a means of attainment and perfection, and our essence desperately needs it. Prayer is not done for worldly purposes because worldly purposes are causes for the prayer. We must pursue Allah's good pleasure through worship, affirm our weakness in our prayer, and seek refuge with Allah through prayer. We should never abandon prayer, for it is the key to the treasury of compassion. We should hold on to it.

Allah has commanded us to remember Him always and forever: "O you who believe, celebrate the praises of Allah, and do so often; and glorify Him morning and evening" (33:41).

After belief, prayer is our essential duty and the basis of worship; we are exposed to endless misfortunes and innumerable enemies. We suffer limitless needs and demands.

Our regular worship gives us an extraordinary spirit; the five daily prayers allow us to repeat and refresh our faith five times a day. While praying, we withdraw ourselves from our worldly engagements and turn to Allah with all our being.

Reciting the Holy Qur'an elevates us to a state as if we were receiving it directly from the Lord of the Worlds. We request divine help to enable us to follow His chosen way, refresh our belief, and remind ourselves that one day we will have to account for our deeds, unburden ourselves, and ask Allah to help us throughout our lives.

Thus the daily prayers strengthen our faith, prepare us for a life of virtue and obedience to Allah, and refresh our belief from which spring courage, sincerity, purposefulness, spiritual purity, and moral enrichment.

In Hadith al-Qudsi, the Messenger narrated, "Allah says: I am to My servant as he expects of Me, I am with him when he remembers Me. If he remembers Me in his heart, I remember him to Myself; if he remembers Me in an assembly, I mention him in an assembly better than his; if he draws nearer to Me a hand's span, I draw nearer to him an arm's length; if he draws nearer to Me an arm's length, I draw nearer to him a fathom length; and if he comes to me walking, I rush to him with great speed."

بِسْمِ ٱللَّهِ ٱلرَّحْمَٰنِ ٱلرَّحِيمِ

With Allah's name, the merciful Benefactor, the merciful redeemer

May the prayers and the peace be upon Allah's noble and kind messenger, Muhammad.

Religion Should Cultivate Moral Qualities

Imam Omar Hazim

The gift of reasoning is one of the greatest gifts Allah (SWT) has given to human beings. The ability to think and ponder, then initiate action based upon those thoughts is what has elevated humans above other creatures. It is in accepting moral and social responsibilities that leads us to moral excellence.

Islamic views on social responsibilities are based on kindness and consideration of others, not only to one's immediate family, parents, relatives and neighbors, but to all mankind and the animals, birds, trees, and plants.

The Arabic word *jihad* is greatly misunderstood. It is not synonymous with war. Jihad means struggling against a visible enemy, against Satan, and against self. The greatest struggle we may ever have is within self, or good versus evil.

We all need to concern ourselves with ethics and upright conduct as exemplified by the prophets and messengers of Allah (SWT) for human guidance. Racism is not the biggest problem anymore. Other kinds of problems caused by human behavior are more prevalent.

These include ignorance, neglect of family, immorality, spiritual blindness, violence, senseless murder, greed, fraud, sexual perversion, dishonesty, injustice, white-collar crime, corruption, drugs, babies having babies, etc. They are the product of faithlessness in Allah (SWT) and the lack of fear of accountability for one's actions.

We have the potential to be much better than we are. The human being is born the weakest creature on the earth, but he/she grows to become the strongest mentally and the most wise. In Islam, we believe Allah (SWT) has given man and woman the potential to achieve human excellence. The real human being is within. The body is only the vehicle for certain physical needs and goals.

We must take care of the body and the mind to achieve our goals of excellence, and we must use our best reasoning for sincere self-evaluations. This should lead to self-improvement, self-discipline, self-management, and self-control and improve morality for ourselves, family, and community.

We cannot blame society or our mothers or fathers for our shortcomings. In Islam, we do not believe men and women are born in sin; we believe the human being was born free of it and is responsible for his/her deeds after the age of discretion (puberty) if and when a sin is committed.

We believe the family structure that begins with male and female is the cornerstone of society and should be protected. Muslims accept the tree that the Bible and Holy Qur'an speak of as being the tree of immorality. We do not accept that the woman tempted man to eat fruit from it and thus began immorality for the world. We believe men and women are equal in the sight of Allah (SWT) and will be judged on their intentions and actions and not their gender.

The moral qualities that are latent within us remain in a dormant condition unless they are called into action. The role of religion is to bring out the best moral qualities in us and guide the human being to the practical affairs of life. Religion should free our minds so we can advance our thinking and purpose on this earth. Our intellect must grow spiritually to overcome the moral dilemmas of our times, and education should be a priority for our young.

Islam is a systematic way of life, which includes worship of Allah (SWT) and service to humanity, Islamic laws, social life, and an economic and political system that ensures justice and equality for all. It does not recognize any discrimination on the basis of language, color, country, sex, or heritage. Islam stresses that being fair and just is next to piety.

The Islamic Center of Topeka is willing to work with others in our community for the solution of the problems that affect us all. Let's strive for moral excellence.

بِسْمِ ٱللَّهِ ٱلرَّحْمَٰنِ ٱلرَّحِيمِ

With Allah's name, the merciful Benefactor, the merciful redeemer

May the prayers and the peace be upon Allah's noble and kind messenger, Muhammad.

The Muslim Women Eloquently Recite the Holy Qur'an in Topeka

Khalil Green

On Sunday February 28, 2010, the Muslims at the Islamic Center of Topeka gathered for their weekly Sunday Holy Qur'an study class.

The class was led by Imam Omar Hazim and attended by Muslim men and women.

The class began with the Muslim women reading selected verses from the Holy Qur'an. They have the choice of reading in English or Arabic.

All the women present this past Sunday recited the Holy Qur'an in Arabic. They truly showed their expertise and command of the Holy

Qur'anic language as spoken to the early believers by Prophet Muhammad (PBUH).

As such, Prophet Muhammad (PBUH) taught that every Muslim should seek knowledge. He did not say men; he said all Muslims according to Omar and other Muslims in Topeka, Kansas.

Thus, it is a wonderful thing that here in America, Muslim women can fulfill their goals according to their own desires.

Left to right: Sisters Laretta Owens, Aliya Hazim,
Sister Abeera, Maha Yasin

Of the sisters present, the verses that they recited were chapter 4:97-100, which states

إِنَّ ٱلَّذِينَ تَوَفَّىٰهُمُ ٱلْمَلَٰٓئِكَةُ ظَالِمِىٓ أَنفُسِهِمْ قَالُوا۟ فِيمَ كُنتُمْ قَالُوا۟ كُنَّا مُسْتَضْعَفِينَ فِى ٱلْأَرْضِ قَالُوٓا۟ أَلَمْ تَكُنْ أَرْضُ ٱللَّهِ وَٰسِعَةً فَتُهَاجِرُوا۟ فِيهَا فَأُو۟لَٰٓئِكَ مَأْوَىٰهُمْ جَهَنَّمُ وَسَآءَتْ مَصِيرًا (٩٧) إِلَّا ٱلْمُسْتَضْعَفِينَ مِنَ ٱلرِّجَالِ وَٱلنِّسَآءِ وَٱلْوِلْدَٰنِ لَا يَسْتَطِيعُونَ حِيلَةً وَلَا يَهْتَدُونَ سَبِيلًا (٩٨) فَأُو۟لَٰٓئِكَ عَسَى ٱللَّهُ أَن يَعْفُوَ عَنْهُمْ وَكَانَ ٱللَّهُ عَفُوًّا غَفُورًا (٩٩) ۞ وَمَن يُهَاجِرْ فِى سَبِيلِ ٱللَّهِ يَجِدْ فِى ٱلْأَرْضِ مُرَٰغَمًا كَثِيرًا وَسَعَةً وَمَن يَخْرُجْ مِنۢ بَيْتِهِۦ مُهَاجِرًا إِلَى ٱللَّهِ وَرَسُولِهِۦ ثُمَّ يُدْرِكْهُ ٱلْمَوْتُ فَقَدْ وَقَعَ أَجْرُهُۥ عَلَى ٱللَّهِ وَكَانَ ٱللَّهُ غَفُورًا رَّحِيمًا (١٠٠)

"When angels take the souls of those who die in sin against their souls, they say: "In what (plight) were ye?" They reply: "Weak and oppressed were we in the earth." They say: "Was not the earth of Allah spacious enough for you to move yourselves away (From evil)?" Such men will find their abode in Hell, - What an evil refuge! Except those who are (really) weak and oppressed - men, women, and children - who have no means in their power, nor (a guide-post) to their way. For these, there is hope that Allah will forgive: For Allah doth blot out (sins) and forgive again and again. He who forsakes his home in the cause of Allah, finds in the earth Many a refuge, wide and spacious: Should he die as a refugee from home for Allah and His Messenger, His reward becomes due and sure with Allah: And Allah is Oft-forgiving, Most Merciful."

These very important words from the Holy Qur'an were meticulously and carefully recited by the sisters. They needed no correction from each other, or anyone else in attendance.

The Muslim women's recitation of the Holy Qur'an was appreciated by all present. Imam Omar Hazim thanked them and acknowledged their expertise.

بِسْمِ ٱللَّهِ ٱلرَّحْمَٰنِ ٱلرَّحِيمِ

With Allah's name, the merciful Benefactor, the merciful redeemer

May the prayers and the peace be upon Allah's noble and kind messenger, Muhammad.

Holy Qur'an Daily Reading

Imam Omar Hazim

I seek refuge with Allah from Satan, the rejected enemy. If we want to talk to Allah, we should pray; if we want Allah to talk to us, we should read the Holy Qur'an. In Arabic, *Holy Qur'an* means that which should be read, to proclaim or to collect. When we read the Holy Qur'an, we increase our knowledge and our understanding, and we are rewarded by Allah for doing so. The Holy Qur'an is the word of Allah (SWT), revealed to Prophet Muhammad (PBUH). Prophet Muhammad (PBUH) said, "Anyone who reads one single letter from the Book of Allah will have a blessing and reward; and each good thing is equal to ten rewards."

The Prophet (PBUH) memorized Allah's revelation to him totally and lived it every minute of his life and advised his companions and followers to recite, memorize it, and live it.

Abu Umamah narrated that the Messenger of Allah said, "Read the Holy Qur'an so that it will be an intercessor for you on the Day of Judgment." From Muslim

We should remember that the Holy Qur'an is a special message from Allah to each one of us personally. We should do our best to read the Holy Qur'an daily for our spiritual uplifting, nourishment, and guidance. The Holy Qur'an is a permanent miracle. The purity of its text through fourteen centuries is a proof of the external care and protection Allah has provided, and the peace and contentment that it brings to the heart and mind in unpeaceful and disruptive societies show its miraculous effect.

Allah says in chapter (surah) 17:88,

قل لَئِنِ اجْتَمَعَتِ الْإِنْسُ وَالْجِنُّ عَلَىٰ أَن يَأْتُوا بِمِثْلِ هَٰذَا الْقُرْآنِ لَا يَأْتُونَ بِمِثْلِهِ وَلَوْ كَانَ بَعْضُهُمْ لِبَعْضٍ ظَهِيرًا (٨٨)

"Say if the whole of mankind and Jinn's were to gather together to produce the like of this Holy Qur'an, they could not produce the like thereof, even if they backed up each other with help and support."

A report from Ibn Abbas says the Messenger of Allah said, "The one who has nothing from the Holy Qur'an in his heart is like a deserted and demolished house."

With these quotes from the Holy Qur'an and the Messenger of Allah, I hope we will realize our need for the daily reading of the Holy Qur'an.

May Allah guide us and bring us closer to Him by reading His word. Ameen.

Chapter 3

Motherhood in Islam

بِسْمِ اللهِ الرَّحْمَٰنِ الرَّحِيمِ

وَقَضَىٰ رَبُّكَ أَلَّا تَعْبُدُوٓا۟ إِلَّآ إِيَّاهُ وَبِٱلْوَٰلِدَيْنِ إِحْسَٰنًا ۚ إِمَّا يَبْلُغَنَّ عِندَكَ ٱلْكِبَرَ أَحَدُهُمَآ أَوْ كِلَاهُمَا فَلَا تَقُل لَّهُمَآ أُفٍّ وَلَا تَنْهَرْهُمَا وَقُل لَّهُمَا قَوْلًا كَرِيمًا (٢٣) وَٱخْفِضْ لَهُمَا جَنَاحَ ٱلذُّلِّ مِنَ ٱلرَّحْمَةِ وَقُل رَّبِّ ٱرْحَمْهُمَا كَمَا رَبَّيَانِى صَغِيرًا (٢٤)

"And your Lord has decreed that you worship none but Him. And that you be dutiful to your parents. If one of them or both of them attain old age in your life, say not to them a word of disrespect, nor shout at them but address them in terms of honor. And lower unto them the wing of submission and humility through mercy, and pray: "My Lord! Bestow on them Your Mercy as they did bring me up when I was young." (Holy Qur'an, chapter 17:23-24)

Prophet Muhammad (PBUH) said,
"Paradise lies at the feet of your mother."

Imam Omar Hazim's mother is eighty-nine years old,
born October 31, 1921; she has eight children, nineteen grandchildren,
and twenty-two great grand children. Her name is Mrs. Lee Edna
Rollins. She is a lifelong businesswoman and real estate broker.

بِسْمِ اللهِ الرَّحْمَٰنِ الرَّحِيمِ

With Allah's name, the merciful Benefactor, the merciful redeemer

May the prayers and the peace be upon Allah's noble and kind messenger, Muhammad.

Honoring Parents

Imam Omar Hazim

There are many special days set aside to honor and appreciate people, such as Memorial Day, Mother's Day, or Father's Day.

Let's hope they're remembered, however, beyond a single day to every day of the year.

Our parents and elders are the building blocks of our society and should always be treated as great assets to the community. They are the reason for our existence. The Holy Qur'an in chapter 17:23-24 says,

وَقَضَىٰ رَبُّكَ أَلَّا تَعْبُدُوا إِلَّا إِيَّاهُ وَبِالْوَالِدَيْنِ إِحْسَانًا إِمَّا يَبْلُغَنَّ عِندَكَ الْكِبَرَ أَحَدُهُمَا أَوْ كِلَاهُمَا فَلَا تَقُل لَّهُمَا أُفٍّ وَلَا تَنْهَرْهُمَا وَقُل لَّهُمَا قَوْلًا كَرِيمًا (٢٣) وَاخْفِضْ لَهُمَا جَنَاحَ الذُّلِّ مِنَ الرَّحْمَةِ وَقُل رَّبِّ ارْحَمْهُمَا كَمَا رَبَّيَانِي صَغِيرًا

"Thy Lord hath decreed that ye worship none but Allah (SWT), and that ye be kind to your parents. Whether one or both of them attain old age in their life, say not to them a word of contempt, nor repel them, but address them in terms of honor, and out of kindness, lower to them the wing of humility and say: 'My Lord! Bestow on them thy mercy even as they cherished me in childhood.'"

Kindness to parents is an individual act of piety.

When parents are strong and the child weak, parental affection is showered on the child. Then the human baby grows to become the strongest both spiritually and mentally, as well as the wisest, on earth.

When the child grows up and is strong and the parents are old and may be weak or sickly, it is an obligation for the child to show a similar tender care and love for the parents.

We cannot really compensate our parents for all they do for us, but we must approach them with at least gentle humility and compassion. There is too much child abuse in our world and that is a very, very, sad commentary of society. There is also too much neglect of our elderly, so much that it has become a crisis in many cities in our county.

There is a saying in the Islamic tradition: "Any young person who is kind to an elderly person, Allah (SWT) will send someone to him or her who will be kind to them when they become old." And there is a Western saying, "The way you treat people, you will be treated."

Growing old is a natural, beautiful process of life, part of a divine plan. I am sure none of us wants to be deserted, unwanted, or neglected if we become ill in our old age.

The presence of our parents in our homes when they cannot take care of themselves is an honor and blessing. Their presence will bring rewards and peace if we do our best to take care of them; if it is not medically possible to do that, then and only then should other methods be sought.

Many of us wait until our parents have passed on before we realize how much we loved them. Honor them in their life and let them know it. If they have already passed on, we believe in Islam we can continue to honor them by offering prayers for their souls, giving to charities, or distributing Islamic literature on their behalf, and more.

I am sure there is much you can do according to your own religious traditions to respect and honor your parents in life and death. But remember: our parents and the elderly need us more in life than in death.

Our Lord! Help us to love and honor our parents more. Ameen.

بِسْمِ اللهِ الرَّحْمَٰنِ الرَّحِيمِ

With Allah's name, the merciful Benefactor, the merciful redeemer

May the prayers and the peace be upon Allah's noble and kind messenger, Muhammad.

Honoring Motherhood

Imam Omar Hazim

In chapter 31:14, the Holy Qur'an states,

وَوَصَّيْنَا الْإِنسَانَ بِوَالِدَيْهِ حَمَلَتْهُ أُمُّهُ وَهْنًا عَلَىٰ وَهْنٍ وَفِصَالُهُ فِي عَامَيْنِ أَنِ اشْكُرْ لِي وَلِوَالِدَيْكَ إِلَيَّ الْمَصِيرُ (١٤)

"And We have enjoined on man (to be good) to his parents: in travail upon travail did his mother bear him, and in years twain was his weaning: (hear the command), "Show gratitude to Me and to thy parents: to Me is (thy final) Goal."

Thus gratitude toward parents, who were instrumental in one's coming to life, in this verse goes with gratitude toward Allah, who is the ultimate cause and source of our existence.

Kindness and just dealings between man and man and respect for our honoring motherhood are parts of the concept of striving for the good in the life to come. Hakim asked the Prophet (PBUH), "Whom shall I be most kind to?" The Prophet answered, "Your mother three times, your father one time." This shows that the right of the mother upon the children is three times more than the right of the father as far as kindness is concerned.

A father's obligation is to help instill this concept in the children by teaching it to the children and by living the example, the best among you is he who is most kind to his wife. Imam Ali, the fourth caliph, stated, "Women are like flowers; do not burden them with responsibilities they cannot bear."

Muslims consider some ladies to be most noble and pious. They are

- Aasiyah—wife of Pharaoh
- Maryam/Mary—mother of Isa (Jesus) (PBUH)
- Khadijah—wife of Prophet Muhammad (PBUH)
- Fatima—daughter of Prophet Muhammad (PBUH) and leader of all the ladies of paradise
- Musa's mother
- The butcher's mother
- Hajira (Haggar)

The last one is Haggar, the second wife of Ibrahim, who was left in the desert with her son Ishmael along with some food and water. When the provisions Ibrahim had brought for Haggar and their son ran out, she set out in search for water, desperately running seven times between Safa and Marwah with faith in Allah (SWT). Then she saw a stream of water rising at the feet of Ishmael. This miraculous stream is still running today, known as the Zam Zam.

Allah so much loved the spirit of motherhood demonstrated by Hajira (Haggar); he has honored her by commanding the Muslim pilgrims to walk between the two hills when they go on pilgrimage in Mecca, in the memory of Hajira as a loving mother.

Moses' Mother: The Intensity of Her Grief

When Musa's (Moses) mother became so worried and confused at the thought of her son being killed by Pharaoh, it was inspired by Allah (SWT) in her heart and mind what she should do.

In chapter (surah) 28:7-10, the Holy Qur'an states,

وَأَوْحَيْنَا إِلَىٰ أُمِّ مُوسَىٰ أَنْ أَرْضِعِيهِ ۖ فَإِذَا خِفْتِ عَلَيْهِ فَأَلْقِيهِ فِي ٱلْيَمِّ وَلَا تَخَافِي وَلَا تَحْزَنِي ۖ إِنَّا رَادُّوهُ إِلَيْكِ وَجَاعِلُوهُ مِنَ ٱلْمُرْسَلِينَ (٧) فَٱلْتَقَطَهُ ءَالُ فِرْعَوْنَ لِيَكُونَ لَهُمْ عَدُوًّا وَحَزَنًا ۗ إِنَّ فِرْعَوْنَ وَهَٰمَٰنَ وَجُنُودَهُمَا كَانُوا خَٰطِـِٔينَ (٨) وَقَالَتِ ٱمْرَأَتُ فِرْعَوْنَ قُرَّتُ عَيْنٍ لِّي وَلَكَ لَا تَقْتُلُوهُ عَسَىٰ أَن يَنفَعَنَا أَوْ نَتَّخِذَهُ وَلَدًا وَهُمْ لَا يَشْعُرُونَ (٩) وَأَصْبَحَ فُؤَادُ أُمِّ مُوسَىٰ فَٰرِغًا ۖ إِن كَادَتْ لَتُبْدِي بِهِۦ لَوْلَا أَن رَّبَطْنَا عَلَىٰ قَلْبِهَا لِتَكُونَ مِنَ ٱلْمُؤْمِنِينَ (١٠)

"And We inspired the mother of Moses, saying: Suckle him and, when thou fear for him, then cast him into the river and fear not nor grieve. Lo! We shall bring him back unto thee and shall make him (one) of Our messengers. And the family of Pharaoh took him up, that he might become for them an enemy and a sorrow, Lo! Pharaoh and Haman and their hosts were men of sin. And the wife of Pharaoh said: (He will be) a consolation for me and for thee. Kill him not. It may be that he will be of use to us, or we may adopt him for a son. And they perceived not. And the heart of the mother of Moses became void, and she would have betrayed him if We had not fortified her heart, that she might be of the believers."

Upon seeing the babe, Aasiyah's (Pharaoh's wife) heart was filled by Allah (SWT) with love for Musa. She, Aasiyah, wanted to honor him (Moses), so she did take him as a son.

When Moses attained manhood and became the servant of Allah (SWT), he challenged Pharaoh to set the children of Israel free. Musa defeated Pharaoh and won the hearts of some of the very elite in Pharaoh's court.

Aasiyah declared the faith in the message of Allah (SWT) after witnessing the miracle of Moses in the court of Pharaoh. Pharaoh tried to turn her away from the true God (Allah) and Moses. She refused to reject the God (Allah) of Moses. On Pharaoh's order, she was tortured to death. The materialistic life did not matter to her.

In chapter 66:11, the Holy Qur'an states the prayer of Aasiyah, Pharaoh's wife:

وَضَرَبَ ٱللَّهُ مَثَلًا لِّلَّذِينَ ءَامَنُوا۟ ٱمْرَأَتَ فِرْعَوْنَ إِذْ قَالَتْ رَبِّ ٱبْنِ لِى عِندَكَ بَيْتًا فِى ٱلْجَنَّةِ وَنَجِّنِى مِن فِرْعَوْنَ وَعَمَلِهِۦ وَنَجِّنِى مِنَ ٱلْقَوْمِ ٱلظَّٰلِمِينَ (١١)

"My Lord, build for me a house with thee in the paradise, and deliver me from pharaoh and his deeds; and deliver me from the unjust people."

Khadija, the wife of the Prophet, she was truly known as a noble lady and the main pillar of support for the Prophet during the Meccan phase. We say she chose the Prophet for marriage, but the reality is Allah chose her to be the Prophet's wife and to bear his children. The Prophet faced severe opposition in the face of the rejection from his people. Khadija provided great moral support and consulting; she was the first shura (consultant) member.

She placed her wealth at this disposal. Allah has honored and praised her by addressing the Prophet. Holy Qur'an 93:8 states,

$$وَوَجَدَكَ عَائِلاً فَأَغْنَىٰ (٨)$$

"And He found thee in need and made thee independent."

She went through the difficulties of three years of social/economic embargo imposed on the Prophet and his family and followers. Some say the hardships of these three years eventually resulted in her death.

Holy Qur'an chapter 3:8 provides a closing prayer:

"Our Lord! Let not our hearts deviate now after you have guided us on the right path, but grant us mercy from your own presence, for you are the grantor of bounties without measure." Ameen.

بِسْمِ ٱللَّهِ ٱلرَّحْمَٰنِ ٱلرَّحِيمِ

With Allah's name, the merciful Benefactor, the merciful redeemer

May the prayers and the peace be upon Allah's noble and kind messenger, Muhammad.

The Butcher's Mother

Imam Omar Hazim

Prophet Muhammad (PBUH) stated, "And the paradise is under the feet of your mother."

Let me tell you about a sinner who obtained paradise through his mother's prayer as related by Sheikh Muzaffer Ozak Al-Jerrahi:

Allah asked Musa (Moses), "O, Musa, would you like me to introduce you here in this world to the companion you will have in the paradise?"

Moses said, "Yes, my Lord, please do."

"He has many faults, but because of the way he served his mother, I accepted the prayers she makes on his behalf. Through his mother's prayers, he has attained the rank of being your companion in paradise," said Allah (SWT).

So Allah told Musa to go to a certain town and there would be a butcher in the local shop. "Identify yourself to him as a traveler and request a stay at his home for the night."

The butcher welcomed Musa to his home. He said to Musa, "Have a seat, and excuse me for a while. I must attend to an earlier guest." He lowered from the ceiling a hammock in which laid a helpless old woman, too weak to sit up. He sat her up, cleaned her, fed her, kissed her, nuzzled her hair and then laid her down again. She whispered something to the butcher, and he said, "Ameen."

Prophet Moses said, "Who is this lady, and what did she say? Was she making a prayer?"

The butcher answered, "She is my mother, the crown of my head, the consolation of my heart, and she is my guest whom I delight in waiting on. She asked Allah [SWT] every day for something that will never happen, just a foolish mother's prayer."

Musa asked again, "What was the prayer?"

The butcher replied, "She asks Allah [SWT] every night, 'O, Allah, please make my son the companion of your messenger Musa in paradise.'"

The butcher added, "I am just an everyday person, a common sinner, and I am not knowledgeable in religious matters. I don't even know who Moses is, but my mother still offers this prayer."

At that time, the prophet Musa said to the butcher that his mother's prayer had been answered by the almighty Allah (SWT), and "I am Musa, messenger of Allah [SWT] who will be your companion in the next life."

Prophet Muhammad (PBUH) said that "paradise lies at the feet of your mothers."

We pray for Allah's forgiveness and guidance. Ameen.

Our Lord! Give us good in this world and good in the next world, and save us from the torment of the fire. Ameen.

$$\text{بِسْمِ ٱللَّهِ ٱلرَّحْمَٰنِ ٱلرَّحِيمِ}$$

With Allah's name, the merciful Benefactor, the merciful redeemer

May the prayers and the peace be upon Allah's noble and kind messenger, Muhammad.

Love and Respect for Motherhood

Sermon by Imam Omar Hazim

Edited online by Khalil Green

On Friday May 7, 2010, Imam Omar Hazim delivered the Friday sermon and honored mothers by conveying a speech called "Love and Respect for Motherhood."

Imam Omar began by relating a Hadith from Prophet Muhammad (PBUH) that states, "O people I enjoin you to observe the rights of women and fear Allah in this regard. You have taken women as your wives as a trust from Allah and in the name of Allah you have made their honor and virtue lawful to you."

The Prophet (PBUH) is telling us, according to Omar, to observe the rights of women so much so that we should fear Allah if we do otherwise. People should conduct themselves respectfully while transacting all forms of business with women during personal and professional dealings.

Mankind should honor all women as the Holy Qur'an says in chapter 4:1, titled the Women (An-Nisa):

$$\text{يَٰٓأَيُّهَا ٱلنَّاسُ ٱتَّقُوا۟ رَبَّكُمُ ٱلَّذِى خَلَقَكُم مِّن نَّفْسٍ وَٰحِدَةٍ وَخَلَقَ مِنْهَا زَوْجَهَا وَبَثَّ مِنْهُمَا رِجَالًا كَثِيرًا وَنِسَآءً وَٱتَّقُوا۟ ٱللَّهَ ٱلَّذِى تَسَآءَلُونَ بِهِۦ وَٱلْأَرْحَامَ إِنَّ ٱللَّهَ كَانَ عَلَيْكُمْ رَقِيبًا (١)}$$

"O mankind! Reverence your Guardian-Lord, who created you from a single person, created, of like nature, His mate, and from them twain scattered (like seeds) countless men and women; reverence Allah, through whom ye demand your mutual (rights), and (reverence) the wombs (that bore you): for Allah ever watches over you."

Thus, the Holy Qur'an tells us that we should respect our women and hold them in high regard, continued Omar, and further stated that human beings are created as a single soul. When men and women come together in union, they are a single soul created to bring forth more life.

The Arabic word for *womb* (arhams) comes from the root word *rahima*, which means to love, have tenderness, forgiveness, have all that is required for exercising beneficence, stated Omar. He continued that *rahima* is also the root word for two attributes of God, which are *rahman* (merciful) and *rahim* (beneficent).

So within the womb of the mother are mercy, compassion, and that which is beneficial. The woman is the vessel through which comes new life. Thus, God has ordained that humanity respect mothers and all women in general.

Umm is the Arabic word for *mother*. It shares its root with the words *ummat* (community) and *imam* (leader). Omar stated that we should acknowledge the connection that these words have with each other. It shows that the importance of woman cannot be downplayed as God has placed her importance into the very language that the Holy Qur'an was delivered in.

Thus, it is the nature of the mother to reflect on God's love. Quoting Imam W. Deen Mohammed, Imam Omar stated that "you can give without love, but you can't love without giving." So, continued Omar, any who has a deep sense of love must give of himself/herself as his/her mother gave before birth.

The word used for love (hubba) in the Holy Qur'an carries the meaning also of a seed that grows. Just as the seed grows in the ground and multiplies for the benefit of a community, so too does a child grow in the mother's womb with care and love, to one day share that care and love with the world.

Toward the end of his speech, Omar recommended that "if your mother is alive, don't go weeks, months or years without making a connection with her. And if she has passed away don't wait weeks, months, years, without offering a prayer [dua] for God to let her into the best parts of paradise."

In his conclusion, Omar stated,

"Our Lord! Let not our hearts deviate now after you have guided us to the right path, but grant us mercy from Your own Presence; for You are the grantor of bounties without measure."

Ameen.

Chapter 4

Khutbah

(Sermons)

بِسْمِ اللهِ الرَّحْمَٰنِ الرَّحِيمِ
يَٰٓأَيُّهَا ٱلَّذِينَ ءَامَنُوٓا۟ إِذَا نُودِيَ لِلصَّلَوٰةِ مِن يَوْمِ ٱلْجُمُعَةِ فَٱسْعَوْا۟ إِلَىٰ ذِكْرِ ٱللَّهِ وَذَرُوا۟ ٱلْبَيْعَ ۚ ذَٰلِكُمْ خَيْرٌ لَّكُمْ إِن كُنتُمْ تَعْلَمُونَ (٩)

O ye who believe! When the call is proclaimed to prayer on Friday (the Day of Assembly), hasten earnestly to the Remembrance of Allah, and leave off business (and traffic): That is best for you if ye but knew! (Holy Qur'an 62:9)

بِسْمِ ٱللَّهِ ٱلرَّحْمَٰنِ ٱلرَّحِيمِ

With Allah's name, the merciful Benefactor, the merciful redeemer

May the prayers and the peace be upon Allah's noble and kind messenger, Muhammad.

December 15, 2000, *Muslim Journal*

Imam Warith Deen Mohammed Day in Topeka, Kansas

Left to right: Imam Omar Hazim, Imam W. Deen Mohammed

Topeka is the capital city of Kansas and has a population of approximately 175,000 people. It is known for the 1954 Supreme Court landmark decision, *Brown v. Board of Education*, which allowed schools to be physically, racially integrated here in the United States.

In many of our lives, it will also be known for the historical visit on November 3, 2000, of Imam W. Deen Mohammed.

Imam Mohammed started the day in Topeka with an inspirational and informative khutbah at the Islamic Center. There was a packed audience of over four hundred worshippers of various nationalities—men, women, and children. This was the largest crowd ever in the Center since its opening in 1992.

The imam told the listeners, "We have to practice neighborly deeds, and Allah will reward us with what he has promised us. And that is life, and a good life."

He encouraged people to stay away from intoxicants. "If you do anything to affect clear thinking, you are making yourself to all kinds of evils and troubles. You are putting yourself in a position to be taken away from Allah," Imam Mohammed said. His message was inclusive for all good people to fight against the schemes of Satan.

On Friday night, Imam Mohammed delivered a public lecture at Lee Arena on Washburn University Campus. His topic was "Islam: The Establishment of the Individual in the Community, Obligations, and Benefits." The spirit of those in attendance was very enthusiastic.

The event was attended by many dignitaries, elected officials, and many leaders from the Jewish, Christian, Sikh, Baha'I, and other faith groups.

Also in attendance were the mayor of Topeka, the honorable Joan Wagnon; the superintendent of the 501 school district, Dr. Robert McFrazier; and the president of Interfaith Inc. of Topeka, Father John Erickson.

Father Erickson said that Imam W. Deen Mohammed is the embodiment of the interfaith concept.

All listened attentively to the great Islamic leader as he delivered his beautiful global message of tolerance and forgiveness. This was a very successful event.

The banquet dinner, which was held at the beautiful Bradbury Thompson Center, was sold out. Mayor Joan Wagnon presented Imam Mohammed with the proclamation declaring November 3, 2000, Warith Deen Mohammed Day in the city of Topeka.

As an added surprise, the mayor presented Imam Mohammed with a medallion of the city of Topeka that has only been presented to a very few dignitaries. This brought the audience to its feet in rousing applause.

Entertainment was provided by Luqman Hamza.

May Allah continue to guide and bless our Imam in every way.

$$\text{بِسْمِ اللهِ الرَّحْمَٰنِ الرَّحِيمِ}$$

With Allah's name, the merciful Benefactor, the merciful redeemer

May the prayers and the peace be upon Allah's noble and kind messenger, Muhammad.

The Swallows Come Back to Capistrano

Imam Omar Hazim

"The Birds in the sky held poised is a sign for those who have faith."

We are to be reminded of the teachings of the prophet: his lifestyle, the code of ethics he laid down for us, his attitude of love, forgiveness, mercy, and kindness, his undying faith, his patience and perseverance.

We are to study his life history in order to adopt as much as possible his wonderful character and personality.

The Holy Qur'an in chapter (surah) 33:21 states that

$$\text{لَقَدْ كَانَ لَكُمْ فِى رَسُولِ اللَّهِ أُسْوَةٌ حَسَنَةٌ لِمَن كَانَ يَرْجُوا اللَّهَ وَالْيَوْمَ الْآخِرَ وَذَكَرَ اللَّهَ كَثِيرًا (٢١)}$$

"Ye have indeed in the apostle of Allah (SWT) a beautiful pattern of conduct for anyone whose hope is in Allah (SWT) and the last day, and who engages much in the praises of Allah (SWT)."

Trust in Allah, He knows our needs before they come into existence. Faith in Allah (SWT) holds us up in times of hardship and distress. Sometimes, it is not our knowledge or experience nor our wealth or influence that brings us out of difficulty; many times it is only our faith in Allah (SWT).

What made them, the Prophet and his followers, brave enough to face ten years of oppression, opposition, and cruelty? It was their faith in Allah (SWT) that held them up. So verily with every difficulty there is relief, every failure brings with it the seeds of a success. Muhammad never gave up because of opposition. Faith and belief are the only known antidote to failure.

The Holy Qur'an in chapter (surah) 21:107 states,

$$وما أرسلناك إلا رحمة للعالمين (١٠٧)$$

"O Muhammad, We sent thee not but as a mercy for all creatures."

The appointment of the Holy Prophet is indeed a blessing and a mercy of Allah to the whole world.

The Holy Qur'an states in chapter (surah) 16:79 that

$$ألم يروا إلى الطير مسخرات في جو السماء ما يمسكهن إلا الله إن في ذلك لآيات لقوم يؤمنون (٧٩)$$

"Do they not look at the birds held poised in the midst of the air and sky? Nothing holds them up but the power of Allah. Verily in this are signs for those who have faith."

Allah tells His servants to look at the birds held in the sky, between heaven and earth, and how He, Allah, has caused them to fly with their wings in the sky. They are held up only by Him. It is He and only He who gave them the strength and ability to do that, subjecting the air to carry them and support them.

Chapter (surah) Al-Mulk 67:19 states,

$$أولم يروا إلى الطير فوقهم صافات ويقبضن ما يمسكهن إلا الرحمن إنه بكل شيء بصير (١٩)$$

"Do they not observe the birds above them spreading their wings and folding them in?"

None can uphold them except Allah, most Gracious. Truly it is He that watches over all things. The flight of birds is one of the most beautiful and wonderful things in nature.

Consider the miracle of the swallows' return to Capistrano. The group motion of birds is a fascinating aspect of nature; synchronized movements of birds are as beautiful as they are intriguing to watch.

Every year around the 19 of March, much of the world pauses momentarily and focuses on that phenomenon of nature known as the return of the swallows to Capistrano. It is a major media event every year. Only Allah knows how long the swallows have been coming back to Capistrano, and some say for centuries.

Every spring, this event has captured the imagination of millions. It is reported that those birds' winter home is in Argentina. They leave San Juan Capistrano about October 23 every year going to Argentina, which is a 7,500 mile flight, and return March 19, another 7,500 miles; a fantastic round-trip flight of 15,000 miles, almost a complete flight around the world. A one-way flight is about 30 days, 7,500 miles. They fly at altitudes above 2,000 feet to take advantage of favorable air current and to stay away from predatory birds along the way. They must do this to fulfill some inner biologic destiny. Allah knows best.

In chapter (surah) 17:13, the Holy Qur'an states,

وَكُلَّ إِنسَٰنٍ أَلْزَمْنَٰهُ طَٰٓئِرَهُۥ فِى عُنُقِهِۦ ۖ وَنُخْرِجُ لَهُۥ يَوْمَ ٱلْقِيَٰمَةِ كِتَٰبًا يَلْقَىٰهُ مَنشُورًا (١٣)

"Every human being has a bird attached to his neck."

Tayra literally means a bird. The Arabs, like the ancient Romans, superstitiously would draw omens from the flight of birds, good or bad. Their idea was to foretell the future from the manner and direction in which birds would fly. They thought that their destiny was in the flight of birds.

Allah speaks of more than one concept here:

1. Our minds fly very swiftly.
2. Destiny and fate
3. Deed and actions

Allah is telling humanity, our destiny and fate are not caused by the direction in which the birds fly. The verse reveals the principle that actions and deeds will produce an effect that is made to cling to a person; that this very effect will be reviewed by Allah on the day of resurrection in the form of a wide-open book. Destiny relates not so much to the external circumstances of events in one's life but to the direction which this life takes as a result of one's moral choices; in other words, it relates to man's spiritual fate, which depends on him.

Since Allah has made humanity responsible for his behavior on earth, Allah speaks of Himself as having tied to every human being a bird (tayra) to his neck.

May Allah accept our prayers and increase us in faith. Ameen.

$$\text{بِسْمِ ٱللَّهِ ٱلرَّحْمَٰنِ ٱلرَّحِيمِ}$$

With Allah's name, the merciful Benefactor, the merciful redeemer

May the prayers and the peace be upon Allah's noble and kind messenger, Muhammad.

The Family Tree

Imam Omar Hazim

Edited online by Khalil Green

On Friday April 9, 2010, at the Islamic Center of Topeka, Imam Omar Hazim delivered the Friday sermon titled "The Family Tree." Omar draws a metaphorical comparison between the growth of a tree and human consciousness. With this Khutbah, Omar expertly wraps up many spiritual lessons into one speech.

Imam Omar began by saying that the Holy Qur'an does not talk, it does not speak, but Muslims should understand that Allah speaks through the Holy Qur'an. Therefore, continues Omar, "this is Allah's Word." So Muslims, and any who read the Holy Qur'an, should appreciate the best that the Holy Qur'an has to offer.

Omar added that Allah is the essence and source of everything that lives. Thus, praise and thanks are given to Him. Everything, like people, trees, and plants, comes from a seed. In this seed is the potential for the fulfillment of the life it will bring forth.

Omar states that Allah says in chapter (surah) 87 verse 1-3,

$$\text{سَبِّحِ ٱسْمَ رَبِّكَ ٱلْأَعْلَى (١) ٱلَّذِى خَلَقَ فَسَوَّىٰ (٢) وَٱلَّذِى قَدَّرَ فَهَدَىٰ (٣)}$$

"Glorify the name of thy Guardian-Lord Most High, Who hath created, and further, given order and proportion; who hath ordained laws. And granted guidance."

This is to say Allah didn't create anything and just leave it, according to Omar. He endowed living things with faculties to become what He created them to turn into. "He equipped each thing with that which is necessary for it to reach its completion," said Omar.

Just like the seed buried in the earth, the flower that grows and shows its beauty, and the tree that brings forth its fruit, so it is with the human who sprouts up, states Omar. He continues by saying that human growth is not just about physical growth; it's also about the spiritual growth. As the old saying goes, "a tree is known by the fruit it bears, and a man is known by his deeds," according to Omar.

The value of a person is known by the depth of deeds he/she performs. Prophet Muhammad (PBUH) has stated that the "best of you are those who are most useful to its community," and the family is the cornerstone of the community, stated Omar.

Imam Omar cites a verse from the Holy Qur'an that metaphorically can be applied to the importance of the family in chapter 7, verse 58, which states,

وَٱلْبَلَدُ ٱلطَّيِّبُ يَخْرُجُ نَبَاتُهُ ۥ بِإِذْنِ رَبِّهِۦ ۖ وَٱلَّذِى خَبُثَ لَا يَخْرُجُ إِلَّا نَكِدًا ۚ كَذَٰلِكَ نُصَرِّفُ ٱلْءَايَٰتِ لِقَوْمٍ يَشْكُرُونَ (٥٨)

"From the land that is clean and good, by the will of its Cherisher, springs up produce, (rich) after its kind: but from the land that is bad, springs up nothing but that which is niggardly: thus do we explain the signs by various (symbols) to those who are grateful."

The family has to grow in soil that is rich and allows the family unit to thrive where it can grow and produce. To do this, Muslims have to be rooted in their spiritual practices. They have to realize that the same food that causes us to thrive can cause us to decay. All things have to be taken in due measure and proportion.

Toward the end of his speech, Imam Omar stated, "If we take the basic lessons we learn in the family structure of honor, decency, trust, honesty, and respect for our brother, our sister, our mother and our father then we go a long way in the greater and outer society."

Omar ended by stating that all children are born alike in need and innocence. If a baby needs something, it will cry. No matter if that baby is in Africa, China, Europe, Arabia, or America, they all cry the same; no matter what language or culture they are born into, they all sound the same.

They were all created from the same soul. As such, humanity is also one. There is a oneness of all humanity who came into this world as babies, and as innocent ones with the natural capacity to learn. As such, all humanity is one, created from the soul of humanity's original parents. Humanity is one family tree created in the best of molds and having the highest capacity for being honorable on this earth.

Our Lord! Give us good in this world and good in the next world, and save us from the torment of the fire. Ameen.

بِسْمِ ٱللَّهِ ٱلرَّحْمَٰنِ ٱلرَّحِيمِ

With Allah's name, the merciful Benefactor, the merciful redeemer

May the prayers and the peace be upon Allah's noble and kind messenger, Muhammad.

Keys to a Good Life: Salat (Prayer)

Dr. Ashraf Sufi

In *chapter (surah) 2:238, the Holy Qur'an states,*

حَٰفِظُوا۟ عَلَى ٱلصَّلَوَٰتِ وَٱلصَّلَوٰةِ ٱلْوُسْطَىٰ وَقُومُوا۟ لِلَّهِ قَٰنِتِينَ (٢٣٨)

Observe the regular prayers and the prayer in the best way; and stand before Allah as devout people.

أَقِمِ ٱلصَّلَوٰةَ لِدُلُوكِ ٱلشَّمْسِ إِلَىٰ غَسَقِ ٱلَّيْلِ وَقُرْءَانَ ٱلْفَجْرِ إِنَّ قُرْءَانَ ٱلْفَجْرِ كَانَ مَشْهُودًا (٧٨) وَمِنَ ٱلَّيْلِ فَتَهَجَّدْ بِهِۦ نَافِلَةً لَّكَ عَسَىٰ أَن يَبْعَثَكَ رَبُّكَ مَقَامًا مَّحْمُودًا (٧٩) وَقُل رَّبِّ أَدْخِلْنِى مُدْخَلَ صِدْقٍ وَأَخْرِجْنِى مُخْرَجَ صِدْقٍ وَٱجْعَل لِّى مِن لَّدُنكَ سُلْطَٰنًا نَّصِيرًا (٨٠)

"Perform the regular prayer in the period from the time the sun is past its zenith till the darkness of the night, and recite the Qur'an at dawn—dawn recitation is always witnessed—and during the nigh wake up and pray as an extra offering of your own, so that your Lord may raise you to a highly praised status. Say, "My Lord, make me go in truthfully and come out truthfully, and grant me supporting authority from You." (Al-Isra, 17:78-80)

وَأَقِمِ ٱلصَّلَوٰةَ طَرَفَىِ ٱلنَّهَارِ وَزُلَفًا مِّنَ ٱلَّيْلِ إِنَّ ٱلْحَسَنَٰتِ يُذْهِبْنَ ٱلسَّيِّـَٔاتِ ذَٰلِكَ ذِكْرَىٰ لِلذَّٰكِرِينَ (١١٤)

"Perform the regular prayer at both ends of the day, and during parts of the night, for good things drive bad away—this is a reminder for those who are aware." (Hud 11:114)

Salat or regular prayer is the command of Allah. It is one of the most important pillars of Islam. It distinguishes between the believers and nonbelievers. Salat is not an option; it is obligatory (fard). It is not done once a week or few times a week. Salat is obligatory five times a day. All prophets of Allah told their people to pray; Islam, however, made it a very essential part of religion. The Prophet, peace be upon him, called the salat as the "pillar of religion" (imad al-din), and in one Hadith, he is reported to have said that there is no good in a religion in which there is no ruku' or bowing (meaning prayer).

The Prophet, peace be upon him, said that the key of Jannah is salat (Al-Tirmidhi, chapter on Purification, Hadith no. 4). This means that the sincere and devoted salat helps a person to enter Jannah; but it also means that salat is the key to everything that is good. The benefits of salat are many both in this world and in the hereafter.

Salat is our link, our bond, and our communication with Allah. If you love Allah and you want Allah to love you, then you should pray. The Prophet, peace be upon him, called the salat "the coolness of my eyes" (Qurrat 'aini). When he wanted Bilal, may Allah be pleased with him, to give *adhan* for salat, he used to say to him, "Give us comfort by it, O Bilal" (Arehna biha, ya Bilal). He used to spend a long time in his nightly prayers. Sometimes, he used to pray one-third of the night and sometimes half of the night, sometimes even more than that. He used to find great comfort and joy in salat.

Salat has many benefits. Its benefits are spiritual, moral, physical, individual, and social. Its rewards are here in this world and in the hereafter. The whole structure of salat is so beautiful and so remarkable that there is nothing like it or comparable to it in any religion. Salat is not just meditation or recitation or physical movements. Salat involves mind, soul, and body, all the three together in a most harmonious way. Salat is done both individually and collectively. Salat is done both in public and in private. If we observe our salat as it should be observed, then everything in our lives will become better. Our relations with Allah will be good because we shall be living fully conscious of Allah all the time. Our relations with our families, our coworkers, our neighbors, and with everyone and everything will be very good. We shall be clean from sin, corruption, and aggression as much as a person who takes a bath five times a day will be clean from every kind of dirt.

Allah says in the Qur'an that the salat restrains from all kinds of evils, vulgarities, and indecencies.

اتْلُ مَا أُوحِيَ إِلَيْكَ مِنَ الْكِتَابِ وَأَقِمِ الصَّلَوٰةَ إِنَّ الصَّلَوٰةَ تَنْهَىٰ عَنِ الْفَحْشَاءِ وَالْمُنكَرِ وَلَذِكْرُ اللَّهِ أَكْبَرُ وَاللَّهُ يَعْلَمُ مَا تَصْنَعُونَ (٤٥)

"Recite what is revealed to you of the Scripture and keep up the prayer: prayer restrains from shameful and evil (behavior). Remembering Allah is great. Allah knows everything you are doing." (Al-Ankabut, 29:45)

Allah says in the Qur'an that the salat saves from distresses and fears, and it helps people during the time of difficulties:

إِنَّ الْإِنسَانَ خُلِقَ هَلُوعًا (١٩) إِذَا مَسَّهُ الشَّرُّ جَزُوعًا (٢٠) وَإِذَا مَسَّهُ الْخَيْرُ مَنُوعًا (٢١) إِلَّا الْمُصَلِّينَ (٢٢) الَّذِينَ هُمْ عَلَىٰ صَلَاتِهِمْ دَائِمُونَ (٢٣)

"Man was truly created anxious: he is fretful when misfortune touches him, but tight-fisted when good fortune comes his way. Not so are those who pray and are constant in their prayers." (Al-Ma'arij, 70:19-23)

Allah says in the Qur'an that salat brings success in this life and in the life to come:

"Successful are the believers. Those who pray humbly ... and who keep up their prayers, they shall be the heirs who shall inherit the Paradise and they shall be there forever." (Al-Mu'minun 23:1-11)

Salat requires *taharah* (cleanliness of the body, clothes, and the place of prayer). The people who are conscious of taharah five times a day, their bodies, their clothes, their environment—everything should be clean. Salat is to be performed at appointed times. The people who are conscious of their appointments five times a day should be time conscious always. In salat, Muslims stand together without any distinction of race, color, economic status, or political position. The people who perform prayer in *jama'ah* (congregation) regularly they learn equality, solidarity, and brotherhood. Salat in jama'ah is performed behind an imam, and everyone has to follow the imam. The people who pray regularly, they learn discipline, order, and organization. If the imam makes any mistake, any person can correct him. This is the most democratic way. The benefits of salat are countless, but it must be performed with full consciousness.

Let us pray regularly and pray in the best way so that its benefits and beauty may reflect in our lives.

Mu'adh reported that one day, the Prophet took my hand and said, "By Allah, I love you."

Mu'adh said, "By the honor of my mother and father, O Messenger of Allah, I also say this by Allah that I love you."

He said, "I advice you, O, Mu'adh, do not leave to say this after every prayer, 'O, Allah, help me to remember You, to thank You, and to worship You in the best way.'" Ameen.

بِسْمِ ٱللَّهِ ٱلرَّحْمَٰنِ ٱلرَّحِيمِ

With Allah's name, the merciful Benefactor, the merciful redeemer

May the prayers and the peace be upon Allah's noble and kind messenger, Muhammad.

ALLAH's Plan

By Imam Samuel Ansari

From Islamic Center AL Mu' Muminun St. Louis, Mo.

ALLAH'S plan for the life of man is universal in its form and structure. Allah encourages us to study the external world symmetry and order, so as to help us better understand our own internal and external structure. Allah's creation is based on principles driven by a systemic order that creates consistency. Studying the external or material creation offers us direction and order that is necessary for establishment.

The Qur'an provides a logic that supports life and compliments man's growth and purpose. The Qur'an is an idea for perfect guidance. Iblis (Satan), attempts give man a clone of that perfect guidance that is offered us in the Qur'an. Iblis wants to influence us to reduce the significance of that perfect guidance in man's life. This is why we are constantly reminded that the greatest prayer is the remembrance of Allah. Thinking on Allah is a prayer itself.

ALLAH makes everything that He has created as a utility to assist us on toward our purpose and destiny. This is why as Believers, we seek to inherit what ALLAH wills. This utility that Allah has provided us with is also a charity that advances life and opportunity. Allah (SWA) says in the Qur'an: "We have bestowed raiment upon you to cover your shame, as well as to be an adornment to you, but the raiment of righteousness is the best." In another Ayat, Allah says, "Verily the most honored of you in the sight of Allah is (he who is) the most righteous of you. And Allah has full knowledge and is well acquainted (with all things)."

"Our Lord! Let not our hearts deviate now after you have guided us on the right path, but grant us mercy from your own presence, for you are the grantor of bounties without measure." Ameen

بِسْمِ اللهِ الرَّحْمَٰنِ الرَّحِيمِ

With Allah's name, the merciful Benefactor, the merciful redeemer

May the prayers and the peace be upon Allah's noble and kind messenger, Muhammad.

The Diversity that Allah Has Created

Imam Omar Hazim

Brothers and sisters, the verse I would like to read from the Holy Qur'an is in chapter (surah) 5, verse 48, which states,

وَأَنزَلْنَا إِلَيْكَ ٱلْكِتَٰبَ بِٱلْحَقِّ مُصَدِّقًا لِّمَا بَيْنَ يَدَيْهِ مِنَ ٱلْكِتَٰبِ وَمُهَيْمِنًا عَلَيْهِ فَٱحْكُم بَيْنَهُم بِمَا أَنزَلَ ٱللَّهُ وَلَا تَتَّبِعْ أَهْوَآءَهُمْ عَمَّا جَآءَكَ مِنَ ٱلْحَقِّ لِكُلٍّ جَعَلْنَا مِنكُمْ شِرْعَةً وَمِنْهَاجًا وَلَوْ شَآءَ ٱللَّهُ لَجَعَلَكُمْ أُمَّةً وَٰحِدَةً وَلَٰكِن لِّيَبْلُوَكُمْ فِى مَآ ءَاتَىٰكُمْ فَٱسْتَبِقُوا۟ ٱلْخَيْرَٰتِ إِلَى ٱللَّهِ مَرْجِعُكُمْ جَمِيعًا فَيُنَبِّئُكُم بِمَا كُنتُمْ فِيهِ تَخْتَلِفُونَ (٤٨)

"And unto thee have We revealed the Scripture with the truth, confirming whatever Scripture was before it, and a watcher over it. So judge between them by that which Allah hath revealed, and follow not their desires away from the truth which hath come unto thee. For each We have appointed a divine law and a traced-out way. Had Allah willed He could have made you one community. But that He may try you by that which He hath given you (He hath made you as ye are). So vie one with another in good works. Unto Allah ye will all return, and He will then inform you of that wherein ye differ."

This verse is very well connected to the prior four verses. These verses are talking about divine scriptures that were revealed to some of the divine messengers of Allah (SWT), including Prophet Musa (Moses) and Esau (Jesus); peace be upon them.

The connection with these verses have some key words for us to understand as Muslims, as to the sacredness of the words concerning

Allah creating humanity and not leaving us on our own to stray, but yet giving guidance and enlightenment to the prophets of Allah (SWT) so that they would relay this information in word form or book form so that humanity can safeguard and check themselves, which is a wonderful blessing for Allah (SWT) to do.

If you make something, then it only stands to reason that you should keep it, preserve it, maintain it, and guide it; this is what Allah (SWT), through his wisdom and his mercy, has done for humanity, the whole of what he has created. Whatever it is that Almighty Allah (SWT) has created, even if it is a microscopic germ, he has provided sustenance for that germ.

When it comes to humanity, not only has he provided the physical sustenance for us to maintain ourselves in the earth, but he has provided the spiritual nourishment, the word that will help humanity advance in the way he wants us to advance, as was given to the previous prophets.

Dear Muslims, in these first few words of this verse, it reads to thee we sent the scripture, the book in truth in various places in Holy Qur'an. The word *un-zalna*, which means sending down iron and cattle and other substances, is used.

In-zalna and *un-zalna* are used. The word is also used in the first revelation to the Prophet, meaning having been sent down, but not for us to imagine in our minds that Allah (SWT) the Creator is up in some high place or throne or chair physically above us, and he sends down the rain or cattle or revelation in the form of a book dropping from the sky. The meaning there is that whatever exists in Allah's (SWT) creation or in the earth, it exists by Allah's (SWT) command. Allah (SWT) has commanded it to exist like He has commanded the wind, rain, and other elements in the earth.

Nothing just appeared by itself; neither did the cattle or other things in the earth that are here for our sustenance. It means that Allah (SWT) desired it, willed it, created it, and made it manifest.

Kursi is used in the Holy Qur'an to mean the chair or throne. This seat does not actually mean a physical seat or throne somewhere in this creation that is higher than anything else that Allah (SWT) has created. However, there are many scholars, including Imam Warith Deen Mohammed, that take it to mean that it is as a symbol that means power, authority, and knowledge above all. That Allah is above all that he has created in this earth.

Allah (SWT) further states that He sent the book in truth confirming the book—not books, but book—that came before it and guarding its safety.

Language of Al-Kitab, the books, but in previous verses, it is clear he is talking about, in our understanding or language, more than one book because he is referring to Prophet Musa (AS) and the scripture that he bought and Prophet Essau (AS) and the book he bought. If we examine what Allah's (SWT) message is and what his message has always been from the time of Adam to the time of Mohammed, it has been consistent: the message of Tauheed, the message of Oneness of Allah (SWT), the message of piety and righteousness, the message of service to humanity, the message of doing of good, and the message that brought certain types of rules and regulations and laws to the people that the message came to. These messages came to humanity to keep humanity morally and spiritually intact. Without this message that Allah (SWT) sent to all the Prophets, including the last Prophet, Prophet Mohammed then the world of mankind would be in a state of spiritual insanity.

Many are spiritually insane; what would it have been like without the teachings of Almighty Allah (SWT) through his prophets?

As we continue this khutbah, the verse I am concentrating on is Holy Qur'an chapter (surah) 5, verse 48.

This verse shows something about diversity, that if Allah (SWT) had desired, He could have made us all one nation, one single people. We also want to keep in mind as we walk through this that there are other passages such as chapter (surah) 4, verse 1, which states,

يَٰٓأَيُّهَا ٱلنَّاسُ ٱتَّقُوا۟ رَبَّكُمُ ٱلَّذِى خَلَقَكُم مِّن نَّفْسٍ وَٰحِدَةٍ وَخَلَقَ مِنْهَا زَوْجَهَا وَبَثَّ مِنْهُمَا رِجَالًا كَثِيرًا وَنِسَآءً وَٱتَّقُوا۟ ٱللَّهَ ٱلَّذِى تَسَآءَلُونَ بِهِۦ وَٱلْأَرْحَامَ إِنَّ ٱللَّهَ كَانَ عَلَيْكُمْ رَقِيبًا (١)

"O mankind! Reverence your Guardian-Lord, who created you from a single person, created, of like nature, His mate, and from them twain scattered (like seeds) countless men and women; - reverence Allah, through whom ye demand your mutual (rights), and (reverence) the wombs (That bore you): for Allah ever watches over you."

Also chapter (surah) 49, verse 13 that Allah (SWT) tells us,

يَٰٓأَيُّهَا ٱلنَّاسُ إِنَّا خَلَقْنَٰكُم مِّن ذَكَرٍ وَأُنثَىٰ وَجَعَلْنَٰكُمْ شُعُوبًا وَقَبَآئِلَ لِتَعَارَفُوٓا۟ إِنَّ أَكْرَمَكُمْ عِندَ ٱللَّهِ أَتْقَىٰكُمْ إِنَّ ٱللَّهَ عَلِيمٌ خَبِيرٌ (١٣)

"O mankind! We created you from a single (pair) of a male and a female, and made you into nations and tribes, that ye may know each other (not that ye may despise (each other). Verily the most honored of you in the sight of Allah is (he who is) the most righteous of you. And Allah has full knowledge and is well acquainted (with all things)."

Allah (SWT) created humanity into many nations from one single being, one single soul. As we look at this, we don't see any contradiction as how humanity was made both female and male. Some men don't like to understand that language in its correct sense because oftentimes men think that they are so much superior to women. They tend to think that women are made from another substance, but not according to the Holy Qur'an.

However, as we try to understand the language of Allah (SWT), Allah (SWT) is clearly telling us in chapter (surah) 5, verse 48 that these books that he referred to as one book, the scripture that he revealed to Mohammed, is a safeguard and a check and a confirmation to the previous books. So what he gave the Prophets prior to Prophet Mohammed was some portion of what he would reveal to Mohammed, the last messenger and the last book in its completed form.

So those previous books in their correct context, not in the context that man with his so-called wisdom and his corrupt mind, got into those books of divinity and began to change them around to suit his own desires and fancies. Therefore, Allah (SWT) sent the Holy Qur'an to check that the Divine Word has been guarded for all times as it confirms the good words and good ideology of the books that came before it. One book, not many books.

That is to show that even though the language was different, from the prophets before Prophet Mohammed, that the location and areas geographically were different, there was a sense of acknowledging diversity but yet the same type of guidance. To show that all the books that came before were books designed to address a certain people at a certain time and age but would not separate the good of those books from the good of the Holy Qur'an.

So the good of the Holy Qur'an is a check of all those books revealed before it. That is a form of diversity that we Muslims in this day and time need to be aware of and conscious of because we can see how the society is growing consciously, as far as religion is concerned, in America and throughout the world. Demands are being put on the thinking people, the world, and society that they must take a careful and serious look at the Holy Qur'an and al-Islam because Islam and the Holy Qur'an will protect and safeguard the truth that is in their books.

If we become hard-liners and try to completely separate the religious scriptures or the book that Allah has sent and degrade the books that came before the Holy Qur'an, we could be traveling in an area that could be dangerous as far as condemning the word of Almighty Allah (SWT). We must use the Holy Qur'an to determine what is correct in the other books. The word here, which is referred to as the Holy Qur'an, *muhaiman* means one that safeguards, watches over, stands as a witness, one who upholds.

This word is used because this is the position that Allah (SWT) has placed the Holy Qur'an, to be a safeguard and check and stand as a witness to the scriptures before it pertaining to the truth and the originality of those scriptures, not the corruption but just as it stands as a witness and upholds the truth of the scriptures before it. It also stands as an indictment to the wrong and corruption of those scriptures that man has added to.

Diversity is the language of the various books. We still have yet to form unity in diversity; just as though we see a form of unity in the diversity of humanity. Allah goes on to talk about the law in an open way. Allah says, "To each among you we have prescribed a law and an open way, if Allah had so willed he would have made you a single people." But this is not what Allah willed. He did not will that we become a single people in the form of thought, mentality, ideas, and desires because if we were single in those matters, then there would be no beautiful diversity, and what a boring and unuseful life that would be if everybody was the same.

Even in the diversities of countries and nations, if all the nations of the earth produced oil, then what would really be the value of that oil; or if all the nations produced sugar? But the diversity is there for all the nations to produce different products so that a state of trade and commerce can exist and the people can come to know one another.

Chapter (surah) 49:13 is talking about the diversity in the way where we come to know one another. It is also talking about the same essence from the point of view that all humans are made basically, and I am not talking about birth defects or deformity, I'm talking about the general rule where man and woman has a head, brain, a heart, digestive system, two legs, and two arms. This is the type of sameness as far as biological birth is concerned and also from the same essence, one soul.

Allah (SWT) states that He would have made you a single people, but His plan is to test you in what He has given you. So He gave some of the people throughout periods of time certain laws, various prescriptions for their conduct based on the geographical area that the people lived in. A lot of the tests are based on the economic condition of the people and the environment.

There are different rules, different laws that have evolved over periods of time to what we have today in the Holy Qur'an. What we have today is the *shariah*, the law that rules the practical conduct that has been laid down by Allah, but He also mentions in this same verse that He not only prescribed a law, but He prescribed an open way; in Arabic, that is called *minhaj*. The law or shariah means the way to a watering place, a direction to get to a place of water so that both humans and animals can drink from an element that is very necessary for human existence and the existence of animals.

Allah uses this term of shariah in the Holy Qur'an to denote a system of law that is necessary for a community's social and spiritual development and welfare. Minhaj, in this same verse, deals with more of a custom, a culture, or a way that a people have established to live with each other based on the environment and the other economic and social conditions of where those people are from.

Oftentimes, in the Western society, many people tend to get the minhaj confused with Islamic law. They often get culture confused with religion, and that presents a problem that many of us must spend time on trying to correct so that those that are learning about Islam can learn true Islam and not necessarily be mistaken by a person's culture to be the religion. All of us know this, and I'm sure none of us here are guilty of putting culture before the religion, or taking the culture and saying that because of the culture it is also religion. I'm sure that all of us are more knowledgeable than that.

Allah points out again in these verses that His plan of not making us a single people, and when we talk about a single people, we are speaking of in thought. Surely we are one humanity, which we clearly understand, I'm sure.

But making up the same thought, He has given us a choice of discretionary powers, which make all the difference in the world as to whether we are a single people or whether Allah (SWT) has created us in diversity. If this had not been done, we would be just like the trees or certain animals or like the oceans or mountains—we wouldn't have a choice to make certain decisions to move in certain directions or go to certain places.

If we were oppressed in one country or masjid, we would not have the ability to leave that place and go to another if we were planted like flowers in the earth. Allah has given us those discretionary powers, and that is what has made us above all the other creatures that He has created.

This is the real diversity in humanity that we all have, different houses that we have made, worked on, or purchased. If all of them in one city would look just alike, how boring it would be. If every businessman would have a restaurant and there were no grocery stores the diversity, beauty that Allah (SWT) has created in these discretionary powers that He has given man. If a man's nature had been made to make him unable to use these discretionary powers, then all men and women would have been a single people.

It would have been impossible for the better qualities in human beings to advance. This is why Allah (SWT), through his mercy and wisdom, chose us not to be one single people.

Our Lord! Give us good in this world and good in the next world, and save us from the torment of the fire. Ameen.

بِسْمِ ٱللَّهِ ٱلرَّحْمَٰنِ ٱلرَّحِيمِ

With Allah's name, the merciful Benefactor, the merciful redeemer

May the prayers and the peace be upon Allah's noble and kind messenger, Muhammad.

The Spiritual and Moral Health of the Heart

Article by Dr. Muzammil H. Siddiqi

Presented at Jumuah by Dr. Ashraf Sufi

In chapter (surah) 3:8, the Holy Qur'an states,

رَبَّنَا لَا تُزِغْ قُلُوبَنَا بَعْدَ إِذْ هَدَيْتَنَا وَهَبْ لَنَا مِن لَّدُنكَ رَحْمَةً إِنَّكَ أَنتَ ٱلْوَهَّابُ (٨)

"Our Lord, Let not our hearts deviate after You have guided us. Grant us your mercy. Indeed you are the Giver always."

Heart is a very important part of the human body. A lot depends on the heart; not only our physical health but also our spiritual and moral health depends on the soundness of the heart. Someone said rightly, "The problem of the heart is the heart of the problem." Individual problems, family problems, social problems, economic problems, political problems, national and international problems—all these problems stem from the problems of the hearts.

Heart indeed has a physical function; but there is no evidence to prove that it has no spiritual or moral functions. The soul probably resides in the heart or is attached to it. Soul is the inner dimension of our being. It is related to the body and mind as well, but it has its own existence, most probably in or near the heart.

Our physical heart is an amazing organ. Its size is no more than the size of your clenched fist. The average heart weighs between 8 oz. and 12 oz. It sits just to the left of the center of your chest cavity. The heart is a hollow, muscular organ, and its rhythmic contractions pump and circulate the blood throughout the body. The heart pumps more than four quarts of blood a minute, about 5,760 quarts a day, and about 36,288,000 gallons in 70 years. The heart beats on average 72 times a minute 24 hours a day. It does not sleep when you sleep. It does not rest when you rest. Every heartbeat is a gift of Allah, and there comes a day when your heart will quietly stop.

I am not going to talk about the physical problems of the heart. That is the subject for cardiologists to discuss, but I shall talk about the moral and spiritual aspect of the heart. In the Qur'an, the words *qalb* and *fu'ad* are used. The word *qalb* (plural *qulub*) occurs 132 times, and the word *fu'ad* (plural *af'idah*) occurs sixteen times. *Qalb* is used both in its physical and spiritual sense, while *fu'ad* is used more in the spiritual sense. Both mean heart; and heart is the seat of awareness, consciousness, feelings, and thought. It could be good or bad, healthy or unhealthy.

Believers are required to pay special attention to their hearts. We pay attention to the physical health of our hearts; we should also pay attention to the spiritual and moral health of our hearts.

Abu Hurairah reported that the Prophet, peace be upon him, said, "Allah does not look at your bodies or possessions but He looks at your hearts and actions" (Muslim 4651).

Allah, of course, looks at everything and He knows everything, but the point of the hadith is that the real thing that matters to Allah is not whether you are young or old, tall or short, fat or skinny, white or black, Arab or non-Arab, rich or poor, upper class, middle class, lower class, etc. What matters in the sight of Allah is whether your heart is sincere, truthful, and honest or not and whether your actions are good or not.

Allah tells us in the Qur'an that He has prepared Jannah only for those who are good at heart, not those who have a big tribe, power, or wealth:

يَوْمَ لَا يَنفَعُ مَالٌ وَلَا بَنُونَ (٨٨) إِلَّا مَنْ أَتَى ٱللَّهَ بِقَلْبٍ سَلِيمٍ (٨٩) وَأُزْلِفَتِ ٱلْجَنَّةُ لِلْمُتَّقِينَ (٩٠)

Imam Omar Hazim

The Day when neither wealth nor children can help. But only he (will prosper) that comes before Allah with a sound heart. To the righteous, the Garden will be brought near. (Al-Shu'ara' 26:88-90)

وَأُزْلِفَتِ ٱلْجَنَّةُ لِلْمُتَّقِينَ غَيْرَ بَعِيدٍ (٣١) هَـٰذَا مَا تُوعَدُونَ لِكُلِّ أَوَّابٍ حَفِيظٍ (٣٢) مَنْ خَشِيَ ٱلرَّحْمَـٰنَ بِٱلْغَيْبِ وَجَاءَ بِقَلْبٍ مُّنِيبٍ (٣٣) ٱدْخُلُوهَا بِسَلَامٍ ذَٰلِكَ يَوْمُ ٱلْخُلُودِ (٣٤) لَهُم مَّا يَشَاءُونَ فِيهَا وَلَدَيْنَا مَزِيدٌ (٣٥)

"And the Garden will be brought nigh to the Righteous; no more a thing distant. (A voice will say:) "This is what was promised for you, for everyone who turned (to Allah) in sincere repentance, who kept (His Law), "Who feared (Allah) Most Gracious unseen, and brought a heart turned in devotion (to Him): "Enter ye therein in Peace and Security; this is a Day of Eternal Life!" There will be for them therein all that they wish, and more besides in Our Presence." (Qaf 50:31-35)

Types of Hearts:

From the spiritual and moral point of view, there are different types of hearts. These types are related to their awareness and consciousness. The Prophet, peace be upon him, is reported to have said this:

> *The Prophet—peace be upon him—said, "There are four types of hearts: a pure heart that shines like a lamp, the covered up and closed heart, the upside down heart and the mixed up heart. The pure heart is the heart of the believer. The covered up heart is the heart of the non-believer. The upside down heart is the heart of the hypocrite who knows and then denies. The mixed up heart is the heart in which there is both faith and hypocrisy. The example of faith in it is like a small plant that grows with good water and the example of hypocrisy in it is like a wound that grows with pus and blood. So whichever grows bigger takes over the heart. (Musnad Ahmad ibn Hanbal 10705)*

Diseases of the Heart:

Imam Ghazali in his book *Ihya'* says that every organ of our body has a function; when it fails to do its functions, it means it is not well. The function of the soul or the spiritual heart is to know its Creator, to love

Him, and to seek closeness to Him. If the heart fails in this function, then we must know that it is sick.

It is important to know the ailments that make the heart weak and sick. In the language of the Qur'an, it is not only the eyes that get blind; the hearts also become blind.

$$\text{أَفَلَمْ يَسِيرُوا فِى ٱلْأَرْضِ فَتَكُونَ لَهُمْ قُلُوبٌ يَعْقِلُونَ بِهَا أَوْ ءَاذَانٌ يَسْمَعُونَ بِهَا فَإِنَّهَا لَا تَعْمَى ٱلْأَبْصَارُ وَلَكِن تَعْمَى ٱلْقُلُوبُ ٱلَّتِى فِى ٱلصُّدُورِ (٤٦)}$$

"Do they not travel through the land, so that their hearts may thus learn wisdom and their ears may thus learn to hear? Truly it is not their eyes that are blind, but their hearts that are in their breasts." (Al-Hajj 22:46)

The Qur'an has spoken in many places about the sickness (marad) of the hearts. Allah says in the Qur'an,

$$\text{فِى قُلُوبِهِم مَّرَضٌ فَزَادَهُمُ ٱللَّهُ مَرَضًا وَلَهُمْ عَذَابٌ أَلِيمٌ بِمَا كَانُوا يَكْذِبُونَ (١٠)}$$

"In their hearts is a disease; and Allah has increased their disease: and grievous is the penalty they (incur), because they are false (to themselves)." (Al-Baqarah, 2:10)

When the heart gets sick, it loses its desire and ability to do right and good deeds. This affects the morals and manners of a person and his/her general behavior.

What are the major diseases that affect the hearts, and how to take precaution, and what are the cures in case one is affected with these ailments? Scholars have spoken about seven major diseases of the heart:

1. Arrogance and conceit (al-kibr wa al-ghurur)
2. Ostentation (al-riya')
3. Jealousy or envy, hate, and deceit (al-hasad, al-hiqd, al-ghish)
4. Suspicion (su' al-zann)

5. Anger (al-ghadab)
6. Stinginess (al-bukhl)
7. Love of power, money, position, and fame (hubb al-jah)

These are called diseases of the heart (amrad al-qalb), and they lead to major sins if they are not controlled and carefully treated. In the Qur'an and Sunnah and in the spiritual writings of Muslim scholars, such as al-Ghazali and Ibn al-Qayyim al-Jawziyah, we find a lot of discussion on the treatment of these ailments.

Arrogance and conceit stem from egotism and overestimation of oneself and one's abilities or merits. This leads sometimes to the denial of the Creator, as it happened to Satan. The best treatment of this disease is to cultivate modesty. We have to remind ourselves always that we are the servants and slaves of Allah. We totally depend on Him for our being and existence.

ostentation is called hidden idolatry (al-shirk al-khafiyy). It is a desire to show off and seek praises from others. It takes away sincerity and seriousness to pursue one's goals and objectives. When a person becomes too much involved with ostentation, he/she becomes shallow and superficial. It may also lead to hypocrisy. The best cure for it is to check the "intention" (niyyah) before any action. A believer must remind oneself that his/her work is for the sake of Allah alone.

Jealousy or envy, hate, and deceit stem from lack of respect, mercy, and love for others. A jealous person does not like to see others happy, successful, and prosperous. Very often, jealousy and envy lead to hate, deceit, and violence. The best treatment is to have positive envy by competing with others in acts of goodness and use this as an incentive to achieve more and better.

suspicion comes from lack of trust and confidence in others. Allah says in the Qur'an, "Some suspicion is sin." Suspicion creates cynicism and takes away hope and optimism. Suspicious persons or cynics are those who, when they see actions and hear some words that have the possibility of being positive or negative, they take the negative and evil. Suspicion sometimes also leads to violence. It is good to be cautious and careful, but we must keep our attitude positive. If we want to be trusted, we must trust others as well.

Anger is given to human being as a mechanism for self-defense, but if it is not properly controlled, it becomes very destructive. In the hadith, it is called fire. The Prophet, peace be upon him, said that when you get angry, change your environment, change your position, and drink some water. Imam Ghazali said, "Love of Allah extinguishes the fire of anger."

stinginess is a terrible disease. The Prophet, peace be upon him, taught us to seek Allah's refuge from stinginess. Stinginess stems from selfishness, materialism, and too much love of this world. It means lack of care and consideration for others. It holds people from fulfilling their duties and recognizing the rights of others. It leads sometimes to cheating and dishonesty. The Prophet, peace be upon him, said, "Be aware of stinginess. It destroyed many nations before you. It made them to shed the blood of each other and misappropriate what was sacrosanct" (Muslim, 2578).

extreme desire for money, power, position, and fame: this is called in Arabic *hubb al-jah*. It is another major disease of the heart. This is also called in the Qur'an and hadith as "love of this world" (hubb al-dunya). In a Hadith, it is reported that the Prophet, peace be upon him, said, "Two hungry wolves in a herd of sheep are not as destructive and harmful as the love of the money and extravagance are for the religion of a person" (Al-Tirmidhi, 2376). The cure for this is to remind oneself always that this world is *fitnah* (a test and trial) and the real world is the hereafter.

Duties of the heart:

Some scholars say that in the Shariah there are things that are obligatory (fard), recommended (mustahabb), forbidden (haram), not recommended (makruh), and permissible (mubah). But these are not only in the external laws that we observe, they are also in the internal matters of the hearts. There are duties of the bodies and there are duties of the hearts. It is thus:

1. Obligatory (fard): It is obligatory for the heart to have sincerity (ikhlas), trust (tawakkul), awe and reverence of Allah (khauf), hope (raja'), and repentance (tawbah).
2. Recommended (mustahabb): It is recommended for the heart to have contentment and satisfaction (rida), humbleness (khushu'), desire to meet Allah and be close to Him (shawq and uns).

3. Forbidden (haram): It is forbidden for the heart to have belief in the divinity of anyone other than Allah (shirk) and to doubt in Allah's existence or in the truth of His Prophets (shakk), show off (riya'), have arrogant pride (kibr), jealousy (hasad), and hypocrisy (nifaq).
4. Undesirable (makruh) for the heart is to have the desire for sinful acts (shahwat al-dhunub), to feel much attachment to the world and worldly things (al-ishtighal al-za'id bi-umur al-dunya).
5. Permissible (mubah) is to like and care for worldly and material things without neglecting one's duties or committing anything that is forbidden.

According to many scholars, the following Hadith contains one-third of Islam:

> **nu'man ibn Bashir reported that he heard the prophet saying: "halal is clear and haram is clear and between the two of them are doubtful matters about which not many people know. Thus he who avoids doubtful matters clears himself in regard to his religion and his honor, but he who falls into doubtful matters falls into that which is forbidden, like the shepherd who pastures around a boundary line, almost crossing it. Truly every king has a boundary and truly Allah's boundaries are his prohibitions. Truly in the body there is a morsel of flesh which, if it be whole, all the body is whole and which, if it be diseased, the whole body is diseased. Truly it is the heart. (Bukhari 50)**

(Khutbah at ISOC—Dhul Qi'dah 10, 1427/ December 1, 2006)

$$\text{بِسْمِ ٱللَّهِ ٱلرَّحْمَٰنِ ٱلرَّحِيمِ}$$

With Allah's name, the merciful Benefactor, the merciful redeemer

May the prayers and the peace be upon Allah's noble and kind messenger, Muhammad.

Darkness of Arrogance and the Light of Reasoning

Edited online by Khalil Green

On Friday, May 14, 2010, Imam Omar Hazim gave a very provocative speech during the Friday sermon at the Islamic Center of Topeka, titled the "Darkness of Arrogance and the Light of Reasoning."

Omar began by giving supplications to God and honoring Prophet Muhammad as the last prophet to humanity.

Imam Omar began his speech by stating that within reasoning is humility. Thus, if we reason properly, we develop humility, stated Omar. He continued that it is for this purpose that reasoning is mentioned over 811 times in the Holy Qur'an.

Quoting the Holy Qur'an, Omar stated that in chapter (surah) 51, verse 55, it is related to us that "surely we advance by the power of thought."

Also in the Holy Qur'an, faith is mentioned exactly the same number of times as reasoning; thus, the two go together. As such we pray to God because we reasonably understand the need and, through faith, crave His forgiveness, related Omar; this is the opposite of arrogance.

Chapter 7, verse 40 of the Holy Qur'an states,

$$\text{إِنَّ ٱلَّذِينَ كَذَّبُوا بِـَٔايَٰتِنَا وَٱسْتَكْبَرُوا عَنْهَا لَا تُفَتَّحُ لَهُمْ أَبْوَٰبُ ٱلسَّمَآءِ وَلَا يَدْخُلُونَ ٱلْجَنَّةَ حَتَّىٰ يَلِجَ ٱلْجَمَلُ فِى سَمِّ ٱلْخِيَاطِ ۚ وَكَذَٰلِكَ نَجْزِى ٱلْمُجْرِمِينَ (٤٠)}$$

"To those who reject Our signs and treat them with arrogance, no opening will there be of the gates of heaven, nor will they enter the garden, until the camel can pass through the eye of the needle: Such is Our reward for those in sin."

Omar states that this verse is not talking about wealth or material things. Instead, it refers to a problem inherited within human beings that go far deeper than physical concerns: arrogance. As such, as taught in Islam, Muslims are to stay away from arrogance of race, gender, wealth, and birth (caste), continued Omar.

Human beings are to abstain from the prideful boasts of (Satan) who caused Adam and Eve to slip from the Garden. They succumbed to the dark ugliness taught to them by Satan.

However, Adam and Eve then repented and submitted to God, and Adam became a messenger of God.

Omar further quoted Sheikh Muzaffer Ozak Al-Jerrahi by stating that in teaching Adam about his role as caretaker of the world, God caused Adam to see three lights. Adam thus looked to his right and asked the first light to indentify itself. The light replied, "I am reason, and I reside in the head where I distinguish good and evil. And as I reside in the head of the human being, I manifest all kinds of skills in those who have me in their skull. I am the means by which they will be able to go to paradise." Adam prayed that God bless those who have this quality, said Omar.

Then did Adam look to the second light and asked, "Who are you?" The second light said, "I am modesty, and I live here inside the eye of human beings, which recognizes the attributes of God, and also, I am a discriminating eye."

The third light said, "My name is compassion. And I reside in the heart of those who believe. And in the heart in which I reside, there is modesty and compassion."

God instructed Adam to choose which light he would possess. He chose reasoning, said Omar. The other lights complained, stating that they go along with reasoning and are inseparable. They stated that they are intertwined with reasoning. So the one who has reasoning by way of default also has modesty and compassion in which there is love and humility. So Adam picked all of them, continued Omar.

Then God caused Adam to look to the left, and he saw three forms of darkness. He questioned the first. The first darkness stated that it was arrogance. "My function is to make men suffer the wrath of God, and I reside in the head." However, Adam informed the darkness that reasoning resides there. The darkness replied that when "reasoning leaves the human being, I take its place."

The second darkness stated that it was greed, and "I reside in the eye, and any who have me becomes like and animal and looses conscious discrimination. Thus, when modesty leaves the eye, I take over."

The third darkness stated that it was envy, and "I reside in the heart. When I am there, I burn my host, and he/she becomes lower than animals and worst than the devil. Thus, when compassion leaves the heart, I take its place."

Omar stated that "we can't be arrogant like Satan without also having greed and envy because all those are connected to darkness," so we should stay away from these grave sins that can consume us from the inside.

Omar concluded by quoting a statement from Prophet Muhammad (PBUH): "A person who repents from a sin becomes like one who is sinless; and as many as our sins may be, they cannot exceed the mercy of our Lord."

Our Lord! We have heard the call of one calling us to Faith, Believe ye in the Lord, and we have believed. Our Lord! Forgive us our sins, blot out from us our iniquities, and take to Thyself our souls in the company of the righteous (chapter [surah] 3:193).

Ameen.

$$\text{بِسْمِ ٱللّٰهِ ٱلرَّحْمٰنِ ٱلرَّحِيمِ}$$

With Allah's name, the merciful Benefactor, the merciful redeemer

May the prayers and the peace be upon Allah's noble and kind messenger, Muhammad.

Created in Pairs

Imam Omar Hazim

In chapter 36, verse 36, the Holy Qur'an states,

$$\text{سُبْحَٰنَ ٱلَّذِى خَلَقَ ٱلْأَزْوَٰجَ كُلَّهَا مِمَّا تُنۢبِتُ ٱلْأَرْضُ وَمِنْ أَنفُسِهِمْ وَمِمَّا لَا يَعْلَمُونَ (٣٦)}$$

As Yusuf Ali translates it, "Glory to Allah, the creator, who created in pairs all things that the earth produces as well as their own kind and other things which they have no knowledge."

Muhammad Asad translates it in a very similar way; he uses limitlessness as the meaning stating that there is no limit to Allah (SWT)'s creation. He says limitlessness is Allah, who created opposites of all things in the earth that He produces, as well as the human being and other things that He has created, which as yet they have no knowledge. I think his interpretation of "that which they have no knowledge of" is significant in this verse because he points out the things that will come that man has no knowledge of, and we are aware that this Holy Qur'an was revealed some 1,426 years ago.

Even at that time, when Allah first revealed these messages to his Prophet Muhammad (PBUH), the things we knew of as pairs as far as human beings generally consisted of the human pair of male and female. The general knowledge is that the female is opposite of the male in so many biological respects, and that through the coming together through marriage and nonmarital relationships, the result will be reproduction to continue the population of the earth.

This was a fact well-known since the time of Adam, but Allah (SWT), speaking in this verse of chapter (surah) 36, verse 36, is speaking of something broader than that, as well as the pairs of humanity. Allah is speaking of inanimate objects as well as of animate existence in Allah's (SWT) creation; he is speaking of sexuality in human beings, animals, and sexuality in plants, meaning that pollen would be blown by the wind from plant to plant and this would also cause reproduction in plants. The plants themselves are also created in pairs.

Maybe at the time of Prophet Muhammad (PBUH), the general scientific community may not have had that knowledge, so Allah says that which they have no knowledge of is also created in pairs. This is showing the knowledge of the Creator, who knows His creation and is also speaking of the relationship of the opposite pairs: darkness and light, heat and cold, positive and negative charges from electricity, positive forces and negative forces within ourselves as human beings, and also that of the atom in the Holy Qur'an.

Allah speaks of knowing the parts of the atom and knowing that the atom is the smallest particle in the earth and creation. Allah (SWT), in the Holy Qur'an, talks about pairs, meaning both a pair, the togetherness of two, and also one of a pair, and that is how the Arabic translates it. This verse, which was given to humanity some 1,400 years ago, shows the importance of the wisdom of the Creator.

In the world we live in, we find that a few years back, one of the great scientists discovered that every particle has an antiparticle or opposite charge, even the smallest particles of matter in this creation. This was Paul Derek, who won a Nobel Prize for this discovery. He was a scientist of physics who studied movement and positive and negative charges of the atom as well as others; such as Sir Isaac Newton, who had studied before Paul Derek.

Sir Isaac Newton was the second person in all history, following Prophet Muhammad (PBUH), to be considered the most influential of the top one hundred people of the history of the world. He also studied this same philosophy or the same idea about particles and the materials that are in space and in our world, as Paul Derek has done more recently.

Paul Derek's discovery, which was dealing with the pairing of the matter and the opposite matter, and through this discovery, he won a Nobel Prize for what the Western world calls a great discovery.

We may think of a vacuum as being vacant and empty, but some of the discoveries show space is not empty itself; particles in space form a field of energy.

The scientific discovery of matter reminds us Muslims to what Allah has said 1,400 years ago in chapter (surah) 41, verse 11, which states,

ثُمَّ ٱسْتَوَىٰٓ إِلَى ٱلسَّمَآءِ وَهِىَ دُخَانٌ فَقَالَ لَهَا وَلِلْأَرْضِ ٱئْتِيَا طَوْعًا أَوْ كَرْهًا قَالَتَآ أَتَيْنَا طَآئِعِينَ (١١)

"Moreover He comprehended In His design the sky, And it had been (as) smoke: He said to it And to the earth; Come ye together, willingly or unwillingly they said: We do come (together), in willing obedience."

As the scientists look at this creation, they are sending ships to Pluto and other planets to land and study. It may help them to understand how this vast creation came into being.

But still yet we respect the scientists for their studies because we know that whatever they find, it will be in accord with whatever has been stated in the Holy Qur'an. Before Allah told the heavens and earth to come into existence, He comprehended what he wanted; it had been smoke and gases, and then He directed them to transform and take shape in the way He wanted. The scientist studied the gases of the whole universe today, and they determined that hydrogen gas is regarded as the primal element of which all material particles of the universe have evolved from and are still evolving. It is not that Allah said "Be" and it is right now, but He said "Be" and it is, meaning if it wasn't going to be at that moment it would eventually come to pass by His will.

Allah tells us in another verse of the Holy Qur'an that this creation of His is still expanding, not that when He first created it that it would stop and come to its completion but is ever expanding.

In chapter 51, verse 47, the Holy Qur'an states,

وَٱلسَّمَاءَ بَنَيْنَـٰهَا بِأَيْيْدٍ وَإِنَّا لَمُوسِعُونَ (٤٧)

"With power and skill did We construct the Firmament: For it is We Who create the vastness of Space."

As we continue this Khutbah, we are talking about pairs. Allah created everything in pairs. We noted about the discovery of Paul Derek, which is dealing with matter and antimatter, components of atoms, positive and negative charges created by none other than Allah.

With Allah (SWT) is the reasoning that when He wants something to be, He simply says "Be," and it is. When He said to the heavens and the earth "Come willingly or unwillingly" and they said "We do come willingly in obedience to our Lord," this is a metaphor of Allah's (SWT) power. So that anything Allah wants to come into existence than this expression of "Be," and it will be so. Thus, Allah saying to the creation to come willingly means that in time, whatever his will is, the universes could not resist, hold back, and not form in the way that Allah (SWT) intended it to form; and that the destiny of the physical creation is to submit to the will of Allah.

Recently we had some discussion in our Sunday class on free will and limited free will of humanity, which is a complete different subject than the destiny of the creation; the creation of Allah (SWT) has no choice.

However, Allah (SWT) has given humanity, the human being, a choice, has given him free will, the ability to plan, to think, to weigh, to ponder a way to initiate certain actions and be disciplined based on this concept of free will.

Talking about pairs, Allah created the animate and inanimate in pairs of opposites to produce certain actions and results in Allah's (SWT) creation. For example, before electricity was discovered, before man was able to take from the atom the negative and positive forces to produce electricity, much of the world was in darkness. By Allah's (SWT) inspiration and guidance to man, man discovered some of the energies and forces of nature to produce electricity so that humanity would have a better life. This is something we take for granted until we are out of electricity. For example, if the power goes out and you go home, you have no lights or electricity in your house; all the food has spoiled in your refrigerator and freezer. Then you begin to realize the real value of electricity because you have been harmed by not having it.

There are many nations and countries in the world that don't have the luxury that we have in this country. It was the pair of the positive and the negative, the electrons and protons, that came together to produce this electricity, the wonderful result.

Chapter (surah) 4, verse 1 states,

يَا أَيُّهَا ٱلنَّاسُ ٱتَّقُوا رَبَّكُمُ ٱلَّذِى خَلَقَكُم مِّن نَّفْسٍ وَٰحِدَةٍ وَخَلَقَ مِنْهَا زَوْجَهَا وَبَثَّ مِنْهُمَا رِجَالًا كَثِيرًا وَنِسَاءً وَٱتَّقُوا ٱللَّهَ ٱلَّذِى تَسَاءَلُونَ بِهِۦ وَٱلْأَرْحَامَ إِنَّ ٱللَّهَ كَانَ عَلَيْكُمْ رَقِيبًا (١)

"O Mankind reverence your guardian Lord, Who created you from a single person created, of like nature, His mate, and from them twain scattered (like seeds) countless men and women."

Allah is telling us something about the nature of both male and female. The essence or seed of which Allah (SWT) created humanity, or human beings, has both the male and female potential, like that in the inanimate world of the neutrons and the electrons coming together to produce something that is significant, important, and valuable for the world.

This verse of the Holy Qur'an, the same seed but in a different form, Allah (SWT) has created it in you and me so that human beings can reach their great potential. Surely the properties in the seed may be different in the male and the female; the properties are different, but yet the potential for excellence and greatness in both lies within the seed.

Just like the seed of the tree, everything that the seed is to be is found in that seed. The potential for growth, the leaves, the trunk, the blossoms, and the fruit—everything is there because Allah (SWT) has created it. Allah (SWT) has put the potential there for every human being to achieve its goals. We should not feel that we are incapable of accomplishing something that other human beings were able to accomplish because the seed of greatness is in all of us.

As we conclude and we talk about the pairs in which Allah has created everything in this creation, many of you may have received this e-mail by Dr. Tariq Al Swaidan. He looked in the Holy Qur'an and found something very interesting. He said that the Holy Qur'an mentioned that one thing is equal to another, the number of times that various things appear in the Holy Qur'an still representing a duality of pairs. For example, in the Holy Qur'an, the number of times *man* and *woman* appear is an equal amount of times. Although it makes sense grammatically, the astonishing fact is that the number of times *man* appears in the Holy Qur'an is 24 and *woman* is 24; therefore, not only is this phrase correct in the grammatical sense, but also, it is true mathematically. Upon further analysis, he indicated that throughout the Holy Qur'an, the same idea and concept is consistent. *Dunya* (this world) and *Akhira*, which is the next life, are mentioned 115 times. *Malaka*, or angels, and *Satan* are mentioned both eighty-eight times each. *Life* and *death* are mentioned both 145 times each, and *benefit* and *corrupt* are mentioned fifty times each. *Iblis* and *seeking refuge from Iblis* are mentioned 11 times each. This idea goes on and on. I am not going to try to mention all of them for the sake of closing this Khutbah. But this concept that this person studied in his analysis of pairs and equality of certain words with opposite meanings and how they are paired in a unique way is interesting.

Our Lord! Give us good in this world and good in the next world, and save us from the torment of the fire. Ameen.

بِسْمِ ٱللَّهِ ٱلرَّحْمَٰنِ ٱلرَّحِيمِ

With Allah's name, the merciful Benefactor, the merciful redeemer

May the prayers and the peace be upon Allah's noble and kind messenger, Muhammad.

Restraining Anger

Imam Omar Hazim

"To Allah belongeth the dominion of the heavens and the earth and Allah hath power over all things."

"La illa ha ill Allah" (There is no deity but Allah). This is the bedrock of Islam; it is Islam's foundation and its essence. No just estimate have they made of Allah, for Allah is He who is powerful and able to carry out His will. All that has ever been said or written about Allah's power and might is insufficient; it is but a drop in the ocean.

In chapter 3:133, the Holy Qur'an states,

وَسَارِعُوٓا۟ إِلَىٰ مَغْفِرَةٍ مِّن رَّبِّكُمْ وَجَنَّةٍ عَرْضُهَا ٱلسَّمَٰوَٰتُ وَٱلْأَرْضُ أُعِدَّتْ لِلْمُتَّقِينَ (١٣٣)

"Be quick in the race for forgiveness from your Lord, and for a Garden whose width is that (of the whole) of the heavens and of the earth, prepared for the righteous."

Be quick, don't hesitate, and don't wait. Be quick in the race for forgiveness from your Lord, your cherisher, your sustainer, the one who evolves you and I from our earliest state to our highest state of completion. Be quick in asking for forgiveness from your Lord and for a garden whose width is that of the heavens and the earth.

Who is the garden prepared for? It is prepared for the *muttaqin* (those who have *taqwa*), Allah consciousness and Allah awareness, those who strive to do Allah's (SWT) work. Islam is a call to worship Allah and a call to cultivate the garden of your own soul.

In the call to prayer, it is said come to prayer, come to success. "Hayya Al Salat, Hayya Al-Falah." *Hayya* means life, Allah is *al-Hayyu*, the forever living. Prayer brings us to life. Allah wants us to have the garden He has prepared for us, but we must work and cultivate the garden of our souls first to develop taqwa within.

Falah means to till a thing. It means come to prosperity, come to success; to be successful in this life and in the next, *falah* means to unfold something in order to reveal its intrinsic properties, till and break open the surface of the earth and make its productivity powers active. To work out our own evolution and to bring out what our creator has placed in us (the best).

We know the Prophet was tested by stubborn and the most ignorant people around Him. He and His followers were oppressed and unjustly punished for accepting Islam. The Prophet Muhammad (PBUH) is an example and a sign for human beings who find themselves in the most unfavorable circumstances or hardships. He is an example and a sign that says you must keep to patience, you must keep your human excellence intact, you must preserve the original patterns that Allah (SWT) has created you in. Allah wants us to have this garden, paradise. He gave us Ramadan so that we can gain self-restraint, discipline, control, mastery over our biological appetites.

The Messenger of Allah said,

> If a man gets angry and says: "I seek refuge with Allah," his anger will go away.

> If any of you becomes angry, let him keep silent.

Allah wants us to have taqwa so we can qualify for the garden, paradise. Allah gave us Hajj; take your provisions with you, but the best provision to take is taqwa. Allah gave us garments to wear, but the best garment is taqwa. Allah really wants us to have this garden; He gave us the glorious Holy Qur'an through His messenger to help us.

In chapter 2:1-2, the Holy Qur'an states,

Imam Omar Hazim

الٓمٓ (١) ذَٰلِكَ ٱلْكِتَٰبُ لَا رَيْبَ ۛ فِيهِ ۛ هُدًى لِّلْمُتَّقِينَ (٢)

"Alif Lam Mim. This is the Book; in it is guidance sure, without doubt, to those who fear Allah."

This is the book of guidance and greatness, the book you were asking for in your prayer, Al-fatiha; the book that humanity needs. As you give water to a thirsty person, saying, "Here it is, this is what you need." The book of guidance, the book of knowledge is your water and guide.

Don't be like Iblis, he rebelled against Allah. Iblis said, "I'm not going to submit to him [man], I am better than he. You created me from fire, thou created him from clay." Iblis became angry and lost his mind, he was puffed up with pride and arrogance, and he was the leader of the angels. His anger caused him to become the big Satan or devil.

In chapter 3:134, the Holy Qur'an states,

ٱلَّذِينَ يُنفِقُونَ فِى ٱلسَّرَّآءِ وَٱلضَّرَّآءِ وَٱلْكَٰظِمِينَ ٱلْغَيْظَ وَٱلْعَافِينَ عَنِ ٱلنَّاسِ ۗ وَٱللَّهُ يُحِبُّ ٱلْمُحْسِنِينَ (١٣٤)

"Those who spend (freely), whether in prosperity, or in adversity; who restrain anger, and pardon (all) men; for Allah loves those who do good."

A Hadith relates to us that a man went to the Prophet and asked for advice. The Prophet said to the man "Don't get angry" three times. "No one does anything more excellent in the sight of Allah than restraining his anger. The strong is not the one who overcomes people by the use of their strength; rather he is the one who controls himself in anger," stated the Prophet.

Anger is like a raging fire out of control; it's destructive to the inner and outer self. A raging fire destroys everything in its path. It has no regard for life or property. Fire has no regard for the past, the present, or the future. You can work hard to build your house, your family, life, and your community life, long years of labor with much struggle and sacrifice. If a fire breaks out, you can lose it all. Anger, uncontrolled, is the same way.

The Messenger of Allah said, "If any of you becomes angry and he is standing, let him sit down, so that his anger will go away. If it does not go away, let him lie down."

Al-Imam al-Khattabi said, "One who is standing is in a position to strike and destroy, while the one who is sitting is less likely to do that, and the one who is lying down can do neither. It is possible that the Prophet told the angry person to sit down or lie down so that he would not do something that he would later regret and Allah knows best."

After the call was made to the public when the Prophet announced his mission, his uncle said, "Mayest thou perish, was it for this that thou didst call us for?" He then threw stones at the Prophet. He would follow the Prophet when he went out to preach, saying to the people that the Prophet was a mad relative of his.

"Perish the hands" or "breaking of the hands" means a person failing in his aim and object, which he/she exerted him/herself. He exerted himself to his utmost to defeat Islam, to frustrate the messenger (PBUH), but he failed, as will the opponents of Islam today will fail. His wife used to lay thorns in the Prophet's pathway. She sold her necklace and other jewelry to have the expense to satisfy her enmity, anger, and hatred against the Prophet. One of the richest men of the Quraish died from a fire within his own soul because of anger and envy, consumed with grief. His own children accepted al-Islam.

O, Allah, please help us to restrain our anger. Accept our prayers and grant us paradise. Ameen.

بِسْمِ ٱللَّهِ ٱلرَّحْمَٰنِ ٱلرَّحِيمِ

With Allah's name, the merciful Benefactor, the merciful redeemer

May the prayers and the peace be upon Allah's noble and kind messenger, Muhammad.

Seizing Opportunities

Imam Omar Hazim

In chapter 103, the Holy Qur'an states,

وَٱلْعَصْرِ (١) إِنَّ ٱلْإِنسَٰنَ لَفِى خُسْرٍ (٢) إِلَّا ٱلَّذِينَ ءَامَنُوا۟ وَعَمِلُوا۟ ٱلصَّٰلِحَٰتِ وَتَوَاصَوْا۟ بِٱلْحَقِّ وَتَوَاصَوْا۟ بِٱلصَّبْرِ (٣)

"By the declining day, Lo! man is in a state of loss, save those who believe and do good works, and exhort one another to truth and exhort one another to endurance."

Also the Prophet Muhammad (PBUH) said,

> Seize the opportunity of five things before the occurrence of five things, your youth before your old age, your health before your illness, your wealth before your poverty, your free time before being occupied and your life before your death. The Prophet urges us to take the opportunity to enjoy our youth and wealth. An old proverb says; "It is better to be a living donkey than a dead lion.

Youth before Old Age

The young people should seize the opportunity of their youth while they are strong and healthy in body and mind. Young people should take the opportunity to get a good education. Young people who are morally and spiritually conscious develop a sense of their own self-worth. Helping their children develop a healthy self-esteem is one of the most important things that parents can do for them; it is the foundation of their faith and commitment to Allah.

A healthy feeling about one's self or a high self-esteem is best started in the home, and this needs to be cultivated in our children from birth. When we do this, we help them to seize the best opportunity of their youth, to develop strong moral and spiritual values.

When you are young, strive for the cases you believe in, even your own life career, a plan, a goal, a purpose.

Your Health before Illness

Health is a crown on the heads of healthy people; nobody sees it as clearly as the sick. The Prophet urges us to take care of our health; we only get one physical body. Most of us eat too much and exercise too little. The food we eat keeps us alive, and it also helps to take us away from this life. The Prophet said the worst things that the children of Adam overfeed are their stomachs. He said to fill it one-third with food, one-third with liquid, and leave one-third empty.

A proverb: a good mind is through a good body.

Let us make sure that we protect our health from the pollution of junk food, cigarettes, alcohol, and drugs.

Exercise three to five times a week. When we become ill, we may not be able to use our physical and mental capabilities as much in the service of humanity and Allah. Remember this maxim of wisdom: "An ounce of prevention is better than a pound of medicine."

Your Time before Being Busy

Time can be our best friend or our foe. Time can be used and time can be wasted. No matter what we do, one thing is always happening: time is passing. The way that we should spend our time is in positive ways, the ways that please Allah (SWT). Once time has passed, it can never be regained. Once we have done something, it is in the past. It can never be changed. If we waste our time, that time can never be used again.

There is a time to pray, time to go to school, time to sleep, time for meals, time to seek knowledge—young and old—leisure time with spouses, family, and loved ones, time for masjid, and time for service to others and community life.

The Prophet said,

> An Angel says to the Children of Adam that, "I am a new day so make the best of me for you will not see me again until the Day of Judgment."

Your Wealth before Poverty

In chapter (surah) 3:14, the Holy Qur'an states,

زُيِّنَ لِلنَّاسِ حُبُّ ٱلشَّهَوَاتِ مِنَ ٱلنِّسَاءِ وَٱلْبَنِينَ وَٱلْقَنَاطِيرِ ٱلْمُقَنطَرَةِ مِنَ ٱلذَّهَبِ وَٱلْفِضَّةِ وَٱلْخَيْلِ ٱلْمُسَوَّمَةِ وَٱلْأَنْعَامِ وَٱلْحَرْثِ ۗ ذَٰلِكَ مَتَاعُ ٱلْحَيَوٰةِ ٱلدُّنْيَا ۖ وَٱللَّهُ عِندَهُۥ حُسْنُ ٱلْمَآبِ (١٤)

"Fair in the eyes of men is the love of things they covet: Women and sons; Heaped-up hoards of gold and silver; horses branded (for blood and excellence); and (wealth of) cattle and well-tilled land. Such are the possessions of this world's life; but in nearness to Allah is the best of the goals (to return to)."

We must admit that wealth, money, properties, and affluence are all blessings from Allah, who grants His bounties to whom He pleases. He wants us to use them properly and effectively. He wants us to spend some of this for His love to help others in terms of charity, donations, grants for education, *zakat*, and interest-free loans. Those who spend in His way will be rewarded in this life and the next.

Remember Prophet Sulaiman who was granted the greatest wealth in the history of mankind.

In chapter 38:30, the Holy Qur'an states,

$$وَوَهَبْنَا لِدَاوُۥدَ سُلَيْمَٰنَ ۚ نِعْمَ ٱلْعَبْدُ ۖ إِنَّهُۥ أَوَّابٌ ﴿٣٠﴾$$

"To David We gave Solomon (for a son) - How excellent in Our service! Ever did he turn (to Us)!"

Your Life before Your Death

Allah has made our life sacred. Humans did not create themselves, not even one single cell. Our life is a trust given to us by Allah (SWT) Almighty. We are not allowed to diminish it, let alone to harm or destroy it.

We should not kill ourselves or take our lives. Islam requires Muslims to be resolute in facing hardships. We are not permitted to give up and run away from life's tragedies. We must always have hope and faith. Our mind is our spiritual estate; don't be careless with your thoughts. We progress by the power of thought.

We pray for Allah's forgiveness and guidance. Ameen.

بِسْمِ ٱللَّهِ ٱلرَّحْمَٰنِ ٱلرَّحِيمِ

With Allah's name, the merciful Benefactor, the merciful redeemer

May the prayers and the peace be upon Allah's noble and kind messenger, Muhammad.

Transforming Spiritual Growth into What Is Practical

Sermon by Imam Hanif Khalil

Edited online by Khalil Green

On Friday, March 19, 2010, Imam Hanif Khalil delivered the Friday sermon at the Islamic Center of Topeka. His captivating sermon about transforming spiritual growth into community action was delivered to a large crowd of Muslims and guests.

After supplications, Imam Khalil began by reminding those in attendance that Allah (God) gave something from Himself to humanity called *ruh* (Spirit from God). He gave it to humanity while they were still in the womb of their mothers.

This ruh, continued Imam Khalil, distinguishes human beings from other created things. This distinguishing characteristic is called a soul (*nafs*). Through each individual's spiritual journey, the soul seeks the satisfaction of its Lord. It will not be satisfied until it reaches the level that God has commanded it to attain. It will remain uneasy until it finds tranquility (*sakina*).

Imam Khalil stated that the soul seeks its satisfaction in community. It starts by looking for fulfillment in its mate, seeking sakina (tranquility). It seeks within its mate a God-fearing quality that creates peace and understanding between the two souls who have made a commitment to travel on their spiritual journey together. Thus begins the basis for community.

Progression began in the garden, said Imam Khalil, with the blessing that everything in it was a favor to humanity. However, honor (*karima*) above all was given to mankind. "We have honored the sons of Adam; provided them with transport on land and sea" (Holy Qur'an, 17:70).

This honor was given to humanity so they could seek their bounty, on land and sea, for the purposes of meeting other people and engaging in commerce. Thus, man must transverse the waters in order to establish himself and his community in the land.

As spiritual beings housed in material bodies, Muslims turn to their Lord five times a day in prayer, asking God to "show us the straight way" (Holy Qur'an, 1:6).

The answer and promise from God that the Muslim will receive this favor from Him is found in the last verse He sent to Prophet Muhammad (PBUH), which states,

حُرِّمَتْ عَلَيْكُمُ ٱلْمَيْتَةُ وَٱلدَّمُ وَلَحْمُ ٱلْخِنزِيرِ وَمَا أُهِلَّ لِغَيْرِ ٱللَّهِ بِهِۦ وَٱلْمُنْخَنِقَةُ وَٱلْمَوْقُوذَةُ وَٱلْمُتَرَدِّيَةُ وَٱلنَّطِيحَةُ وَمَا أَكَلَ ٱلسَّبُعُ إِلَّا مَا ذَكَّيْتُمْ وَمَا ذُبِحَ عَلَى ٱلنُّصُبِ وَأَن تَسْتَقْسِمُوا۟ بِٱلْأَزْلَـٰمِ ذَٰلِكُمْ فِسْقٌ ٱلْيَوْمَ يَئِسَ ٱلَّذِينَ كَفَرُوا۟ مِن دِينِكُمْ فَلَا تَخْشَوْهُمْ وَٱخْشَوْنِ ٱلْيَوْمَ أَكْمَلْتُ لَكُمْ دِينَكُمْ وَأَتْمَمْتُ عَلَيْكُمْ نِعْمَتِى وَرَضِيتُ لَكُمُ ٱلْإِسْلَـٰمَ دِينًا فَمَنِ ٱضْطُرَّ فِى مَخْمَصَةٍ غَيْرَ مُتَجَانِفٍ لِّإِثْمٍ فَإِنَّ ٱللَّهَ غَفُورٌ رَّحِيمٌ (٣)

"This day have I perfected your religion for you, completed My favor upon you, and have chosen for you Islam as your religion." (Holy Qur'an, 5:3)

Thus, the bases for good community are families living in tranquility and God-consciousness (taqwa). In such a community, schools hospitals and an overall healthy lifestyle are promoted.

Toward the conclusion of his discussion, Imam Khalil informed the Topeka community about a man from Yemen who ordered a jihad—erroneously translated as Holy War, actually it means *struggle*—against America.

Imam Khalil stated during Friday service that this call is a false one and should not be heeded. He cautioned all Muslims to study their religion from the Holy Qur'an and avoid all violent actions.

He further stated that the principles laid down by America are good ones, and said, "We hold these truths to be self-evident, that all men are created equal, that they are endowed by their Creator with certain unalienable Rights, that among these are Life, Liberty and the pursuit of Happiness."

Commenting later, Imam Omar Hazim stated that all acts of violence and terrorism are rejected and Muslims should stand up in defiance to the terrorist and hate mongers.

بِسْمِ ٱللَّهِ ٱلرَّحْمَٰنِ ٱلرَّحِيمِ

With Allah's name, the merciful Benefactor, the merciful redeemer

May the prayers and the peace be upon Allah's noble and kind messenger, Muhammad.

The Cycle of Good Deeds

Imam Omar Hazim

مَّن ذَا ٱلَّذِي يُقْرِضُ ٱللَّهَ قَرْضًا حَسَنًا فَيُضَٰعِفَهُ لَهُ أَضْعَافًا كَثِيرَةً وَٱللَّهُ يَقْبِضُ وَيَبْصُۜطُ وَإِلَيْهِ تُرْجَعُونَ (٢٤٥)

"Who is he that will loan to Allah (SWT) a beautiful loan which Allah will amply repay and multiply many times? It is Allah (SWT) that giveth want or plenty, and to Him shall be your return."

Spending in the cause of Allah (SWT) is called, metaphorically, a beautiful loan. It shows a beautiful spirit of self-denial and helping others, humanity at large. *Cycle* is defined as a series of recurring events or phenomena—the cycle of the seasons, an orbit of the heavens or planets.

A period of time occupied by a set of events which will go on recurring in similar periods of time, an ordered series of phenomena in which some process is completed. Chemistry and physics are any series of changes that restore a system to its original state, such as a ring, wheel, and an alternating electric current.

The Water Cycle

The water is drawn up from the earth in a fine mist that the eye cannot always see. It is drawn up by the moon and the sun's attracting power over the water. Once it reaches a certain height and weight, then it returns back to the earth in the form of rain, snow, or sleet and brings great benefits to the earth and all its creatures. Good works also recycle and return in beneficial ways for the doer of good.

In the Holy Qur'an 55:60, Allah says,

$$\text{هَلْ جَزَاءُ ٱلْإِحْسَٰنِ إِلَّا ٱلْإِحْسَٰنُ (٦٠)}$$

"Is there any reward for doing good other than good?"

This is a very short but powerful verse in the Holy Qur'an that expresses a great phenomenon of equity and more. The return of goodness for goodness, the return of service to Allah (SWT) and humanity increases in the status of bounties. This effect is in accord with Allah's laws in nature; if you plant a seed in the ground, much more than you plant will return to you.

Allah has written down the good deeds and the bad deeds. A hadith from the Prophet states,

> He who has intended a good deed and has not done it, Allah writes it down as a full good deed. If he/she has intended it and has done it, Allah writes it down out of His mercy as 10 to 100 times or more as good deeds. If one intends a bad deed and does not do it, it is recorded as a good deed. If one intends a bad deed and carries it out it is written as one bad deed.

Good deeds and actions will benefit the doer of the deed as much or more than the receiver. Our good deeds will help us enter the paradise along with Allah's forgiveness and mercy.

Good deeds help return us to the best nature in which we were created. The Holy Qur'an encourages us to spend in Allah's (SWT) way for the benefit of mankind. The best motive for or the best kind of spending in Allah's (SWT) way should be to help others stand on their own feet, not to keep them permanently in the beggar's seat. Indeed, to help another person in a way which makes him to look for help all the time is inherently ill motivated. Give a man a fish; you feed him for a day. Teach him how to fish, and you feed him for a lifetime (Confucius).

The Prophet said, three things will continue to benefit man after his death:

1. A useful knowledge
2. A perpetual charity
3. The prayer of a righteous child

The Prophet further stated that three things follow the dead person to the grave, two return, and one remains with him: his wealth, his loved ones, and his deeds. There is absolutely nothing from the life of this world that endures and lasts beyond death except good or bad deeds, not your fame, fortune, or wealth.

I am reminded of the story told by H. Jackson Brown Jr.:

Decades ago in Scotland, a young boy cried for help, "Someone please help me." A poor Scottish farmer heard the cry and ran to help. He found a boy sinking in thick black mud. The poor farmer saved the boy. Later, the poor farmer was visited by a wealthy gentleman in a stately carriage. He said, "You saved my son yesterday, and I am here to reward you." The poor farmer would not accept any of the money offered to him. The gentleman wanted to give a gift of gratitude to the man. The wealthy man saw a boy in the house and said, "Since you helped my son, I will help yours. I will see that your son will receive the finest education available in the country."

Later, the farmer's son graduated from St. Mary's Hospital Medical School of London. The poor farmer's son in turn gave a gift to the world. He discovered penicillin. His name was Alexander Fleming. The wealthy man's son's life would be threatened for a second time. Now grown, he lay dying of pneumonia. It was the poor farmer's son who saved him this time when penicillin was prescribed. The wealthy man, Randolph Churchill, provided for the education of Alexander Fleming. That education saved his son, Sir Winston Churchill.

We pray for Allah's forgiveness and guidance. Ameen.

بِسْمِ ٱللَّهِ ٱلرَّحْمَٰنِ ٱلرَّحِيمِ

With Allah's name, the merciful Benefactor, the merciful redeemer

May the prayers and the peace be upon Allah's noble and kind messenger, Muhammad.

The Future is Bright for Muslims in America

Imam Omar Hazim

Edited online by Khalil Green

This past Friday, Imam Omar Hazim delivered the Morning Eid Prayer. The Morning Eid Prayer is performed by the Muslims that don't go on pilgrimage to Mecca. The title of the sermon delivered by Omar was "The Future Is Bright for Muslims in America."

Imam Omar mentioned how the pilgrims were finishing up their pilgrimage to Mecca on Friday. He stated that they were busy with completing the rituals, such as sacrificing an animal. However, as Imam Omar points out, the Holy Qur'an states that "it's not the meat or blood that reaches Allah, but the piety of the worshipper." This lets the Muslim know, as did the sacrifice of Abraham's first son, that Allah (SWT) cares nothing about blood sacrifice. He merely wants us to perform a spiritual sacrifice and complete our religious development.

Omar further stated that human and animal sacrifice is irrelevant because life is sacred to the Muslims, as is stated in the Holy Qur'an, "If a person kills someone it's as if they have killed the entire human race." Thus, abortion is an ongoing problem in today's society as women of all ages opt to end the life of an unborn child simply due to inconvenience. However, Islam does not negate the necessity for such an act in cases where the women's life is in jeopardy.

Life to the Muslim begins at conception, not birth. The crime of murder is thus twofold: ending the life of something that has done no harm and by killing something Allah (SWT) has given life to.

Imam Omar continued that according to the sayings of Prophet Muhammad (PBUH), Muhammad was asked by the Angel Gabriel what will the signs of the end of days be. Prophet Muhammad (PBUH) responded that the sun will rise from the west instead of the east.

Imam Omar stated that this means that Islam, which once prospered in the east, will begin anew in the west. Today it can be seen that many Muslims have travelled from the east to the west in search of higher education and a better, more peaceful life. The light of Islam is thus rising in the west.

Now today, Muslims are thriving in the west as civil servants, businessmen and businesswomen, and health-care professionals. With the spiritual life, these individuals bring with them and the Muslims sprung from western soil, Imam Omar believes that, the future is indeed bright for Islam and the western society.

May Allah guide us and accept our prayers. Ameen.

بِسْمِ ٱللَّهِ ٱلرَّحْمَٰنِ ٱلرَّحِيمِ

With Allah's name, the merciful Benefactor, the merciful redeemer

May the prayers and the peace be upon Allah's noble and kind messenger, Muhammad.

The Caretaker of Allah's Earth

Imam Omar Hazim

Allah is Allah in the heavens and in the earth, He is just and true, there is no weakness or unrighteousness in Him. He is free from every flaw. He never sleeps nor does He slumber, time has no effect on Him. He separates the night from the day and the day from the night, He does not age, He is the Creator of space and time. He brings to birth but is not born, He causes death, yet he does not die. He has no need for anything, yet everything needs Him. He is the Ever-Living, the source of life, self-subsistent, the Eternal, forever standing.

Khalifa means people reproducing generation after generation, century after century to come from behind.

Khalif means succession in time, place, or degree or status. The night succeeds the day; one succeeds the other in ownership of something in office or in authority or status. The root letters and forms have been used in the Holy Qur'an 127 times. The three basic letters are *K* (kaf), *L* (lam), *F* (fah). From these roots come many words like a tree with roots, trunk, branches, fruit, leaves, etc. They are connected in some way. Khalifa—caretaker, supreme chief, successor, ruler, children of Adam, the whole of mankind, to come from behind, alternate-replace representative by Allah (SWT)'s permission, vicegerents, agent, ambassador-position of authority.

Bashara-Bishr means significant news. A joyful continence, good news, stupendous news, fine-looking appearance, the outer and visible part of the skin. *Mubashashir*—one who announces good news. The Prophet said, "I am a mortal just like you."

Allah said to the Angels:

> Behold I will create a Khalifa on Earth." As an open declaration of Allah (SWT)'s independent will and decision. Khalifa signifies that earlier a species other than mankind had the upper hand or rule ship on earth. Then Allah decided to supercede them with human beings. The response of the angels makes it clear that the species before man had created much corruption and disorder.

The Holy Qur'an, chapter 15:27 states,

$$\text{وَٱلْجَانَّ خَلَقْنَٰهُ مِن قَبْلُ مِن نَّارِ ٱلسَّمُومِ (٢٧)}$$

"And the jinn did We create aforetime of essential fire."

This suggests that before man was created, the jinn inhabited the earth.

They the Angels said in chapter (surah) 2:30:

> Will you make a successor on Earth who will create corruption and who will shed blood? Allah said: "I know what you know not."

Please note this, brothers and sisters: while angels do not commit sin, they may make mistakes. Everyone besides Allah has shortcomings. Only Allah is free of all imperfections, every one other than Allah is liable to error. What the angels said may have been induced from an earlier observation. But they made a hasty judgment with incomplete knowledge. They lacked knowledge about the potential of the khalifah (man).

In chapter (surah) 2:31, Allah (SWT) speaks to Adam and says,

> "O Adam tell them their names."

Adam was an intellectual type. He and his mate, Eve, were not only to produce children and populate the earth; they were to build a world, a society of moral and intellectual advancements.

In chapter (surah) 2:32, the angels say,

$$\text{قَالُوا۟ سُبْحَٰنَكَ لَا عِلْمَ لَنَا إِلَّا مَا عَلَّمْتَنَا إِنَّكَ أَنتَ ٱلْعَلِيمُ ٱلْحَكِيمُ (٣٢)}$$

Imam Omar Hazim

Glory to Thee of knowledge, we have none save what Thou have taught us.

Their mistake was what they knew of the past and, from this perspective of their observations of the jinn and other creatures, assumed they knew what man would do. They looked at the dark side of humanity.

In chapter (surah) 3:190, the Holy Qur'an states,

إِنَّ فِى خَلْقِ ٱلسَّمَٰوَٰتِ وَٱلْأَرْضِ وَٱخْتِلَٰفِ ٱلَّيْلِ وَٱلنَّهَارِ لَءَايَٰتٍ لِّأُو۟لِى ٱلْأَلْبَٰبِ (١٩٠)

Behold! In the creation of the heavens and the earth, and the alteration of night and day, there are indeed signs for men of understanding.

This alternation, this rotation, is as natural as the creation itself. The khalifah is as connected to the creation as is the changing of the night and the day is to the changing of the seasons. Allah gives it to us like in this verse to let us know that we, the khalifah, will come from behind one another. We will alternate like the night and the day.

The prophets, the greatest khalifahs that ever walked the earth, came one behind the other from Adam to Muhammad in succession, in rotation, and alternation.

In chapter (surah) 38:71, the Holy Qur'an states,

إِذْ قَالَ رَبُّكَ لِلْمَلَٰٓئِكَةِ إِنِّى خَٰلِقٌۢ بَشَرًا مِّن طِينٍ (٧١)

"Behold thy Lord, said to the angels I am about to create man from clay."

The Prophet said, "We all come from Adam and he from Clay!" We are walking, talking earth, moving earth upon the earth. The khalifah is in the clay that walks the walking, talking earth in you and me.

The khalifa is a mind-set, Allah-given faculties like knowledge, will, discretion, understanding, reasoning, judgment, love, compassion, ability to know right from wrong, repenting ability, remorsefulness. The khalifa is put on the earth to establish the best moral and spiritual life to build an ideal society based on Allah's (SWT) law for the benefit of all people.

May Allah guide us and accept our prayers. Ameen.

$$\text{بِسْمِ اللهِ الرَّحْمَٰنِ الرَّحِيمِ}$$

With Allah's name, the merciful Benefactor, the merciful redeemer

May the prayers and the peace be upon Allah's noble and kind messenger, Muhammad.

The Parable of a Good Word

Imam Omar Hazim

The Holy Qur'an states in chapter (surah) 33:70 that

$$\text{يَٰٓأَيُّهَا ٱلَّذِينَ ءَامَنُوا۟ ٱتَّقُوا۟ ٱللَّهَ وَقُولُوا۟ قَوْلًا سَدِيدًا (٧٠)}$$

"O Ye who believe, fear Allah, and always say a word directed to the right."

We should speak in a straightforward manner, with no crookedness or distortion. Allah promises those who do that, He will reward them by making their deeds righteous and forgiving them their past sins. We all depend on the proper use of words to convey our thoughts and feelings to one another.

We, as Muslims, must understand the power of words, and we must harness that power in order to serve our wider responsibilities. Words are the means by which we can study history, and words are the means in which we can leave a legacy for the future. Words can be weapons; words can wound, humiliate, and inflict pain far greater than physical violence. Words can be used to inflame passions, arouse anger, to declare war, and to destroy.

Also, words can heal wounds and relationships. They can bring happiness and peace to humanity. The Prophet said if you can't say a good word, then you should remain silent.

Martin Luther King said, "Injustice anywhere in the world is a threat to justice everywhere in the world."

The fortieth year after Dr. Martin Luther King Jr.'s assassination, we found out that in the late '50s and early '60s that J. Edgar Hoover of the FBI wiretapped his phones, and he stated that Martin Luther King was the most dangerous man in America. Martin Luther King stated that the greatest war criminals in the world are in the United States of America. These were powerful words used as devices that kept blacks and whites apart.

The racism of the white church led to the black church's birth. The Black Liberation theology in America was created because of the racism in the white church but also in that same time period of violence (racial). Words have always influenced people in a positive or negative way; dear Muslims, let us be a force for the positive in this world.

Many African Americans, myself included, heard the words "The earth belongs to Allah; there is no Allah but Allah. You are a free man in this city."

The Holy Qur'an states in 14:24-25 that

أَلَمْ تَرَ كَيْفَ ضَرَبَ ٱللَّهُ مَثَلًا كَلِمَةً طَيِّبَةً كَشَجَرَةٍ طَيِّبَةٍ أَصْلُهَا ثَابِتٌ وَفَرْعُهَا فِى ٱلسَّمَآءِ (٢٤) تُؤْتِىٓ أُكُلَهَا كُلَّ حِينٍۭ بِإِذْنِ رَبِّهَا ۗ وَيَضْرِبُ ٱللَّهُ ٱلْأَمْثَالَ لِلنَّاسِ لَعَلَّهُمْ يَتَذَكَّرُونَ (٢٥)

"Seest thou not how Allah sets forth a parable? A goodly Word like a goodly tree, whose root is firmly fixed, And its branches (reach) to the heavens. It brings forth its fruit, at all times, by the leave of its Lord. So Allah sets forth parables for men, in order that they may receive admonition.

It is through the tree, the oldest living thing on earth, that Allah has given us many signs to study that we may learn about the oldest institution on earth, the family.

The Family Tree

The tree is a symbol of society and speaks to the development of society. The society feeds from the earth for its material development like the tree gets water out of the earth to feed its body.

The roots of the tree go deep in the earth to support itself and receive water. The water goes up through the body of the tree and feeds the branches and the leaves. At the very top of the tree, there is also a kind of feeding taking place. The leaves also feed on sunlight and carbon dioxide and produce oxygen, like the human beings feed on oxygen and produce carbon dioxide. The tree gets its life from the material body and the heavenly body.

A Good Picture of the Human Society

Some people only feed themselves from the ground, the materialist. Some feed from both the ground and from the higher moral values, from the light of truth, from the light of Allah (SWT), and from righteousness (the sun).

The good word is testifying there is no Allah but Allah! The good tree, whose root is firmly fixed, is the firm and unshakeable faith in the heart of the believer.

And its branches reach to the sky—the believers' works are ascended to heaven. Good deeds—good statements and actions.

The Prophet said, Three will continue to benefit man after his death: A useful knowledge, a perpetual charity, and the prayer of a righteous child.

Giving its fruit at all times by day and night, a tree that always has fruits, summer, winter, spring and fall.

Words can heal wounds and make peace, words can be soothing to those in grief, words can offer hope to those in despair, and words have a power and a beauty that can project well beyond a lifetime. Who can forget when Umar, the second khalifah, first heard the words of al-Holy Qur'an (Allah's word)? He had just been told his sister had joined the Muslims. He went to her house with his sword in hand. As he passed her open window, he heard the words of Allah being recited. These words carried such a powerful, persuasive beauty that it stopped an angry and aggressive man in his tracks and melted his heart.

May Allah have mercy on us all and give us guidance. Ameen.

بِسْمِ ٱللَّهِ ٱلرَّحْمَٰنِ ٱلرَّحِيمِ

With Allah's name, the merciful Benefactor, the merciful redeemer

May the prayers and the peace be upon Allah's noble and kind messenger, Muhammad.

The Verse of Light

Khalil Green

The verse of light has many symbolic features, utilizing a lamp and what lights the lamp as its major features of a metaphor designed as a focus for contemplation.

The verse of light found within the pages of the Holy Qur'an has sparked many narrations over the last 1,400 years. Mystics, philosophers, and the most mundane of narrators have written volumes about this one particular verse found in the pages of the Holy Qur'an.

The verse of light (ayat an-nur) states in the Holy Qur'an 24:35,

ٱللَّهُ نُورُ ٱلسَّمَٰوَٰتِ وَٱلْأَرْضِ ۚ مَثَلُ نُورِهِۦ كَمِشْكَوٰةٍ فِيهَا مِصْبَاحٌ ۖ ٱلْمِصْبَاحُ فِى زُجَاجَةٍ ۖ ٱلزُّجَاجَةُ كَأَنَّهَا كَوْكَبٌ دُرِّىٌّ يُوقَدُ مِن شَجَرَةٍ مُّبَٰرَكَةٍ زَيْتُونَةٍ لَّا شَرْقِيَّةٍ وَلَا غَرْبِيَّةٍ يَكَادُ زَيْتُهَا يُضِىٓءُ وَلَوْ لَمْ تَمْسَسْهُ نَارٌ ۚ نُّورٌ عَلَىٰ نُورٍ ۗ يَهْدِى ٱللَّهُ لِنُورِهِۦ مَن يَشَآءُ ۚ وَيَضْرِبُ ٱللَّهُ ٱلْأَمْثَٰلَ لِلنَّاسِ ۗ وَٱللَّهُ بِكُلِّ شَىْءٍ عَلِيمٌ (٣٥)

"Allah is the Light of the heavens and the earth. The Parable of His Light is as if there were a Niche and within it a Lamp: the Lamp enclosed in Glass: the glass as it were a brilliant star: Lit from a blessed Tree, an Olive, neither of the east nor of the west, whose oil is well-nigh luminous, though fire scarce touched it: Light upon Light! Allah doth guide whom He will to His Light: Allah doth set forth Parables for men: and Allah doth know all things."

The lamp

Within the crude matter of a niche sits a beautiful lamp. Lamps are a combination of various materials from the earth, which are brought together to produce the ability to carry fire for the purpose of lighting an area, a room, or the way. To carry the metaphor further, the fire is lit in such a way as to light an entire room to produce little or no areas of darkness. This lighting allows that which was in darkness to now be revealed. The glass of the lamp is polished to allow for the best transmission of the light to flow and reveal.

The Tree

The tree has been used in many spiritual circles as a symbol of peace and growth. There was one at the center of the Garden from which Adam was to draw his substance. Other traditions use the palm branch in religious ceremonies. There are even flags carried by different countries with a tree as its centerpiece. In the Kabbalah, the symbol of spiritual progression resembles a tree. Here in the Holy Qur'an, it represents the potential for feeding that which is involved with the development of positive qualities. Thus, the oil from the tree to light the lamp is of a pure source without any deficiency. Not degraded by poor soil or uneven sunlight, created in the best possible manner.

The Fire

The fire is the source of the light that is lit from oil so pure that it glows before the flame touches it. Thus, the fire cannot claim that it is the source from which the light springs. But it is in itself a tool used for the transmission of the light.

The lesson

There are many lessons taught from the parable of the lamp. As such the source of all true light comes from the Divine. No one or thing within the confines of creation can claim that he or she is the discoverer of truth and understanding. The light is simply reflected through sources that have been polished to transmit the light as clear as possible to anyone desiring a release from the darkness of their own lower self.

Imam Omar Hazim

Thus, the light flows from its source, Allah, through His angel Jibreel and into Prophet Muhammad (PBUH). As such, Prophet Muhammad (PBUH) is the polished source from which we receive our religion. The message is finished and completed in our holy book, the Holy Qur'an. In it does the believer find all the clarity needed for faith, belief, and spiritual growth.

May Allah have mercy on us all and give us guidance. Ameen.

$$\text{بِسْمِ ٱللَّهِ ٱلرَّحْمَٰنِ ٱلرَّحِيمِ}$$

With Allah's name, the merciful Benefactor, the merciful redeemer

May the prayers and the peace be upon Allah's noble and kind messenger, Muhammad.

Social Connections

Sermon by Imam Omar Hazim

In chapter (surah) 16, verses 68-69, Allah revealed the chapter on "The Bee" to tell the Prophet, even after all his hardships in Mecca, "you will be successful in your mission. Success and failure are related to the habits we form. You will be of great benefit to humanity, all humanity."

In-Sanna, basically meaning human being, is used by Allah to address us in the Holy Qur'an. Its root, *inisa*, includes woman and man—humanity—to be companionable, sociable, nice, and friendly, man, Homo sapiens with a highly developed brain.

The Prophet said, "I am a mortal like you." Basher—mortal, also good news.

We are further told in the Holy Qur'an that all creatures have communities like you.

In this chapter, Allah shows his signs in the rain-bringing cloud, the cattle that gives milk, the bee that produces honey, the wonderful relations of family and social life.

The Holy Qur'an in chapter 16, verse 68 states,

$$\text{وَأَوْحَىٰ رَبُّكَ إِلَى ٱلنَّحْلِ أَنِ ٱتَّخِذِى مِنَ ٱلْجِبَالِ بُيُوتًا وَمِنَ ٱلشَّجَرِ وَمِمَّا يَعْرِشُونَ (٦٨)}$$

"And thy Lord taught the bee to build its cells in hills, on trees, and in men's habitations."

The Holy Qur'an in chapter 16, verse 69 states,

ثُمَّ كُلِى مِن كُلِّ ٱلثَّمَرَٰتِ فَٱسْلُكِى سُبُلَ رَبِّكِ ذُلُلًا ۚ يَخْرُجُ مِنۢ بُطُونِهَا شَرَابٌ مُّخْتَلِفٌ أَلْوَٰنُهُۥ فِيهِ شِفَآءٌ لِّلنَّاسِ ۗ إِنَّ فِى ذَٰلِكَ لَءَايَةً لِّقَوْمٍ يَتَفَكَّرُونَ (٦٩)

"Then to eat of all the produce (of the earth) and find with skill the spacious paths of its Lord, there issues from within their bodies a drink of varying colors, wherein is healing for man. Verily in this is a sign for those who give thought."

Allah created it, inspired it, caused something to come from it that is a healing, a cure for humanity.

Shi-fi-oon means to make better, to heal, to improve upon, and to cure. We know about the value of the honey. We are not talking about the honey today; maybe next week or another time we will talk about the honey. It is more than just a physical healing. Today we are talking about the social connections. It is a sign for those who think and reflect. What are some of the qualities of honey and bees? Naturally sweet, loved ones-sweet, it adheres—sticky, clings—attaches, bees stay close together, a strong community life, connections, family and community closeness.

Social Affections

Consider tender feelings, friendly feelings of attachment, the aspect of consciousness manifested in feeling and emotions. A phone call—an illness or disease is often helped with just a show of concern. A person may be depressed or feeling bad, sometimes just needing someone to talk to.

The Prophet said, "Visit the sick, feed the hungry and release the captive." The rights of a Muslim over another are five:

1. Answering the greeting
2. Visiting the sick
3. Going to the funeral
4. Accepting the invitation
5. Blessing for the sneezers

The Bee Dance

A fascinating behavior in animal life: if the food source is sixty degrees to the left of the sun, the waggle run will be sixty degrees to the left or vertical in the hive. There are different locations in the hive for closeness and distance. As the bee is industrious and productive, it is in us, all humans, to be productive. Much of the advancement of this country is from Islamic teaching and the Holy Qur'an.

The founders of this country were Freemasons. A secret order of thirty-three-degree Shriners and third-degree masons. The writers of the Declaration of Independence, they studied the Bible, Torah, and Holy Qur'an. Listen to this language.

As quoted by Imam Mustafa al-Amin:

> The beehive is an emblem of industry and recommends the practice of this virtue of being industrious to all created beings from the highest angels in heaven to the lowest reptile of the dust. It teaches us that we come into the world naturally, rational and intelligent beings, so should we be ever industrious ones, never sitting down contented while our fellow creatures around us are in need or want, when it is in our power to relieve them without inconvenience to ourselves. This is Holy Qur'an, they studied it!

This knowledge from Allah is what has driven them, and what drives many of them today. It is divine knowledge to be industrious and productive, and to establish social connections. It would be illogical to think that the masons did not look at this in the Holy Qur'an before they made the bee and beehive their emblem.

The Holy Qur'an in chapter 17:82 states,

وَنُنَزِّلُ مِنَ ٱلْقُرْآنِ مَا هُوَ شِفَاءٌ وَرَحْمَةٌ لِّلْمُؤْمِنِينَ وَلَا يَزِيدُ ٱلظَّالِمِينَ إِلَّا خَسَارًا (٨٢)

"We send down in the Holy Qur'an that which is a healing and a mercy to those who believe."

The Philosophy of Service

If one removes a hardship of a believer in this life, Allah (SWT) will relieve a hardship from him or her on the Day of Judgment. Charity is prescribed for every person every day the sun rises.

Patience

The patient person will be paid back their reward in full without measure. As the Holy Qur'an states in 39:10;

قُلْ يَٰعِبَادِ ٱلَّذِينَ ءَامَنُوا۟ ٱتَّقُوا۟ رَبَّكُمْ لِلَّذِينَ أَحْسَنُوا۟ فِى هَٰذِهِ ٱلدُّنْيَا حَسَنَةٌ وَأَرْضُ ٱللَّهِ وَٰسِعَةٌ إِنَّمَا يُوَفَّى ٱلصَّٰبِرُونَ أَجْرَهُم بِغَيْرِ حِسَابٍ (١٠)

"Say: O My bondmen who believe! Observe your duty to your Lord. For those who do good in this world there is good, and Allah's earth is spacious. Verily the steadfast will be paid their wages without stint."

The disabled should be cared for and respected. This is a test for society.

May Allah help us to be productive in this life and bless us with the best in the next life. Ameen.

بِسْمِ ٱللَّهِ ٱلرَّحْمَٰنِ ٱلرَّحِيمِ

With Allah's name, the merciful Benefactor, the merciful redeemer

May the prayers and the peace be upon Allah's noble and kind messenger, Muhammad.

Chapter (Surah) Najm—The Star—Chapter 53 in the Holy Qur'an

Sermon by Imam Omar Hazim

Edited online by Khalil Green

On Friday, March 26, 2010, Imam Omar Hazim spoke at the Islamic Center of Topeka during the Friday jumuah service. Imam Omar gave a charismatic speech during the Friday service.

Omar spoke on the chapter (surah) called the Star (al-Najm), which is the fifty-third chapter of the Holy Qur'an.

Omar began with supplications by saying, "All praises are due to Allah, and we seek his aid and crave his forgiveness. To Allah belongs the dominion of the heavens and the earth and to Him is all power. Allah states that no just estimate have they made of Him; for Allah is he who is powerful and able to carry out His will. God but says, 'Be,' and it is."

Omar states that there are two powerful books: one is the revelation from God (Holy Qur'an and previous scriptures) and the other is the Book of Creation (the created world). God created the heavens and the earth, states Imam Omar, for the purpose of serving or stimulating the intellect of humanity. That is why all through the Holy Qur'an, God draws mankind's attention to creation. It has been made subjected to humanity according to the Holy Qur'an.

The sun, moon, and earth become servants to man by God's command; thus, do they yield of their utilities for humanity, continued Omar.

The stars also, which are far away, are also under this subjugation. They are far away and generate no heat energy like the sun. They are too far away for such a purpose, but they help the traveler at night, who uses them for navigation.

We know that stars don't have human desires, stated Omar, but humans who fail to rise above their selfish desires fall like stars. So our attention is drawn to the metaphor of the star to show that the worst of people can appear like stars. In the time of Prophet Muhammad (PBUH) as well as today, such people are driven by selfish motives and ignorance but soon become destitute in spirit.

There are stars on the flags of many countries. The American flag has many stars. Some Muslim countries have stars on their flags also. Sports figures and movie personalities are also known as stars. The Pharaohs in Egypt thought they were the only true stars and all should worship them.

Yet stars set and go down, especially those without a good moral foundation. As Imam Omar further quoted from the Holy Qur'an,

وَٱلنَّجْمِ إِذَا هَوَىٰ (١) مَا ضَلَّ صَاحِبُكُمْ وَمَا غَوَىٰ (٢) وَمَا يَنطِقُ عَنِ ٱلْهَوَىٰ (٣)

By the Star when it goes down,-
Your Companion is neither astray nor being misled.
Nor does he say (aught) of (his own) Desire. (Holy Qur'an, 53:1-3)

God in this particular verse swears by the star that Muhammad is not in the category of the destitute of spirit.

The Muslims present at Jumuah were warned by Omar not to be among those in the fallen star category. Muslims should pray; "truly my prayer, my service, my sacrifice, my life, and death are all for Allah the Lord of all the worlds, the Lord of all systems of knowledge," stated Omar.

Prophet Muhammad (PBUH) was a companion to mankind and a citizen of Mecca. The Meccans knew him as truthful and trustworthy. So truthful and dependable was Prophet Muhammad (PBUH) that before he became the Messenger of Allah, he was known as al-Amin (the trustworthy) by his people, the Meccans. The Meccans would even leave their valuables with al-Amin when they went on journeys.

However, most of them turned their backs on him when he brought them revelation from God. They disbelieved, but God chose Prophet Muhammad (PBUH) to be His Messenger nevertheless.

Prophet Muhammad (PBUH) spoke only what God gave him to say. It is well known that Muhammad had no desire to become a leader, continued Omar. His goals were simply to promote the good of humanity. Thus, Prophet Muhammad (PBUH) remains humanity's unwavering star.

The Holy Qur'an delivered remains in the same form, with the same wording as was given to man from God through Prophet Muhammad (PBUH). It continues to guide humanity to all that is true and trustworthy.

"Our Lord! Let not our hearts deviate now after you have guided us on the right path, but grant us mercy from Your own Presence, for you are the grantor of bounties without measure." Ameen.

بِسْمِ اللهِ الرَّحْمَٰنِ الرَّحِيمِ

With Allah's name, the merciful Benefactor, the merciful redeemer

May the prayers and the peace be upon Allah's noble and kind messenger, Muhammad.

Stages of Human Development: Part I

Sermon by Imam Omar Hazim

Edited online by Khalil Green

On Friday, February 19, 2010, Imam Omar Hazim delivered the Friday sermon titled "Stages of Human Development: Part I."

His speech was very inspirational and full of information for those who seek knowledge of the Holy Qur'an's verse that describes the process of fetal development.

Chapter 23, verses 12-16 of the Holy Qur'an contains a powerful description of fetal development for a book over 1,400 years old. A book given to humanity during a time when there were no microscopes to verify such statements. Yet the Holy Qur'an gets it right!

It states,

وَلَقَدْ خَلَقْنَا ٱلْإِنسَٰنَ مِن سُلَٰلَةٍ مِّن طِينٍ (١٢) ثُمَّ جَعَلْنَٰهُ نُطْفَةً فِى قَرَارٍ مَّكِينٍ (١٣) ثُمَّ خَلَقْنَا ٱلنُّطْفَةَ عَلَقَةً فَخَلَقْنَا ٱلْعَلَقَةَ مُضْغَةً فَخَلَقْنَا ٱلْمُضْغَةَ عِظَٰمًا فَكَسَوْنَا ٱلْعِظَٰمَ لَحْمًا ثُمَّ أَنشَأْنَٰهُ خَلْقًا ءَاخَرَ فَتَبَارَكَ ٱللَّهُ أَحْسَنُ ٱلْخَٰلِقِينَ (١٤) ثُمَّ إِنَّكُم بَعْدَ ذَٰلِكَ لَمَيِّتُونَ (١٥) ثُمَّ إِنَّكُمْ يَوْمَ ٱلْقِيَٰمَةِ تُبْعَثُونَ (١٦)

"Man We did create from a quintessence (of clay); Then We placed him as (a drop of) sperm in a place of rest, firmly fixed; Then We made the sperm into a clot of congealed blood; then of that clot We made a (fetus) lump; then we made out of that lump bones and clothed the bones with flesh; then we developed out of it another creature. So blessed be Allah, the best to create! After that, at length ye will die. Again, on the Day of Judgment, will ye be raised up."

Imam Omar makes it clear that people remember none of the time they existed as any of the above-mentioned stages. However, if it can be acknowledged that everyone has proceeded forth from the darkness of the womb, then surely it is possible that the afterlife, although unseen, is very real and at present unknowable.

Imam Omar explains that the sperm cell exists in the male body and is part of the essence that makes up each human being. Within the seed of human beings resides the totality of what a person will become. Yet no one remembers the time they existed as a sperm or ovum.

Further, the seed lodges in its place within the uterus of the mother. Here it develops from a clot that clings to a creature of bones clothed with flesh. Yet again, the human remembers none of this time spent developing in the womb.

Yet each child comes forth from his/her mother into a new world that it never knew could have possibly existed. All it knew was the warm darkness of the womb. Now it is aware of the physical world.

It then proceeds to go through the stages of development outside of the womb; until at length she/he will die and return to God.

In the future existence when all are raised up from the dead, continued Omar, human beings will not have a body like the present one. It will be a new creation as mentioned above.

All humanity, according to the Holy Qur'an, travels from stage to stage. The human being is of the earth—a walking, talking earth. God causes the human, who is made of dirt and water, to develop and change into forms of which they know not. However, all will receive these new forms in the future world.

"Our Lord! Let not our hearts deviate now after you have guided us on the right path, but grant us mercy from Your own Presence, for you are the grantor of bounties without measure." Ameen.

Imam Omar Hazim

بِسْمِ ٱللَّهِ ٱلرَّحْمَٰنِ ٱلرَّحِيمِ

With Allah's name, the merciful Benefactor, the merciful redeemer

May the prayers and the peace be upon Allah's noble and kind messenger, Muhammad.

Stages of Human Development: Part II

Sermon by Imam Omar Hazim

Edited online by Khalil Green

On Friday, February 26, 2010, Imam Omar Hazim delivered the Friday khutbah (sermon) titled "Stages of Human Development: Part II."

This sermon was in continuation of the Friday khutbah from February 19, 2010.

Imam Omar Hazim began the sermon with salutations and recognition of the birthday of Prophet Muhammad (PBUH). However, Imam Omar pointed out that Muslims are not, and should not be, in the practice of revering the Prophet, or his birthday, in the sense that he is raised to the position of worship. Islam forbids the worship of anyone but God.

Imam Omar continued that we honor the prophet in the vein of emulating his spiritual character, and Muslims should develop theirs accordingly. The process is found in the very Holy Qur'an given to humanity by God through Prophet Muhammad (PBUH).

The Holy Qur'an states,

لَقَدْ كَانَ لَكُمْ فِى رَسُولِ ٱللَّهِ أُسْوَةٌ حَسَنَةٌ لِّمَن كَانَ يَرْجُوا۟ ٱللَّهَ وَٱلْيَوْمَ ٱلْأَخِرَ وَذَكَرَ ٱللَّهَ كَثِيرًا

(٢١)

"Ye have indeed in the Messenger of Allah a beautiful pattern (of conduct) for any one whose hope is in Allah and the Final Day, and who engages much in the Praise of Allah." (Holy Qur'an, 33:21)

As such, the previous sermon was about how the physical self develops and grows, whereas this khutbah deals with the development of the inner self or soul (nafs).

Imam Omar stated that although we have no control over the physical growth of ourselves, we do have control over the development of the soul.

Muhammad had a good character for Muslims to learn from, as God states in the Holy Qur'an,

فَلَا أُقْسِمُ بِمَا تُبْصِرُونَ (٣٨) وَمَا لَا تُبْصِرُونَ (٣٩) إِنَّهُ لَقَوْلُ رَسُولٍ كَرِيمٍ (٤٠)

"But nay! I swear by that which you see, and that which you do not see. Most surely, it is the Word brought by an honored Messenger." (Holy Qur'an 69:38-40)

Imam Omar goes on to say that the formula for spiritual and moral progression is to understand the three levels of soul outlined in the Holy Qur'an; these are

- *Ammarah* (the state of being when one operates their life through the weaker part of the soul, which is prone to evil deeds)
- *Lawwamah* (state of consciousness or the inner voice that speaks to the self and encourages it to do good)
- *Mutma'innah* (the state where the soul develops to the point where it becomes at peace with itself and Allah).

All people exist at one of these levels. However, only through devotion and righteous deeds do people progress to higher states. This is further strengthened in the Holy Qur'an when God says,

وَنَفْسٍ وَمَا سَوَّاهَا (٧) فَأَلْهَمَهَا فُجُورَهَا وَتَقْوَاهَا (٨) قَدْ أَفْلَحَ مَن زَكَّاهَا (٩) وَقَدْ خَابَ مَن دَسَّاهَا (١٠)

Imam Omar Hazim

"By the Soul, and the proportion and order given to it;
And its enlightenment as to its wrong and its right;
Truly he succeeds that purifies it,
And he fails that corrupts it!" (Holy Qur'an, 91:7-10)

Imam Omar states that if you purify and develop the soul, it becomes clean; if you neglect it, it becomes corrupt. All mankind has potential for both. God gave everyone the faculty between right and wrong so they can recognize both paths.

In regard to the lower self (ammarah), Omar said, "If that part is not checked in myself, and in you, by a higher consciousness [lawwamah] you and I can fall by the wayside into corruption. But through spiritual education can we hold ourselves to higher moral standards."

Imam Omar states toward his closing remarks that when people first get ready to do a terrible wrong or evil, the conscious self shouts at the person in an attempt to prevent the wrongdoing, but if the voice goes unheeded, then it begins to speak more softly during future episodes of that particular wrongdoing. Until it finally gives up and the soul falls back into Nafsi Amara.

Imam Omar encourages the Muslims and guests to listen to that voice so that the soul may become mutma'innah and rest in a state of perfection where God is well pleased with it.

May Allah help us to be productive in this life and bless us with the best in the next life. Ameen.

$$\text{بِسْمِ ٱللَّهِ ٱلرَّحْمَٰنِ ٱلرَّحِيمِ}$$

With Allah's name, the merciful Benefactor, the merciful redeemer

May the prayers and the peace be upon Allah's noble and kind messenger, Muhammad.

Dressing for the Battlefield

Sermon by Imam Rudolph Muhammad

Edited online by Khalil Green

On April 16, 2010, Imam Rudolph Muhammad of Al-Inshirah Islamic Center in Kansas City, Missouri, delivered a captivating sermon at the Islamic Center of Topeka titled "Dressing for the Battlefield."

Imam Muhammad began with supplications and praises to God. He proceeded with the sermon by sharing with the congregation that the mantle or garment that the Prophet (prayers and peace be upon him) was wrapped in is the example that we should pattern our lives after. Having good character and the drive to get Allah's work done.

Citing chapter 74, verses 1-7, Imam Muhammad stated,

$$\text{يَٰٓأَيُّهَا ٱلْمُدَّثِّرُ (١) قُمْ فَأَنذِرْ (٢) وَرَبَّكَ فَكَبِّرْ (٣) وَثِيَابَكَ فَطَهِّرْ (٤) وَٱلرُّجْزَ فَٱهْجُرْ (٥) وَلَا تَمْنُن تَسْتَكْثِرُ (٦) وَلِرَبِّكَ فَٱصْبِرْ (٧)}$$

"O thou wrapped up (in the mantle)! [Prophet Muhammad (PBUH)] Arise and deliver thy warning! And thy Lord do thou magnify! And thy garments keep free from stain! And all abomination shun! Nor expect, in giving, any increase (for thyself)! But, for thy Lord's (Cause), be patient and constant!"

Imam Muhammad stated that Prophet Muhammad (PBUH) is an example to us for doing the work that continuously needs to be accomplished. The Holy Prophet was known as Al-Muzzammil, which is translated as "enfolded one" because he was wrapped in garments, garments that Prophet Muhammad (PBUH) kept free from stain by maintaining moral excellence.

The word for garments in Arabic is *thiab*. *Thiab* comes from the verb *thaba*, which means moral behavior, purehearted, good character, one who has been endowed with good character. As such, Prophet Muhammad (PBUH) (prayers and peace be upon him) remained in such a state, says Imam Muhammad. We should enfold ourselves in the same taqwa or regard for Allah!

Imam Muhammad further points out that the Holy Qur'an, through the story of Adam and Eve, shows the believer the necessity of following Prophet Muhammad (PBUH), when it states in chapter 7, verses 26-27 that,

يَٰبَنِىٓ ءَادَمَ قَدْ أَنزَلْنَا عَلَيْكُمْ لِبَاسًا يُوَٰرِى سَوْءَٰتِكُمْ وَرِيشًا ۖ وَلِبَاسُ ٱلتَّقْوَىٰ ذَٰلِكَ خَيْرٌ ۚ ذَٰلِكَ مِنْ ءَايَٰتِ ٱللَّهِ لَعَلَّهُمْ يَذَّكَّرُونَ (٢٦) يَٰبَنِىٓ ءَادَمَ لَا يَفْتِنَنَّكُمُ ٱلشَّيْطَٰنُ كَمَآ أَخْرَجَ أَبَوَيْكُم مِّنَ ٱلْجَنَّةِ يَنزِعُ عَنْهُمَا لِبَاسَهُمَا لِيُرِيَهُمَا سَوْءَٰتِهِمَآ ۗ إِنَّهُۥ يَرَىٰكُمْ هُوَ وَقَبِيلُهُۥ مِنْ حَيْثُ لَا تَرَوْنَهُمْ ۗ إِنَّا جَعَلْنَا ٱلشَّيَٰطِينَ أَوْلِيَآءَ لِلَّذِينَ لَا يُؤْمِنُونَ (٢٧)

"O ye Children of Adam! We have bestowed raiment [Libas] upon you to cover your shame, as well as to be an adornment to you. But the raiment of righteousness, - that is the best . . . O ye Children of Adam! Let not Satan seduce you, in the same manner as He got your parents out of the Garden, stripping them of their raiment [libas], to expose their shame."

Imam Muhammad stated that *libas* has been translated as "raiment" but it also means "to dress, to cover up, and to obscure." The best adornment, he continued, is that of righteousness, and thus our mantle is taqwa (Allah-consciousness).

The Prophet is our pattern of conduct and the best role model for all human beings. Muslims should model themselves accordingly and set the best example for humanity.

Imam Muhammad, quoting from Imam W. D. Mohammed's (may God grant him paradise) book *Life: The Final Battlefield*, states that "life itself is the last battlefield, human life is the core life of humanity, human essence is what counts for that core life, human life is as a seed for plant life ... from ... seed lost, future lost. Where people are found not conscious of what it means to be human or have human life, life goes down, not up."

As Muslims, we have to realize that this is the battlefield upon which we have to stand and fight. As Imam Muhammad states, quoting from chapter 100, verses 1-5 of the Holy Qur'an,

وَٱلْعَٰدِيَٰتِ ضَبْحًا (١) فَٱلْمُورِيَٰتِ قَدْحًا (٢) فَٱلْمُغِيرَٰتِ صُبْحًا (٣) فَأَثَرْنَ بِهِۦ نَقْعًا (٤) فَوَسَطْنَ بِهِۦ جَمْعًا (٥)

"By the (Steeds) that run, with panting (breath), strike sparks of fire, and push home the charge in the morning, and raise the dust in clouds the while, and penetrate forthwith into the midst (of the foe) en masse."

Imam Muhammad explained that the horse running with panting breath refers to the Muslim warrior/worker, who, like the Arabian horse, is peaceful yet powerful, living in peace but always ready to go forth for a righteous cause.

The panting breath, Imam Muhammad continues, is how the horse draws in energy and applies it to its powerful legs. The air and breath both symbolize the spirit; in the martial arts, it is called *chi*.

So running with panting breath is something Muslims need to do today, according to Imam Muhammad. As Prophet Muhammad (PBUH) and his companions did—and in this era so did Imam W. Deen Mohammed—we too must run with panting breath while striking sparks of fire. As such, the sparks of fire represent moving with a logical purpose and direction, a direction that is controlled, calculated, and beneficial to humanity.

The pioneers of our community, mentioned above, pushed home the charge in the morning, creating a path for us to follow. They pushed home the charge by laying the groundwork for Muslim warriors and workers to tread upon in this day and time.

In conclusion, Imam Muhammad stated that Muslims must raise the dust and charge into the work of community building with a group effort. Muslims must support all good community efforts by being the Thoroughbred and not the lazy and slow-moving donkey. Let us establish a community pleasing to God, and one in honor of our predecessors and pioneers, with good character and strength of steed.

We pray for Allah's forgiveness and guidance. Ameen.

بِسْمِ ٱللَّهِ ٱلرَّحْمَٰنِ ٱلرَّحِيمِ

With Allah's name, the merciful Benefactor, the merciful redeemer

May the prayers and the peace be upon Allah's noble and kind messenger, Muhammad.

Excerpts from the Sermon "Identity"

Zaid Hayyeh

Edited by Khalil Green

Brother Zaid gave a very informative sermon about, "Identity," At the Islamic Center of Topeka.

After supplications, Zaid quoting Quran stated that, "Abraham gave advice to his son . . . Allah has chosen for you the religion, the way of life, do not perish except as Muslim."

"We are Muslims first nothing after that really matters," stated Zaid. As such, we should say to those who ask us, that we believe in Allah, and what has been given to us, through Ishmael, and Isaac. We believe in the prophets Moses and Jesus and what has been given to them. As Muslims, Zaid continued, we should make no distinction between any of the Prophets.

We are Muslim and every example in the Quran shows that the prophets did not come from one caste, one race, or even one place, affirmed Zaid. But they came from every race and level. But man created caste. First, there were the landowners vs. non land owners, race, now it is becoming the arrogance that can stem from national pride among Muslims.

There are always things that divide people into different groups. But Muslims should be concerned about one identity alone; their Muslim identity, encouraged Zaid.

Quoting the Prophet, Zaid stated that "different colors are like the different colors of rock, what you care about the color of rocks." Bilal, the

African Muslim, who was a slave, was tortured by his pagan master. He was whipped and stoned nearly to death by his master so that he would give up Islam. Yet he kept saying "Ahad" meaning One, saying God is One. And if you go read this story about Bilal's suffering and you have the slightest degree of emotions, it will make you cry.

According to Zaid, the Quran states that Muslims are merciful to each other and firm against those who would harm the Muslims. That the Muslims are known by the prostrations marks on their foreheads from prayer. The believers are known by these markings and not their race, finances, or position on the earth.

"None of you will have faith unless he wishes for his brother what he wishes for himself," Zaid quoting Prophet Muhammad (PBUH). So whatever you wish for yourself you should wish for your Muslim brother. Zaid further quoting Prophet Muhammad (PBUH) stated that if a Muslim does not want for his brother what he wants for himself then he is not a true believer.

Quoting Prophet Muhammad Zaid stated that "by him in whose Hands my soul is, none of you will have faith till he loves me more than his father and children." Because that is what ties us together and gives us our identity, continued Zaid. In the end that's all that matters.

Concluding Zaid states that, whoever has these three qualities will have the sweetness of faith;

- The one who Allah and the prophet becomes dearer to him than anything else.
- Who loves a person only for Allah's sake.
- Who hates to revert to Atheism as he hates to be thrown in the fire.

As such, Muslims should know their identity as believers. Nothing else matters; not race, origin, status, etc. We should always strive to be pleasing to Allah and identify ourselves as Muslim.

May Allah help us to be productive in this life, and bless us with the best in the next life. Ameen

$$\text{بِسْمِ اللهِ الرَّحْمَٰنِ الرَّحِيمِ}$$

With Allah's name, the merciful Benefactor, the merciful redeemer

May the prayers and the peace be upon Allah's noble and kind messenger, Muhammad.

Appreciating the Holy Qur'an

Sermon by Imam Omar Hazim

Edited online by Khalil Green

On Friday, February 15, 2010, Imam Omar Hazim delivered the Friday sermon titled "Appreciating the Holy Qur'an." He referenced to the audience three different sets of verses from the Muslim holy book, the Holy Qur'an, that speaks about its importance.

Imam Omar informed worshippers and guests that the Holy Qur'an is a guide from which the belief and culture of the Muslim should be taken. The Muslim should not doubt what is contained in its pages and seek to understand.

$$\text{ذَٰلِكَ ٱلْكِتَٰبُ لَا رَيْبَ ۛ فِيهِ ۛ هُدًى لِّلْمُتَّقِينَ (٢)}$$

"This is the Book; in it is guidance sure, without doubt, to those who fear Allah." (Holy Qur'an, 2:2)

Imam Omar further stated that much appreciation should be given to the Holy Qur'an by Muslims. It is not a book that needs clarification but one that clarifies spiritual and mundane matters.

$$\text{وَٱلْكِتَٰبِ ٱلْمُبِينِ (٢) إِنَّا جَعَلْنَٰهُ قُرْءَٰنًا عَرَبِيًّا لَّعَلَّكُمْ تَعْقِلُونَ (٣)}$$

"By the Book that makes things clear. We have made it a Qur'an in Arabic, that ye may be able to understand (and learn wisdom)." (Holy Qur'an, 43:2-3)

Omar further asserted that the Holy Qur'an was made Arabic because it was the tongue that was spoken by Prophet Muhammad (PBUH) and the Arab people. As such, Arabic should not be overemphasized as being a particularly special language.

If Prophet Muhammad (PBUH) had been born to an English- or Farsispeaking people, for instance, the Holy Qur'an would have been given to humanity in that language. However, given excellent translators like Abdullah Yusuf Ali and others, the Holy Qur'an can be studied in many modern languages.

The Holy Qur'an should be read, "not left to collect dust on a shelf," continued Omar. It is difficult to find wisdom when the Holy Book simply sits on a high shelf in a room for display.

وَٱلْقُرْءَانِ ٱلْحَكِيمِ (٢) إِنَّكَ لَمِنَ ٱلْمُرْسَلِينَ (٣) عَلَىٰ صِرَاطٍ مُّسْتَقِيمٍ (٤) تَنزِيلَ ٱلْعَزِيزِ ٱلرَّحِيمِ (٥)

"By the Qur'an, full of Wisdom, Thou art indeed one of the messengers, on a Straight Way. It is a Revelation sent down by (Him), the Exalted in Might, Most Merciful." (Holy Qur'an, 36:2-5)

Imam Omar tells the crowd that the messenger to whom God was speaking was Prophet Muhammad (PBUH). As such, the Messenger is a walking example of the Holy Qur'an put into practice.

In his conclusion, Imam Omar references a popular movie that is currently playing in theaters called *The Book of Eli*. Denzel Washington plays a man who is in possession of the last Bible on earth. On his way to the archives to preserve the book, he loses it. However, he had memorized the Bible and dictated it to the archive keepers. The keepers of the archives then placed the book on a special shelf alongside a Torah and a Holy Qur'an.

Omar concludes that this memorization that Eli displays for the Bible is the goal of many Muslims who strive to become *hafiz* (one who has memorized the entire Holy Qur'an). As such, striving to become a hafiz and studying the Holy Book shows true appreciation and respect that a Muslim should have for the Holy Qur'an.

May Allah help us to be productive in this life and bless us with the best in the next life. Ameen.

$$\text{بِسْمِ اللهِ الرَّحْمَٰنِ الرَّحِيمِ}$$

With Allah's name, the merciful Benefactor, the merciful redeemer

May the prayers and the peace be upon Allah's noble and kind messenger, Muhammad.

Striving for Excellence

Sermon by Imam Omar Hazim

Edited online by Khalil Green

On Friday, April 23, 2010, Imam Omar Hazim delivered a very motivational khutbah (sermon) at the Islamic Center of Topeka. Imam Omar presented a sermon titled "Strive for Excellence."

After supplications, Imam Omar quoted the Holy Qur'an, verse 2:148, which states that

$$\text{وَلِكُلٍّ وِجْهَةٌ هُوَ مُوَلِّيهَا فَاسْتَبِقُوا الْخَيْرَاتِ أَيْنَ مَا تَكُونُوا يَأْتِ بِكُمُ اللَّهُ جَمِيعًا إِنَّ اللَّهَ عَلَىٰ كُلِّ شَيْءٍ قَدِيرٌ (١٤٨)}$$

"To each is a goal to which Allah turns him; then strive together (as in a race) towards all that is good. Wheresoever ye are, Allah will bring you together. For Allah hath power over all things."

Thus, human excellence is the striving as in a race toward all that is good and wholesome for humanity.

Omar continued by stating that Prophet Muhammad (PBUH) (peace be upon him) has left the believers with two things: the Holy Qur'an and his *Sunna* (his way of life). If Muslims follow these two things, they will attain excellence in this world.

The objective of adhering to the Holy Qur'an and the practices of Muhammad is to "attain to excellence in this life and in the next through

... the life giving teachings of the Holy Qur'an, and the life example of Prophet Muhammad [PBUH]," stated Omar.

Allah states in the Holy Qur'an that He has given us a book full of wisdom and, Omar adds, that the word *Holy Qur'an* comes from the Arabic root *qaraa*. Imam Omar states that the word *qaraa* means "to read, a written thing, recite with or without having a script, proclaim, convey, call, rehearse, transmit, deliver a message." As such, the Holy Qur'an is a book that is meant to be read, conveyed, transmitted, and rehearsed.

In its definition of being rehearsed, Omar continues, the very name of the Holy Qur'an is relating to humanity that it is meant to be read over and over again. Every time it is read, something new is discovered; something different is comprehended. As such, states Omar, the more it is read over and over again, the more wisdom is bestowed on the reader over and over again. "This wisdom will increase us in excellence," Omar completed.

On the walk toward excellence, Omar stated, we will experience something of difficulty and loss on the journey to wisdom. However, Allah states in the Holy Qur'an that with every difficulty there is relief. Those who experience calamity yet who believe in Allah will say that "to Allah we belong and to Him is our return." The ones who understand this will perseveringly press on.

Perseverance, as a form of endurance, transcends patience. "Perseverance includes the dedication necessary to up keep a situation until it can be passed on to future generations even without obtaining the goal ourselves," said Omar. The goal is not just about the person, it is also about the community and future. Thus, should all good works and goals be passed along to future generations to develop and enhance.

Yet still, along the way, a person can lose that which is precious to him or her, as this hadith (sayings of Prophet Muhammad [PBUH]) relates God's conversation with the angels about the death of a child, quoted by Imam Omar, which states, "Allah asked the angels, 'Have you taken away my servants, beloved child?' The angels responded, 'Yes, by your permission.' Allah asked, 'What was my servant's response?' The angels said, 'He praised your name and said, To Allah we belong and to Him is our return.' Allah said, 'How excellent. Build for them both [child and servant] a house in paradise and call it the House of Praise.'"

Thus must everyone strive for excellence by cultivating patience and perseverance, even in the face of tragedy. Omar continued by stating that everyone must teach their children to have patience but set goals for themselves as we, the parents, aid them in the choices they have to make.

We have to teach them that setting high-enough goals for themselves is what will unlock the tremendous potential that lies within them, stated Omar.

As Omar concluded, he stated that Islam teaches us to be balanced, not extreme in any direction. Not to neglect any aspect of our life but be in harmony with all aspects of our religious, intellectual, social, family, personal, and physical goals as we strive toward excellence while maintaining harmony and equilibrium in our lives.

"Our Lord! Let not our hearts deviate now after You have guided us on the right path, but grant us mercy from Your own Presence, for You are the grantor of bounties without measure." Ameen.

بِسْمِ ٱللَّهِ ٱلرَّحْمَٰنِ ٱلرَّحِيمِ

With Allah's name, the merciful Benefactor, the merciful redeemer

May the prayers and the peace be upon Allah's noble and kind messenger, Muhammad.

Cultivating The Garden Of Our Souls

By
Imam Omar Hazim

On January 7, 2011 Imam Omar Hazim gave a very uplifting sermon titled Cultivating the Garden of our Souls, at the Islamic Center of Topeka.

After supplications Imam Omar stated "we want to talk about how faith is deeply rooted in the heart; how it translates into our outward action."

Omar began by stating that, in the adhan (call to prayer) that the brother recited at the beginning of this service, he mentioned "hiyya ala falah;" which means rush lively to success. Hiyya means rush lively, and Falah means success. Together they are calling humanity to cultivate our lives; develop self. Falah further means to unfold something to reveal the properties within, commented Omar. Just as the farmer cultivates his crops for the best produce so most we cultivate what is real within us. So five times a day during the call to prayer we are encouraged to evolve the self by using what Allah has put in us and manifest out potential, stated Omar.

Quoting verses from chapter 36, Omar states "By the Qur'an, full of Wisdom surely thou art indeed one of the messengers. On a Straight Way. It is a Revelation sent down by (Him) the Exalted in Might, Most Merciful."

The Quran is full of wisdom for those looking to be successful. Quoting Imam W.D. Mohammed, Omar states, "we should follow wisdom to its logical conclusion." Quran comes from Qaraa which means to read a written thing. A book which is meant to be read, recited and rehearsed. So we rehearse the Quran over and over again. For if we rehearse and practice it over and over again we will gain some of its wisdom, stated Omar.

This verse also affirms the prophethood Of Prophet Muhammad (PBUH).

Allah uses the word Tanzilul for sent down; He uses the same word for sending down rain. Thus nothing in the creation came down on its own but Allah has sent it and protects it. As he does the Quran, affirmed Omar.

In Chapter 69 38-40 of the Quran Omar quotes "So I do call to witness what ye see, and what ye see not, that this is verily the word of an honored messenger."

Allah swears by all that you see; as in that which we are endowed with understanding to comprehend. Allah is swearing by all that we see and witness as the entire perceivable creation. Then He swears by what we don't see. We don't see Allah, success, or what is in us. Even the scientist state there is ninety percent of the universe that we don't see, continued Omar.

So what is all this swearing about, asks Omar. That this Quran is true and that Prophet Muhammad (PBUH) is an Honorable Messenger.

Quoting Prophet Muhammad (PBUH) Omar said "Every day the sun rises to bring about another Day, The Day says 'oh children of Adam I am a new day and I witness what you do so make the best of me for you will not see me again until the resurrection.'" So whether you are striving for success of forgiveness every new day is a day to work towards your pursuit and start anew, encouraged Omar.

Omar, quoting Quran, says, "Think! For surely you progress by the power of thought." Allah put in the Quran over 811 times dhikr (think). Also in the Quran equally is Amana (Faith). So Allah is telling us to be successful by reasoning and having faith. These two things go together; faith and reasoning. "Success and failure are generally related to the habits we form," stated Omar.

The thoughts that we think they produce our action. Then that action produces a habit. Habits will produce a characteristic and that characteristic will determine our destiny, continued Omar. So if we want a business that is going to be successful then we want to perform the habits for that business to be successful.

In chapter 6:125 of the Quran, Omar continued, when Allah wishes to guide us He expands our chest. The word for chest is sadurr but usually refers to the heart. So Allah puts faith in our hearts. So we all have a gift from Allah called faith that He put in our hearts. So faith is put in out chest as Islam. And the Quran gives us a desire to be successful, stated Omar.

"So Islam is not in our clothes, in our skin, country we originated from, but it is in our hearts," said Omar.

It's important to know that Allah believes in something according to one of His attributes. This attribute is Al -Mumin, the Guardian of Faith. Thus Allah believes in his creation. Allah believes in all of us, and knows what we are capable of said Omar.

When Allah was about to create man the Angels ask Allah if he was going to create something that will spread mischief in the earth. But Allah told them that He knows and they know not and that He created us in the best of molds. We are not created in sin. We are created to bring forth out of us the best. "Not to die with our song still in our hearts," stated Omar.

Often we go into business and have a failure and we are ready to close the door. "Persistence is one of the key ingredients to being successful" and the Quran states that we should be patient and persevere, stated Omar. Allah is with those who are patient and persevere. Even if we don't see the success in our life time we understand that it might be successful in our children's lives.

Thomas Edison failed at creating a lamp that would operate by electricity 10,000 times. But he did not call them failures, he stated that he learned 10,000 lessons why those things did not work, he kept at it until he succeeded. Also the early Muslims stayed in Mecca with Prophet Muhammad ten long oppressive years. Not fighting back until the revelation came to the Prophet (pbuh) to defend them self. It was the mystical power of faith and persistents that allowed them to be that strong.

W.D. Mohammed once received a call from people who stated that if he left his house that day he would be killed. However he had work to do at home and was not planning on leaving. But because of the threat, he left his home, and drove all around town. Something he never does, just to answer that threat and show his faith, how nothing happens unless it's by Allah will.

The importance of possessing some of the Attributes of Allah, is illustrated in this story, began Omar. Adam, after being forgiving for his mistake, was told to look to his right. He saw three lights. He asked the first light, "What is your position and station? The light responded, "My position and station is in the human head, all types of skills are manifested in those who have me inside their skulls. I am the light of reasoning and cause people to go to paradise. The question was asked of the second light, it stated "I am modesty, I reside in the eyes and I see the Attributes of Allah." The third said I am the light of compassion and those who have me in the heart are on their way to an everlasting paradise. Adam choose reasoning to reside in him but the other two rejected that saying "we all go together." So Adam possessed all the lights. Thus the potential of reasoning, modesty, and compassion resides in all of us, continued Omar.

Then Allah caused Adam to look to his left, he saw three darkness's. Adam said, "What a foul creature are you, what is your station?" The first darkness said, my name is arrogance, I reside in the head and my function is to make men suffer the wrath of Allah. When reason leaves I occupy the space there. The second darkness said, "My name is Greed and I reside in the eye. When modesty leaves I take over and I make men and women become lower than animals." The third said "I am envy and I reside in the Heart and when Compassion leaves I take over and drive men and women to hell."

Thus when we become successful by incorporating the three lights mentioned, we have to keep arrogance out of our mind; not allow greed to come into our lives; and stay away from envy. Allah has given us the gift of these lights in order to cultivate our lives with faith and reasoning. We have to un-wrap the gifts that Allah has given us, as great potential. Let us look inward to our own selves and open up that gift, and see what Allah has given us to develop.

May Allah have mercy on us all and give us guidance. Ameen

بِسْمِ ٱللَّهِ ٱلرَّحْمَٰنِ ٱلرَّحِيمِ

With Allah's name, the merciful Benefactor, the merciful redeemer

May the prayers and the peace be upon Allah's noble and kind messenger, Muhammad.

Moving Forward in the Direction of Rasullulah (Prophet Muhammad [PBUH])

Sermon by Imam Sulaiman Z. Salaam Jr.

Edited online by Khalil Green

On June 25, 2010, Imam Sulaiman Z. Salaam Jr. gave an excellent sermon titled "Moving Forward in The Direction of Rasullulah."

Imam Salaam begins by quoting the Holy Qur'an by stating,

يَٰٓأَيُّهَا ٱلنَّاسُ قَدْ جَآءَتْكُم مَّوْعِظَةٌ مِّن رَّبِّكُمْ وَشِفَآءٌ لِّمَا فِى ٱلصُّدُورِ وَهُدًى وَرَحْمَةٌ لِّلْمُؤْمِنِينَ

(٥٧)

"O mankind their comes to you a direction from your lord and a healing of the diseases in your heart and for those who believe a guidance and a mercy." (Holy Qur'an, 10:57)

That direction was Jerusalem. The Muslims during the time of Prophet Muhammad (PBUH) were turning their faces toward Jerusalem for their prayer, the same *qibla* (direction of prayer) as the people of the book. Allah revealed to Prophet Muhammad (PBUH) that he was going to change our direction, states Imam Sulaiman. This represented a change in the direction that Allah was going to take the community toward Islamic life.

Imam Sulaiman continued by saying that if we take the time to look at the Messengers that Allah sent to each particular group of people, we can see that they were responsible for moving their own communities back to guidance. Move them back to guidance because we know that Allah (SWT) has created us in the most excellent of molds. This is to say that "embedded within our own selves is the guidance we need to be successful in life," stated Imam Sulaiman. Children know instinctively the difference between right and wrong. So the guidance is factored in our own being at the time of our creation.

But people have a tendency to move away from guidance, Imam Sulaiman suggested. Yet Prophet Muhammad (PBUH) was sent to be "of the most excellent moral character" as an example to all people. He was trustworthy and honest before receiving revelation. After he received revelation, he was described by his wife, Ayesha, as the walking Holy Qur'an. He lived his life according to the revelation that he received.

However, he was different from other prophets because he was sent "as a mercy for all mankind," stated Imam Sulaiman. He would be the universal prophet or the prophet for all mankind regardless of color, creed, or tribe.

Even though we understand his worth, we attempt to follow him in very small ways like taking on his cultural dress, said Imam Sulaiman. We imitate him and think that's following him.

In truth, we follow him by living our life according to the Holy Qur'an. Prophet Muhammad (PBUH) is reported to have said that the jinn accompany us and urge us to do that which is wrong but he (Prophet Muhammad [PBUH]) caused his jinn to submit and become Muslim. We are human just like Prophet Muhammad (PBUH) was and should strive to do the same, concluded Imam Sulaiman.

Thus when we come across something that is not good for us, we make our jinn submit by moving away from the wrong. We can't take the position that Prophet Muhammad (PBUH) was perfect, for the Holy Qur'an states that he was a human (bashir) just like us. He was made by Allah (SWT) as a model for us to follow. Thus, we should be striving to make our jinn submit to the will of Allah.

Those who believe study the Holy Qur'an as it should be studied. So when we read the stories in the Holy Qur'an, we have to ask ourselves, "Are we like the one in the story who moves toward all that is wrong, or are we like the prophet in the story who strives toward all that is right and moves away from evil?" Do we call other people to do the right thing? asked

Imam Sulaiman. In other words, everyone should ask themselves, "Am I a helper or one who works against all that is good?"

In the Holy Qur'an, Allah is not only speaking to Muhammad but to all mankind. The Kaaba (house of worship in Mecca) is the direction which God turned the Prophet toward and, hence, every believer, continued Imam Sulaiman.

Thus the direction Allah turned man to was the qibla, which is symbolic to the direction to which we should turn our attention; "establishing community life at its finest," stated Imam Sulaiman.

When Adam was correctly focused on his direction, Satan (Satan) made it his business to influence him away from his intention, influencing him toward power and desire instead of building a healthy community life. We stop focusing our attention away from community and become focused on self. "We forget about the bigger picture which is humanity," related Imam Sulaiman.

So we ought to focus on self by getting our souls right in order to strengthen ourselves and become a use to our community, instructed Imam Sulaiman and continued that we should do as Muhammad did to establish community life and be a benefit to humanity and travel in the right direction.

We have to be concerned as to what is good for self, the community, and humanity. Those great Muslim civilizations of the past flourished because they followed the example of Prophet Muhammad (PBUH), taught Imam Sulaiman. They were not just focused on what was good for the Muslims; they were focused on what was good for everyone.

Thus in Medina did Prophet Muhammad (PBUH) establish a place of worship for the Muslims, but he also invited others of different faiths to come and worship at the mosque. And he established a government to protect all the people in Medina.

In looking at the people in Muslim communities, Imam Sulaiman stated that he noticed that most Muslims are fifty or older. That most Muslims who visit the Islamic centers are older, and the younger generations are not visiting the Islamic centers, nor are they establishing family life at the mosque. As people get older and die off, "we [the community] can die off," concluded Imam Sulaiman.

Thus, if we do not fulfill our covenant, we can be replaced as groups and Muslim civilizations of the past can be replaced. Thus, if we believe what the Holy Qur'an says that "we are the best evolved for all mankind," then we have a responsibility to all our extended family. We must fulfill our covenant with Allah by doing all that we can do by being the best example for all to see, stated Imam Sulaiman.

Imam Sulaiman concluded that we should be more mindful that our life as Muslims is not just about the ritual, but by showing Islam in all that we do; by moving forward and following the example of Prophet Muhammad (PBUH). "The best that we can do is to be the best example that Allah [SWT] has called us to be."

بِسْمِ ٱللَّهِ ٱلرَّحْمَٰنِ ٱلرَّحِيمِ

With Allah's name, the merciful Benefactor, the merciful redeemer

May the prayers and the peace be upon Allah's noble and kind messenger, Muhammad.

Protecting Our Life through Protecting Our Behavior

Sermon by Imam Bilal Mohammed

Edited online by Khalil Green

On Friday March 12, 2010, Imam Bilal Mohammed delivered the Friday sermon at the Islamic Center of Topeka, Kansas. Imam Bilal delivered a very dynamic speech to the crowd in attendance.

He began with prayers to God and salutations to Prophet Muhammad (PBUH).

Imam Bilal stated in his salutations that God is the Lord of the Worlds (Alamin). He further stated that because *alamin* also means knowledge, it can also be translated that he is the Lord of all the systems of knowledge.

Thus, everything has a system of knowledge from which humanity can study, learn, and know.

Humanity, Imam Bilal continued, is created from and as one soul. Therefore, humanity is connected to one another here in America, and Muslims have a life in this country.

As such, Muslims have to learn to protect their life in this society. Imam Bilal clarified this by saying Muslims should be "protecting our life in this country by protecting how we behave." For all humanity is one soul and a person's actions impact everyone else.

He cites the following verse from the Holy Qur'an:

$$\text{وَهُوَ ٱلَّذِى يَتَوَفَّىٰكُم بِٱلَّيْلِ وَيَعْلَمُ مَا جَرَحْتُم بِٱلنَّهَارِ ثُمَّ يَبْعَثُكُمْ فِيهِ لِيُقْضَىٰٓ أَجَلٌ مُّسَمًّى ۖ ثُمَّ إِلَيْهِ مَرْجِعُكُمْ ثُمَّ يُنَبِّئُكُم بِمَا كُنتُمْ تَعْمَلُونَ (٦٠)}$$

"It is He who doth take your souls by night, and hath knowledge of all that ye have done by day: by day doth He raise you up again; that a term appointed be fulfilled; in the end unto Him will be your return; then will He show you the truth of all that ye did." (Holy Qur'an 6:60)

Imam Bilal stated that this verse is intended to be mysterious; humanity doesn't understand much about dreams that occur when God takes the souls at night. Some scholars say that "sleep is the twin brother of death," said Imam Bilal.

Imam Bilal stated that although God knows all that a person does by day, the person is not aware of everything they do during the day because "we don't know the consequences of our actions." For example, a person may be driving along on a highway, cut someone off in traffic, and cause a pile up behind him, not knowing that someone died; "but God knows," continued Imam Bilal.

On the other hand, a simple smile may create a wealth of good in a person's life. "We don't know how a smile may affect someone," stated Imam Bilal. It may help a person through hard times or build within them self-worth.

Toward the end of his sermon, Imam Bilal stated that when we are truly raised up from sleep, morality and goodwill toward each other will be the rules of the day. People can be morally and intellectually progressive as humanity prepares to return to their Lord.

Islam is a necessary component of such spiritual growth. It is no mistake that Islam came to the West through the routes in which it appeared. That is why Islam is necessary in this Western society and is here to stay.

May Allah Accept our prayers.

$$\text{بِسْمِ ٱللّٰهِ ٱلرَّحْمٰنِ ٱلرَّحِيمِ}$$

With Allah's name, the merciful Benefactor, the merciful redeemer

May the prayers and the peace be upon Allah's noble and kind messenger, Muhammad.

Moral Accountability in Islam

Sermon by Imam Omar Hazim

Edited online by Khalil Green

On Friday April 2, 2010, at the Islamic Center of Topeka, Imam Omar Hazim delivered a thought-provoking sermon for the Friday service entitled "Moral Accountability in Islam."

He stated that many imams speak about the symbolism of Easter, including the bunny, the egg, etc., during the Friday before Easter. He stated that the speeches are good and thought provoking.

However, on this Friday, Imam Hazim stated that he will speak on what the Holy Qur'an says about moral accountability.

Imam Omar acknowledged that all human beings have the sense of being accountable for their actions in this world, and Allah has given us so many ways to repent from our sins and mistakes directly from Him instead of seeking out another to intercede on behalf of the wrongdoer.

Imam Omar, quoting from chapter 6, verse 164 of the Holy Qur'an, said,

$$\text{قُلْ أَغَيْرَ ٱللَّهِ أَبْغِى رَبًّا وَهُوَ رَبُّ كُلِّ شَىْءٍ ۚ وَلَا تَكْسِبُ كُلُّ نَفْسٍ إِلَّا عَلَيْهَا ۚ وَلَا تَزِرُ وَازِرَةٌ وِزْرَ أُخْرَىٰ ۚ ثُمَّ إِلَىٰ رَبِّكُم مَّرْجِعُكُمْ فَيُنَبِّئُكُم بِمَا كُنتُمْ فِيهِ تَخْتَلِفُونَ (١٦٤)}$$

"What! Shall I seek a Lord other than Allah? And He is the Lord of all things; and no soul earns (evil) but against itself, and no bearer of burden shall bear the burden of another; then to your Lord is your return, so He will inform you of that in which you differed."

Imam Omar said that this is a powerful verse, and people should realize that it is better to believe in God as opposed to not believing. If a person believes in God, it is better to worship God than to worship His servants who have also sinned, or been tempted to sin.

Part of our worship, Omar continued, is realizing that each day is a new day to correct past mistakes and ask for forgiveness. Muslims should concern themselves with the new day, ask for forgiveness, and work to please their Lord.

In the time of Prophet Muhammad (PBUH), said Omar, quoting chapter 29, verse 12 of the Holy Qur'an:

وَقَالَ ٱلَّذِينَ كَفَرُوا لِلَّذِينَ ءَامَنُوا ٱتَّبِعُوا سَبِيلَنَا وَلْنَحْمِلْ خَطَٰيَٰكُمْ وَمَا هُم بِحَٰمِلِينَ مِنْ خَطَٰيَٰهُم مِّن شَىْءٍ إِنَّهُمْ لَكَٰذِبُونَ (١٢)

"And the Unbelievers say to those who believe: follow our path, and we will bear [the consequences] of your faults. Never in the least will they bear their faults: in fact they are liars!"

Imam Omar continued that this verse is talking about two burdens: the burden of the liar's own sins and the burden on the liar for leading others astray.

The wrongdoers even stated that they will accept the burdens of those who follow them. Imam Omar stated further that even if we say we would die for each other, it is only on a practical level. No one can die for or absorb the sins of another.

To Muslims, every Friday is a Good Friday. For it is filled with mercy, kindness, and forgiveness. It is the day that Adam was created. We don't have to reach out to another source other than God, said Omar. We get weak, we make mistakes, but we have a forgiving Lord whom we can approach directly.

Omar quoted the following verse from the Holy Qur'an, which clarifies the Islamic standing on a person's fate when it says,

وَكُلَّ إِنسَٰنٍ أَلْزَمْنَٰهُ طَٰٓئِرَهُۥ فِى عُنُقِهِۦ ۖ وَنُخْرِجُ لَهُۥ يَوْمَ ٱلْقِيَٰمَةِ كِتَٰبًا يَلْقَىٰهُ مَنشُورًا (١٣) ٱقْرَأْ كِتَٰبَكَ كَفَىٰ بِنَفْسِكَ ٱلْيَوْمَ عَلَيْكَ حَسِيبًا (١٤) مَّنِ ٱهْتَدَىٰ فَإِنَّمَا يَهْتَدِى لِنَفْسِهِۦ ۖ وَمَن ضَلَّ فَإِنَّمَا يَضِلُّ عَلَيْهَا ۚ وَلَا تَزِرُ وَازِرَةٌ وِزْرَ أُخْرَىٰ ۗ وَمَا كُنَّا مُعَذِّبِينَ حَتَّىٰ نَبْعَثَ رَسُولًا (١٥)

"Every man's fate We [God] have fastened on his own neck: On the Day of Judgment We shall bring out for him a scroll, which he will see spread open. (It will be said to him) "Read thine (own) record: Sufficient is thy soul this day to make out an account against thee." Who receiveth guidance, receiveth it for his own benefit: who goeth astray doth so to his own loss: No bearer of burdens can bear the burden of another: nor would We visit with Our Wrath until We had sent a messenger (to give warning)." (Holy Qur'an, 17:13-15)

These are very practical words from God, contained in the Holy Qur'an, in regard to moral accountability, according to Omar. They allow no situation where blame for one's sins can be placed on someone else, Omar explained. But all people are responsible for their own sins and should ask God for forgiveness, and do good deeds for compensation of bad deeds.

Toward the end of the Friday service, Omar stated if a person finds himself making a mistake or committing a crime against his own soul, then no blame can be placed on someone else in the form of lies or sacrifice, but that person is accountable for all his own actions.

We pray for Allah's forgiveness and guidance. Ameen.

$$\text{بِسْمِ ٱللّٰهِ ٱلرَّحْمَٰنِ ٱلرَّحِيمِ}$$

With Allah's name, the merciful Benefactor, the merciful redeemer

May the prayers and the peace be upon Allah's noble and kind messenger, Muhammad.

The Jinn

Sermon by Imam Omar Hazim

Edited online by Khalil Green

On Friday December 8, 2010, Imam Omar spoke about the jinn during Jumah service at the Islamic Center of Topeka.

The jinn are one of the most interesting subjects in Islam and one of the most important. There is a lot of misunderstanding about the jinn. Some think that they are equivalent to the demons in the Judeo/Christian tradition. Some think that they are all evil. However, according to Islam, they are simply another creation that was created before the advent of man. Thus, they are older than man.

$$\text{وَلَقَدْ خَلَقْنَا ٱلْإِنسَٰنَ مِن صَلْصَٰلٍ مِّنْ حَمَإٍ مَّسْنُونٍ (٢٦) وَٱلْجَانَّ خَلَقْنَٰهُ مِن قَبْلُ مِن نَّارِ ٱلسَّمُومِ (٢٧)}$$

"We created man from sounding clay, from mud molded into shape; and the Jinn race, We had created before, from the fire of a scorching wind." (Holy Qur'an 15:26-27)

Thus, the jinn were here before man as rulers of this world. They failed in their charge as caretakers of this world and became prideful. They had all the rights and responsibilities of caring for the world and had the ability to rise above their animal nature. One jinn in particular, named Iblis, obtained the station of being over the angels.

As Omar stated in his khutbah (sermon), Iblis was in charge of a contingent of the angels and, at Adam's creation, was directed to bow down to man, along with the angels. The angels all obeyed, bowing to man as the new caretaker of the world; all except Iblis. He refused the word of his Lord, stating,

قَالَ لَمْ أَكُن لِّأَسْجُدَ لِبَشَرٍ خَلَقْتَهُ مِن صَلْصَالٍ مِّنْ حَمَإٍ مَّسْنُونٍ (٣٣)

"'I am not one to prostrate myself to man, whom Thou didst create from sounding clay, from mud mould into shape.'" (Holy Qur'an 15:33)

As such, Iblis—who is now Satan (adversary)—was removed from his station and cast out of the presence of the angels. He thus became man's open enemy.

Omar continued his speech by stating that the jinn who are of the same race as Iblis are not all evil. Some have indicated that they follow Islam and believe in Prophet Muhammad (PBUH) after hearing the recitation of the Holy Qur'an:

وَإِذْ صَرَفْنَا إِلَيْكَ نَفَرًا مِّنَ الْجِنِّ يَسْتَمِعُونَ الْقُرْآنَ فَلَمَّا حَضَرُوهُ قَالُوا أَنصِتُوا فَلَمَّا قُضِيَ وَلَّوْا إِلَىٰ قَوْمِهِم مُّنذِرِينَ (٢٩)

"Behold, We turned towards thee a company of Jinn's (quietly) listening to the Qur'an: when they stood in the presence thereof, they said, "Listen in silence!" When the (reading) was finished, they returned to their people, to warn (them of their sins)." (Holy Qur'an 46:29)

Thus, among the jinn are those who believe in Islam and those who disbelieve in Islam. There are those who go about their lives worshipping God as they were meant to do; and there are those who are an open enemy to the righteous among men.

Toward the end of his speech, Imam Omar mentioned that Prophet Muhammad (PBUH) informed his people that among all mankind, there is a type of jinn attached to each and every person. The jinn side of man makes evil suggestions to his soul. When question by his people, Prophet Muhammad (PBUH) was asked if he had a jinn. He replied to them that he does indeed have one attached but it became Muslim.

Thus, does every person act according to their nature, which is guided by their jinn or their higher self. A person either listens to the jinn (which can lead to wrongdoing) or to the higher side of one's nature that desires only to please their Lord.

We pray for Allah's forgiveness and guidance. Ameen.

$$\text{بِسْمِ ٱللَّهِ ٱلرَّحْمَٰنِ ٱلرَّحِيمِ}$$

With Allah's name, the merciful Benefactor, the merciful redeemer

May the prayers and the peace be upon Allah's noble and kind messenger, Muhammad.

Trials and Temptations

By Imam Omar Hazim

Edited online by Khalil Green

On Friday May 22, 2010, Imam Omar Hazim gave an encouraging sermon titled "Trials and Temptations."

Imam Omar began by stating that there is no way we can come into this world and grow spiritually without some type of trial and temptation.

Omar stated that during the first three years of Prophet Muhammad's (PBUH) mission, he taught Islam in secret. He was commanded by God to teach it at first to a small group. After three years, chapter 74, verse 1-2 was revealed, which states,

$$\text{يَٰٓأَيُّهَا ٱلْمُدَّثِّرُ (١) قُمْ فَأَنذِرْ (٢)}$$

"O thou wrapped up (in the mantle)! Arise and deliver thy warning!"

The Prophet was wrapped up in secrecy by God's command. But when this verse was revealed, it was time for Prophet Muhammad (PBUH) to take this message to everyone, stated Omar.

However, when Prophet Muhammad (PBUH) proclaimed only one God, the trials and tests of the new community began. His uncle threw stones at him; thus, was he tested by the hardship of being the Messenger, as we will be tested, stated Omar.

Imam Omar, quoting chapter 29, verse 2, stated,

$$\text{أَحَسِبَ ٱلنَّاسُ أَن يُتْرَكُوٓا۟ أَن يَقُولُوٓا۟ ءَامَنَّا وَهُمْ لَا يُفْتَنُونَ (٢)}$$

"Do men think that they will be left alone on saying, "We believe", and that they will not be tested?"

"In other words, do people think that verbal declaration is enough for those who believe in God?" asked Omar.

Prophet Muhammad (PBUH) is reported to have said "faith is a conviction that is deep within the heart." Those who believe feel it deeply before it is acknowledged. Then comes the declaration with the mouth, and then come the good works. In the Holy Qur'an, faith and good works are mentioned together as if they are one and the same, said Omar.

The Holy Qur'an is translated into many languages and translated by many scholars and linguists. "But the best translation is translating our faith into good actions, good works and good deeds," stated Omar.

Those who are deepest in faith and belief have the most severe of tests. In order of severity, the Prophet's degree of most severe, then the righteous, then the best of men and women. Thus, "the stronger a person is into their religious convictions the stronger the test," affirmed Omar.

When the message was proclaimed in public by Prophet Muhammad (PBUH), slaves who converted to Islam were beaten. Businesspeople were boycotted. Influential people like Abu Bakr were shunned.

The Ethiopian slave Bilal was dragged in the streets by his pagan master. Hot sand was thrown on him. Yet he refused to renounce Islam. He continued to proclaim Islam until a boulder was placed on him. Then when he was unable to speak, he held up one finger to symbolize the One and only God. He endured until Prophet Muhammad's (PBUH) good friend sent Abu Bakr to purchase Bilal's freedom from his cruel owner.

Today we are also being tested, stated Omar. We were created to worship God and to be tested on this earth. Being tested is nothing new. The Prophets Ibrahim, Moses, Jesus, and others were all tested. Mary, mother of Prophet Jesus, was also tested. It is the same today, continued Omar.

The test comes in the form of foolish and false rhetoric by people who misunderstand Islam. Other right-wing bloggers and radio-show personalities have stated that anyone who has a Middle Eastern name should be scrutinized carefully in a separate line at the airport.

However, Omar responded, Muslims must remember that Prophet Muhammad's (PBUH) life is an example as to how we must exemplify his good human nature in such difficult circumstances. Muslims must do the works necessary to introduce Islam to society at large.

"Your mission as Muslims is not just to come out to the Islamic Center to pray, have dinners and social gathering, certain all that is a part of this work, but we must also have an eye on the future of Islam. We should always be ready to go out to the public, churches, synagogues, and wherever we are invited to tell the truth about Islam and to clear up all the horrible misconceptions that are prevalent in this society," stated Omar.

As the Holy Qur'an states in chapter 21, verse 18,

بَلْ نَقْذِفُ بِٱلْحَقِّ عَلَى ٱلْبَٰطِلِ فَيَدْمَغُهُ فَإِذَا هُوَ زَاهِقٌ وَلَكُمُ ٱلْوَيْلُ مِمَّا تَصِفُونَ (١٨)

"Nay, We hurl the Truth against falsehood, and it knocks out its brain, and behold, falsehood doth perish! Ah! Woe be to you for the (false) things ye ascribe (to us)," quoted Omar.

With all the falsehood out there, God tells us that truth will knock out falsehood. Not weapons of war. Just the simple truth, which God tells us cannot perish. It will always rise as surely as the sun rises, affirmed Omar.

The Holy Qur'an and the Bible are full of stories of how prophets and men and women of faith have suffered some of the hardest and harshest test. They all prevailed, and so must our community. It must prevail against ignorance, misinformation, and downright lies, stated Omar.

In his conclusion, Imam Omar, in acknowledging God's promise, quoted a verse from the Holy Qur'an—chapter 93, verses 1-5—which states,

وَٱلضُّحَىٰ (١) وَٱلَّيْلِ إِذَا سَجَىٰ (٢) مَا وَدَّعَكَ رَبُّكَ وَمَا قَلَىٰ (٣) وَلَلْأَخِرَةُ خَيْرٌ لَّكَ مِنَ ٱلْأُولَىٰ (٤) وَلَسَوْفَ يُعْطِيكَ رَبُّكَ فَتَرْضَىٰ (٥)

"By the Glorious Morning Light, and by the Night when it is still - Thy Guardian-Lord hath not forsaken thee, nor is He displeased. And verily the Hereafter will be better for thee than the present. And soon will thy Guardian-Lord give thee (that wherewith) thou shalt be well-pleased."

بِسْمِ ٱللَّهِ ٱلرَّحْمَٰنِ ٱلرَّحِيمِ

With Allah's name, the merciful Benefactor, the merciful redeemer

May the prayers and the peace be upon Allah's noble and kind messenger, Muhammad.

Purity in Islam (Taharah)

Sermon by Professor Ali Khan

Edited online by Khalil Green

Friday at the Islamic Center of Topeka, Professor Ali Khan gave a thought-provoking speech on purity in Islam (taharah).

Professor Khan began his speech by explaining the importance and need for Muslims to have a desire for purity in their worship at all times during daily life.

He encouraged Muslims to maintain a state of cleanliness before and during worship, and in every moment of life.

يَـٰٓأَيُّهَا ٱلَّذِينَ ءَامَنُوٓا۟ إِذَا قُمْتُمْ إِلَى ٱلصَّلَوٰةِ فَٱغْسِلُوا۟ وُجُوهَكُمْ وَأَيْدِيَكُمْ إِلَى ٱلْمَرَافِقِ وَٱمْسَحُوا۟ بِرُءُوسِكُمْ وَأَرْجُلَكُمْ إِلَى ٱلْكَعْبَيْنِ ۚ وَإِن كُنتُمْ جُنُبًا فَٱطَّهَّرُوا۟ ۚ وَإِن كُنتُم مَّرْضَىٰٓ أَوْ عَلَىٰ سَفَرٍ أَوْ جَآءَ أَحَدٌ مِّنكُم مِّنَ ٱلْغَآئِطِ أَوْ لَـٰمَسْتُمُ ٱلنِّسَآءَ فَلَمْ تَجِدُوا۟ مَآءً فَتَيَمَّمُوا۟ صَعِيدًا طَيِّبًا فَٱمْسَحُوا۟ بِوُجُوهِكُمْ وَأَيْدِيكُم مِّنْهُ ۚ مَا يُرِيدُ ٱللَّهُ لِيَجْعَلَ عَلَيْكُم مِّنْ حَرَجٍ وَلَـٰكِن يُرِيدُ لِيُطَهِّرَكُمْ وَلِيُتِمَّ نِعْمَتَهُۥ عَلَيْكُمْ لَعَلَّكُمْ تَشْكُرُونَ (٦)

"O ye who believe! When ye prepare for prayer, wash your faces, and your hands (and arms) to the elbows; Rub your heads (with water); and (wash) your feet to the ankles. If ye are in a state of ceremonial impurity, bathe your whole body . . . Allah doth not wish to place you in a difficulty, but to make you clean, and to complete his favour to you, that ye may be grateful." (Holy Qur'an 5:6)

According to Professor Khan, Islam, like no other religion, encourages its adherents to stay clean. At least five times a day, the Muslim should be washing his or her exposed skin and taking a bath or shower when necessary before prayer.

Such need for cleanliness induces into the mind of the Muslim the desire to be clean in spiritual ways also; for "Allah loveth those who make themselves pure [Taharah]" (Holy Qur'an 9:108).

Ali Khan continued by stating that cleanliness of the inner self is another way of understanding what God is saying in the Holy Qur'an. He stated that Muslims should be thinking purely as did Prophet Muhammad (PBUH).

Ali Khan referenced a story about Prophet Muhammad (PBUH) where a man came to the mosque in Medina to learn about Islam. The man urinated in the corner of the mosque, which in at that era in history was a sandy floor covered with prayer rugs. This act created a stir among the Muslims. Prophet Muhammad (PBUH) calmed the Muslims down and told them to clean it up, and taught the man through kind words that it is inappropriate to urinate in a place of prayer and worship.

This story shows the need for all Muslims to think about kindness and love toward their neighbors, and collectively come together for the mutual benefit of their fellow humankind.

At the end of the service, a collection was taken up for the relief of the inhabitants in Haiti.

"Our Lord! Let not our hearts deviate now after you have guided us on the right path, but grant us mercy from Your own Presence, for you are the grantor of bounties without measure." Ameen.

بِسْمِ ٱللَّهِ ٱلرَّحْمَٰنِ ٱلرَّحِيمِ

With Allah's name, the merciful Benefactor, the merciful redeemer

May the prayers and the peace be upon Allah's noble and kind messenger, Muhammad.

The Uniqueness of Our Dependency upon Each Other

Sermon by Imam Muhammad Shabazz

Edited online by Khalil Green

On Friday, February 5, 2010, guest speaker Imam Muhammad Shabazz from Kansas City, Missouri, of Masjid Al-Inshura delivered the sermon at the Islamic Center of Topeka.

His dynamic speech touched the hearts of many Muslims present.

In his introduction, Imam Shabazz related to the community the misnomer of attaching the phrase *superpower* to nations on earth. He stated that all nations rise, have their time on earth, and then eventually fail. He continued that the only true superpower is that which never fails and is eternal; that something is God.

Imam Shabazz referenced a verse from the Holy Qur'an that states,

سُبْحَٰنَ ٱلَّذِى خَلَقَ ٱلْأَزْوَٰجَ كُلَّهَا مِمَّا تُنۢبِتُ ٱلْأَرْضُ وَمِنْ أَنفُسِهِمْ وَمِمَّا لَا يَعْلَمُونَ (٣٦)

"Glory to Allah, Who created in pairs all things that the earth produces, as well as their own (human) kind and (other) things of which they have no knowledge." (Holy Qur'an 36:36)

According to Imam Shabazz, this shows not only the uniqueness of creation but that each created thing is dependent on something opposite, or complementary, to it.

The plants were created with male and female parts, and will fail if one part is missing. The seasons were created in pairs, and all life would fail if winter wasn't paired with summer, or spring with fall. Opposites in the seasons are needed to promote life.

Man too was created in pairs, with the male and female gender. As such, these oppositional forces represent the necessary limitation of dependency needed for creation to function properly.

However, within God there exists no such differentiation or limitation. God is the only supreme superpower that exists independently of the need for anything or anyone.

As such, in Islam, there exists no opposite of God. Satan is merely a created being who has chosen to be evil, and is an adversary to humanity.

God created the light and darkness; then He brings forth from the depths of darkness living things into the brightness of day.

God is supreme over all His creation and has created everything with a positive codependency so that everyone can understand their need for each other.

May Allah help us to be productive in this life and bless us with the best in the next life. Ameen.

بِسْمِ ٱللَّهِ ٱلرَّحْمَٰنِ ٱلرَّحِيمِ

With Allah's name, the merciful Benefactor, the merciful redeemer

May the prayers and the peace be upon Allah's noble and kind messenger, Muhammad.

Patriotism

Sermon by Imam Omar Hazim

Edited online by Khalil Green

On Friday July 2, 2010, Imam Omar Hazim delivered a captivating sermon titled "Questioning Patriotism."

After prayers and supplications to God, Imam Omar stated that he will be discussing the questions of patriotism in our homes and community.

Omar began by stating that the Holy Qur'an tells us that Allah is Al-Hayyu, the Living, "he is the author of all that exist in this world." Thus, Allah represents life and living. The word *hayyu* means to live, to fertilize the earth, and let someone live. It is also used in the call to prayer when it says "Come lively to prayer" (hayya ala salah). Furthermore, the prophet John's (yahya) name in the Holy Qur'an means life.

Omar stated that the word *falah*, which is mentioned in the call to prayer (hayyah ala falah), also means success. So God uses this word to tell us to come to success. The word also means to unfold something in order to reveal its intricate properties, till the soil to break up the surface to and make the life therein active and productive.

So coming to prayer, stated Omar, means prosperity and success in this life as well as the next. Thus, prayer is to help the devotee open up and bring forth the latent or inner potential. To bring forth what is best in us. "Whatever that is noble and good within us must come out so as to manifest the potentiality of the greatness that God has put in you and me," stated Omar. As such, we must work out our own evolution.

Jumuah is a part of this evolution, continued Omar, and Muslims attend the Friday prayer in the hope that something is said to aid us in solving our problems. Or if nothing is said, it could be the *rakah* (a unit of prayer involving standing, sitting, and prostrating) that we perform so that God may open that gate for us and answer our prayers.

The Holy Qur'an states in chapter 33:70 that

يَـٰٓأَيُّهَا ٱلَّذِينَ ءَامَنُوا۟ ٱتَّقُوا۟ ٱللَّهَ وَقُولُوا۟ قَوْلًا سَدِيدًا (٧٠)

"O ye who believe! Fear Allah, and (always) say a word directed to the Right."

In lieu of this verse, Omar stated that we should always be truthful and say a word of kindness; and if we do this, Allah states that He will make our conduct whole and sound and forgive our sins.

So with patriotism, the meaning is to have a devotion to a cause and have love for one's country. However, Omar continued, as true Muslims, we will make the best patriots to our country wherever in the world that may be due to our love for justice.

Omar then asked the following questions: So is it wrong to love one's country? Should one love it more than justice and Allah? People want to know if Muslims are patriotic. Can you be a good Muslim and be a good American citizen? Yet in some countries, patriotism can run so high as to blind its people to any injustice their nation may commit.

The poet Ben Johnson stated, "Patriotism is the last refuge of the scoundrel." In his commentary, he remarked that when leaders no longer lead by moral standards, they rouse the people to patriotism in a last attempt to get to the people through their emotions.

When the opposition saw presidential candidate Barack Obama winning his bid for presidency, they began to call him a Muslim, an Arab, and a foreigner and said he was not patriotic because he did not always wear the flag lapel. "They have lost their reasoning," stated Omar.

You can be a patriot to a country without agreeing with everything the government says or does. Calling those who do not agree with certain aspects of governmental policy unpatriotic is unjust. You can have great love for your country and disagree with the current administration, stated Omar.

The Holy Qur'an states that Muslims are the best of people evolved for mankind. Omar asked the question why. He answered by stating it is because Muslims enjoin what is right and forbid what is wrong.

Imam Omar said of Imam W. Deen Mohammed that "sometimes he voted as a democrat and sometimes as a republican." His choice was based on the candidate and the issues. Sometimes, the Republican Party has a better concept; sometimes, the Democrats have a better concept. It has to do with justice and injustice.

During the civil war, a general told President Abraham Lincoln, "Don't worry, Mr. President, Allah is on our side." To which the President retorted, "But what worries me is if we are on Allah's side." Oftentimes, sports figures say Allah was with me. But the true question is, are you on Allah's side?

Imam Omar goes on to say, leaders in some countries want you to be with the government whether the country is right or wrong. Some countries will put you in prison for speaking out. Citizens should speak out. Omar, quoting the Prophet, stated that we should "help our brother when he is oppressed and when he is the oppressor." The people questioned the prophet by asking, "We understand when he is oppressed, but how can we help him when he is the oppressor?" The Prophet replied by saying, "You help him by stopping him from being the oppressor."

If the world adopted this philosophy, then the whole world would be better. Prophet Muhammad (PBUH) said that "speaking the truth in court against an unjust ruler is one of the best jihads."

Many in this country love President Obama, some don't, some think he is making great changes. If we see he is making an error, then, out of love, we should let him know. If you see that the imam or any brother is traveling along the wrong path, then you should go to him with kindness and inform him of his wrongdoing.

In 4:135, the Holy Qur'an states,

يَـٰٓأَيُّهَا ٱلَّذِينَ ءَامَنُوا۟ كُونُوا۟ قَوَّٰمِينَ بِٱلْقِسْطِ شُهَدَآءَ لِلَّهِ وَلَوْ عَلَىٰٓ أَنفُسِكُمْ أَوِ ٱلْوَٰلِدَيْنِ وَٱلْأَقْرَبِينَ ۚ إِن يَكُنْ غَنِيًّا أَوْ فَقِيرًا فَٱللَّهُ أَوْلَىٰ بِهِمَا ۖ فَلَا تَتَّبِعُوا۟ ٱلْهَوَىٰٓ أَن تَعْدِلُوا۟ ۚ وَإِن تَلْوُۥٓا۟ أَوْ تُعْرِضُوا۟ فَإِنَّ ٱللَّهَ كَانَ بِمَا تَعْمَلُونَ خَبِيرًا (١٣٥)

"O ye who believe! Stand out firmly for justice, as witnesses to Allah, even as against yourselves, or your parents, or your kin, and whether it be (against) rich or poor: for Allah can best protect both. Follow not the lusts (of your hearts); lest ye swerve, and if ye distort (justice) or decline to do justice, verily Allah is well-acquainted with all that ye do."

Omar stated that we should go home, read, and think about the powerful words of Allah. We should understand that the command from Allah toward justice is a command. It is not an option.

Omar continued that we have to look at ourselves critically and look outward. Slavery built this nation, and the former slaves lived off Jim Crow laws. Those involved in the civil rights movement were loyal to the country and wanted to see the country change course toward a policy of justice.

In his conclusion, Imam Omar stated that "just because some Muslims support the liberation of Palestine, support Muhammad Ali's refusal to go to Vietnam, or support Nelson Mandela for standing up against apartheid, for which he was incarcerated for twenty-seven years, does not mean that they were not patriotic." But by standing forth for righteousness, they were truly patriotic as we as Muslims are truly patriotic. For we stand up for justice in the country of which we reside.

"Our Lord! Let not our hearts deviate now after You have guided us on the right path, but grant us mercy from Your own presence, for You are the grantor of bounties without measure." Ameen.

Chapter 5

Articles in the Topeka Capital-Journal

Imam Omar Hazim. Reproduced by permission from Jeff A. Taylor of the *Topeka Capital-Journal*.

Islamic Leader Calls on Local Muslims to Devote Their Lives to Their Faith. Reproduced by permission from Phil Anderson of the *Topeka Capital-Journal*.

Speaking before a packed audience Friday afternoon at the Islamic Center of Topeka, Imam W. Deen Mohammed of Chicago urged local Muslims to live out the teachings of their faith for both personal and societal edification.

"We have to practice neighborly deeds," he said, "and Allah will reward us with what he has promised—and that is life, and a good life."

Mohammed, 67, leader of the 2.5 million members Muslim American Society, made his remarks at the jumuah prayer service at the Islamic Center of Topeka. Local Islamic leaders said Mohammad was the highest-ranking Muslim cleric ever to visit Topeka.

Officials estimated attendance at three hundred men, women, and children, with some people coming from as far away as St. Louis; Tulsa, Oklahoma; Dallas; and the Kansas City area.

On Friday night, Imam Mohammed delivered a public lecture at Lee Arena on the Washburn University campus before being honored at a banquet at the Bradbury Thompson Center.

His Topeka appearance was sponsored by the Islamic Center of Topeka, the Muslim Student Association, and the Washburn Student Association.

During his Friday afternoon presentation, Imam Mohammed quoted from the Qur'an, the holy book of Islam, as he exhorted attendees to "give our life, our whole life, in obedience" to God's guidance.

"God is saying to us that you can never have the fullness of blessings and good things he wants for us unless you strive for purification," he said. "God is wanting us to come into a strong moral life."

Mohammed also said individuals must take responsibility for how they live, not allowing themselves to get into situations that could compromise their ability to think clearly.

"If you do anything to affect clear thinking, you are making yourself vulnerable to all kinds of evils and troubles," he said. "You are putting yourself in a position to be taken away from God."

Among those in attendance at Friday afternoon's jumuah prayer service was Bilal Mohammad, forty-two, of Kansas City, Missouri.

"It means a lot to have the imam take time out of his schedule to be here," he said. "This is a man who goes all over the world, and to have him take time to come here does a lot for our spirits and keeps us in the know about where we should be putting our emphasis."

Sallye Wilkinson, of First Congregational church, shows "My Coloring Book of Salah" to guests from the Islamic Center of Topeka.

Christian church, Islamic Center sponsor for Middle East children.
"Building Bridges of Understanding."
Reproduced by permission from Phil Anderson.

Youths at First Congregational United Church of Christ and the Islamic Center of Topeka are finding common ground and increased cultural and religious understanding through a joint project in which they are sponsoring education for two young Middle Eastern children.

In the process, they are building bridges between Christians and Muslims in Topeka.

"We're trying to be peacemakers by building relationships between the church and the mosque," said Sally Wilkinson, an adult organizer of the First Congregational Church effort. "The whole idea is to get the kids to know each other and to help the children in Palestine."

The project began this past fall, when confirmation class students at First Congregational Church, 1701 SW Collins, launched a peacemaking project.

Left to right: Ferdousi Hossain, Sue Walters

The confirmation class linked with a humanitarian program sponsored by the United Church of Christ denomination to sponsor a five-year-old girl named Rand, who attends an interfaith school for Christian and Muslims in East Jerusalem. Arabic and English are taught in the school.

As part of the project, the church youths—who are in middle school—set out to raise funds to pay for two years of schooling for Rand. The fundraising involved a concert and a lock-in, with a collection also taken at a worship service.

The church then began working in partnership with youths from the Islamic Center of Topeka, 1115 SE Twenty-seventh, who sponsored the cost of an education for a kindergartner boy named Khaleel at the same school. Imam Omar Hazim and Ferdousi Hossain helped organize efforts at the Islamic Center.

Parents from both congregations have helped move the partnership forward, Wilkinson said.

The cost for one year of education for each of the children, which already has been covered, is $25 a month, or $300 a year, church leaders said. Fund-raising for a second year is to begin this summer.

Grace Hartzell, fifteen, a Topeka High School sophomore and First Congregational member, said the confirmation class enjoyed being able to help a child in a different part of the world.

She said the class also was benefiting from learning more about Islam from its meetings with Muslim youths in Topeka.

"It gives you a view of what another religion is like," Hartzell said. "You get to experience how they do things and compare it to the way you do it."

Sue Walters, Christian Education director at First Congregational, said the church has been staying in touch with the mosque, letting members there know about "everything we've got going on over here."

Walter said she expected the church and the mosque to do more events together in the future.

Beyond working together to sponsor schooling for the two youngsters in the Mideast, the church and mosque have broadened their efforts and have met together on several occasions.

In early March, about fifty church members—including children and adults—went to the Islamic Center of Topeka on a Sunday afternoon for lunch and a tour of the masjid, or house of worship.

In April, about twenty children and adults from the Islamic Center came to First Congregational to take part in an Easter egg hunt, followed by lunch tours of the church.

In May, thirty-three youths and seven adults from the Islamic Center came to the church to attend Sunday school and talk about their religion.

Shafeen Housain, ten, explained the five pillars of Islam to the Sunday school class and shared a story about Muhammad's compassion for a neighbor who threw trash on his doorstep every day.

Marah Schlingenseipen, twelve, of the church shared Jesus's parable of the Good Samaritan, followed by a discussion of the Golden Rule by youths from both faith groups.

Rehan Reza, president of the Islamic Center of Topeka, said he welcomed the interaction between the congregations.

"We want you to visit the mosque and see what we are doing and what we are teaching our kids," Reza told guests from the church during their March visit. "The Islamic Center is open to everyone."

Reza said he also appreciated it when churches opened their doors to Muslims.

Dr. Ashraf Sufi applauded the combined efforts of the mosque and church.

"It's always a good idea when two groups meet together and help children all over the world," Sufi said. "It does increase understanding because we are working together."

A Spiritual Journey:
Millions of Muslims Take Part in Hajj

by Phil Anderson of the *Topeka Capital-Journal*, 2006

For Dr. Ali Khan, president of the Islamic Center of Topeka, the pilgrimage to Mecca, Saudi Arabia, known as the hajj, is a momentous experience for millions of Muslims around the world.

"It represents the international unity of Muslims," said Khan, "because Muslims from all over the world come together."

The hajj is the fifth pillar of Islam, in addition to the Declaration of Faith, saying five prayers daily, performing acts of charity, and fasting during the month of Ramadan.

All Muslims who are physically and financially able to do so are mandated to go on hajj at least once in their lifetime.

This year, some two million pilgrims are expected to be on hand for the event, which Muslims believe was mandated by Abraham and reintroduced some 1,400 years ago by Muhammad.

Most go on hajj as part of larger groups, and quotas are allocated for various nations worldwide to accommodate as many as possible.

Through television coverage, which has increased in recent years, Muslims who aren't able to go on hajj can witness the event.

"It's no longer abstract," Khan said. "You can actually see it, even if you can't afford to be there."

The hajj began this past Sunday and continues until Tuesday, when the three-day celebration of Id al-Adha begins.

The hajj occurs during the first ten days of Zul-Hijjah, the twelfth month of the lunar calendar, which lasts twenty-nine or thirty days.

Once every thirty-two years, two hajjis occur on the same year on the Western calendar. This is the case in 2006, when the month of Zul-Hijjah began in January 1 and will start again December 22. During the hajj, pilgrims visit holy sites and perform a series of rituals.

One of the rituals is known as the *tawaf*, in which pilgrims march counterclockwise around the Kaaba. Muslims consider the Kaaba to be the first house of worship originally built by Adam and Eve and rebuilt later by Abraham and his son Ishmael.

Pilgrims throw stones at a wall in Mina, representing their rejection of Satan and their desire to fight against evil.

The ninth day of Zul-Hijjah, known as the Day of Forgiveness, is the most significant day of hajj. On this day, Muslims go to Mount Arafat, where they pray for Allah (SWT) to forgive them of their sins.

Regardless of nationality or lot in life, all men on the hajj wear identical clothing composed of two sheets.

"People from all regions and all countries come together to show that Islam is a universal religion," Khan said. "It represents solidarity across cultures and races and classes and customs."

Khan added that both men and women attend hajj without distinction.

Even Muslims who aren't able to attend the hajj are aware it is going on, as many know someone who is participating in any given year.

The hajj can be completed in a three-day or a ten-day period, though some pilgrims stay for longer periods.

Four members of the local Islamic community are known to be on the hajj this year, said Imam Omar Hazim, of the Islamic Center of Topeka.

Hazim, who has been on the hajj in 1977 and 1998, noted that those who stay home, rather than travel to Mecca, are encouraged to perform extra acts of obedience at this time.

"They should participate in more good deeds," Hazim said. "They should pray more and fast more.

"These ten days are important for us to be conscientious of what the Muslim community at large is doing, and we should be encouraged to do more good deeds."

At the conclusion of the hajj, Muslims will celebrate Id Al-Adha, which begins with prayer services at the mosques. In Topeka, an Id Al-Adha prayer service will take place at 8:00 a.m. Tuesday at the Islamic Center of Topeka, 1115 SE Twenty-seventh.

A large gathering will take place Tuesday in a conference room at Bannister Mall in Kansas City, Missouri. Hazim said that the event is expected to attract from ten thousand to twelve thousand area Muslims.

For Id Al-Adha, many Muslims sacrifice an animal such as a goat, cow, or sheep, commemorating Abraham's obedience to Allah (SWT). Meat is shared with the needy in the community.

The Islamic Center of Topeka will have a community dinner and gathering at 5:00 p.m., January 15, after Id al-Adha has concluded.

Muslims Cringe at Terror Tie

Muslims: Imam Says There Has Been No Local Backlash

Phil Anderson of the *Topeka Capital-Journal*

Local Muslims say they condemn terrorism and are displeased when their religion is associated with perpetrators behind the violence.

In particular, local Muslims say they would like to see an end to such terms as "Islamic terrorist" in media reports.

"They should not bring Islam into the picture," said Rehan Reza, president of the Islamic Center of Topeka. "Religion is separate from politics."

Reza said he believed recent terrorist attacks in London were carried out from anger rather than religion.

The fact that terrorist may be Muslims is secondary, he said, and shouldn't be used to detract from the religion, which has an estimated 1.2 billion adherents worldwide, including about six million in the United States.

"Islam is designed for peace," Reza said. "Islam is not designed for terrorism or to destroy and kill innocent people."

While denouncing terrorism, Imam Omar Hazim, of the Islamic Center of Topeka, said foreign policy issues and politics may be a factor in the violence.

Hazim and other members of the Islamic Center of Topeka said Muslims in Topeka haven't been subjected to religious-based backlash in light of recent terrorism.

"I believe people of Topeka understand the beauty of Islam, maybe more so than in other cities," he said, "because we've had so much good interaction with people for so long."

Hazim said Muslims in the United State and other nations are continuing to speak out against terrorism, and many have signed the "Not in the Name of Islam" online petition sponsored by the Council on American-Islamic Relations.

According to www.cair-net.org earlier this week, nearly seven hundred thousand people had signed the petition, which is designed to "correct misperceptions of Islam and the Islamic stance on religiously motivated terror."

Ron Owen Hasan, one of the assistant imams at the Islamic Center of Topeka, said such pronouncements are nothing new. Muslims have been denouncing terrorism for years, he said, but their statements seem to fall on deaf ears.

"We say it all the time," Hasan said. "It's just that people ignore it."

Dr. Samir F. Badawi, of Topeka, said the United States government is making a "major mistake" if it deals with Islam in the same way it did with "communist ideology" decades ago—as a problem it would defeat in a matter of time.

Badawi said the United States should instead do all it can to present Islam in a positive light, especially in educational setting and classroom curriculum.

Dr. Ashraf Sufi said he and his wife, Qaiser, "strongly condemn" attacks, such as the bombing on the London subway.

"No moral person of any faith, whether Christians, Jews, Muslims, or Hindus, will do what they did," said Sufi, of Topeka. "All moderate Muslims, at this time, should get together and help the authorities to find these extremists so this kind of terror does not happen again."

Sufi said the United States also should stabilize the situation in Iraq, withdraw its forces, and find a solution to the Palestinian-Israeli conflict so these situations can't be used as a scapegoat for terrorist attacks.

Amer Safadi, of Lawrence, said those who commit the acts of terrorism "are nothing but murderers and represent no one but themselves and their own created ideology. No one who believes in Allah [SWT] can commit such crimes, and in Islam in particular has no room and will have no room for such people."

Safadi said that rather than confronting terrorists with a similar kind of violence, people need to get together to address issues ranging from "Islamophobia, racism, economic deprivation, social injustice, and other factors that drive those people towards the path of violence."

Chapter 6

Ramadan and Eid

سُورَةُ الْبَقَرَةِ

شَهْرُ رَمَضَانَ الَّذِي أُنزِلَ فِيهِ الْقُرْءَانُ هُدًى لِلنَّاسِ وَبَيِّنَـٰتٍ مِنَ الْهُدَىٰ وَالْفُرْقَانِ فَمَن شَهِدَ مِنكُمُ الشَّهْرَ فَلْيَصُمْهُ وَمَن كَانَ مَرِيضًا أَوْ عَلَىٰ سَفَرٍ فَعِدَّةٌ مِنْ أَيَّامٍ أُخَرَ يُرِيدُ اللَّهُ بِكُمُ الْيُسْرَ وَلَا يُرِيدُ بِكُمُ الْعُسْرَ وَلِتُكْمِلُوا الْعِدَّةَ وَلِتُكَبِّرُوا اللَّهَ عَلَىٰ مَا هَدَىٰكُمْ وَلَعَلَّكُمْ تَشْكُرُونَ (١٨٥)

"Ramadhan is the (month) in which was sent down the Qur'an, as a guide to mankind, also clear (Signs) for guidance and judgment (Between right and wrong). So every one of you who is present (at his home) during that month should spend it in fasting, but if anyone is ill, or on a journey, the prescribed period (Should be made up) by days later. Allah intends every facility for you; He does not want to put to difficulties. (He wants you) to complete the prescribed period, and to glorify Him in that He has guided you; and perchance ye shall be grateful." (Holy Qur'an 2:185)

$$\text{بِسْمِ ٱللَّهِ ٱلرَّحْمَٰنِ ٱلرَّحِيمِ}$$

With Allah's name, the merciful Benefactor, the merciful redeemer

Injustice Anywhere is a Threat to Justice Everywhere

Imam Omar Hazim

It's critical for us to understand that each day is an opportunity for us to be forgiven our mistakes and shortcomings.

Today we chose to talk about justice.

"Injustice anywhere in the world is a threat to justice everywhere." This is a statement by Martin Luther King who made it during the civil rights movement.

It is in accordance with the Holy Qur'anic teachings and with Prophet Muhammad (PBUH).

Let me begin by reading a verse from chapter 3, verse 189 from the Holy Qur'an:

$$\text{وَلِلَّهِ مُلْكُ ٱلسَّمَٰوَٰتِ وَٱلْأَرْضِ ۗ وَٱللَّهُ عَلَىٰ كُلِّ شَيْءٍ قَدِيرٌ (١٨٩)}$$

"To Allah belongs the dominion of the heavens and the earth and Allah has power over all things."

Wallahi is mentioned everywhere and pertains to Allah's (SWT)'s ownership. Allah is saying that He is the owner of heaven and earth. And the last part of the verse contains the word *Allahu*; it pertains to the all-seeing God who sees everything in the heavens and the earth, the light and darkness. What is in darkness to humanity is in full view to Allah.

Reading from the Holy Qur'an in chapter (surah) Hud, the eleventh chapter of the Holy Qur'an, it opens *A, L.R.* These are mystic letters sometimes translated as "Allah the best knower." It is designed to get the reader's attention.

And in most cases, we see after these letters it tells us something about the book. Then it says in chapter 11:1,

الر ۚ كِتَابٌ أُحْكِمَتْ آيَاتُهُ ثُمَّ فُصِّلَتْ مِن لَّدُنْ حَكِيمٍ خَبِيرٍ

"This is a book with verses basic or fundamental of established meaning further explained in detail from one who is wise and acquainted with all things."

So after he gets our attention, he said these are basic or fundamental. There are other verses from the Holy Qur'an that are allegorical and require our research and study and more thinking, more praying over while asking Allah for guidance.

This is telling us by using *ukibat* from the root *hakimah*, and *hakima* has different shades of meaning, but here it is, saying the verses are rooted in wisdom and knowledge; then he uses the word *fusillat*. That it means to make clear, to set apart from, to explain in detail, to narrate a thing with all its particular and divine parts. So everything in the Holy Qur'an contains a reason and a philosophy selected by God to be contained in this divine revelation. It gives a message of hope and warns against evil inspired by their soul or influenced by someone else.

Injustice anywhere is a threat to justice everywhere.

Like those verses in the Holy Qur'an that talks about the basic and fundamental principles of justice, it is basic and fundamental to the nature of human beings and society as a whole that Allah (SWT) placed justice in the Holy Qur'an over thirty-three times and usually four or five times in the same verse. The word is *Al-Mizan*, meaning weight, balance, even, and equally balanced in due proportion. This is the message of the Holy Qur'an. Allah states in the Holy Qur'an in reference to this type of justice that he has given to humanity a sign in his creation in chapter 55 (surah) Rahman, Allah (SWT) says in verses 7-9 that "and the firmament that he has raised high and he has set up the balance of justice; In order that ye may not transgress due balance. So establish just weight and justice and fall not short in the balance."

So Allah is telling us that His very fundamental creation of heaven and earth that we see every day—the sun, moon, and wind that we don't see but feel—is all established in balance so that we won't transgress balance. So we establish our world with balance and justice, then we can have peace in our souls, societies, homes, and in the world. But when justice is missing from our own lives, we have no peace in our souls and surely won't have it in our world.

As we continue, I want to read a few of these basic fundamental *ayat* in the Holy Qur'an that was mentioned in chapter (surah) 5:8:

يَـٰٓأَيُّهَا ٱلَّذِينَ ءَامَنُوا۟ كُونُوا۟ قَوَّٰمِينَ لِلَّهِ شُهَدَآءَ بِٱلْقِسْطِ ۖ وَلَا يَجْرِمَنَّكُمْ شَنَـَٔانُ قَوْمٍ عَلَىٰٓ أَلَّا تَعْدِلُوا۟ ۚ ٱعْدِلُوا۟ هُوَ أَقْرَبُ لِلتَّقْوَىٰ ۖ وَٱتَّقُوا۟ ٱللَّهَ ۚ إِنَّ ٱللَّهَ خَبِيرٌۢ بِمَا تَعْمَلُونَ (٨)

"O ye who believe! stand out firmly for Allah, as witnesses to fair dealing, and let not the hatred of others to you make you swerve to wrong and depart from justice. Be just: that is next to piety: and fear Allah; For Allah is well-acquainted with all that ye do."

We don't need a lot of *tafsir* to understand those basic words rooted in wisdom.

Oftentimes, in our world, we find that people are more just toward the rich and less for the poor. Some tend to lean toward fairness to parents and friends. But Allah tells us to be fair and just to all people.

In chapter (surah) 4:58, the Holy Qur'an states,

إِنَّ ٱللَّهَ يَأْمُرُكُمْ أَن تُؤَدُّوا۟ ٱلْأَمَـٰنَـٰتِ إِلَىٰٓ أَهْلِهَا وَإِذَا حَكَمْتُم بَيْنَ ٱلنَّاسِ أَن تَحْكُمُوا۟ بِٱلْعَدْلِ ۚ إِنَّ ٱللَّهَ نِعِمَّا يَعِظُكُم بِهِۦٓ ۗ إِنَّ ٱللَّهَ كَانَ سَمِيعًۢا بَصِيرًا (٥٨)

"Allah doth command you to render back your trusts to those to whom they are due; And when ye judge between man and man, that ye judge with justice: Verily how excellent is the teaching which He giveth you! For Allah is He Who heareth and seeth all things."

We are approaching the inauguration of Barack Obama. We are seeing a change in America. But we should ask what type of characteristics we want to see in our president. We have seen him campaigning and seen many of his qualities.

We would like to see justice in our new president that is equally balanced, setting himself apart from the last administration: courage to stand up to those who will bring him to corruption. We would like to see him establish a set of new foreign policies and get away from the present and past administration, especially with regard to Middle Eastern policies. We would like for him to step back and get away from the double standards especially toward the relation and policies in the Middle East.

The Prophet said if someone charges you with being unjust, stand back and take a look at yourself and see if there is any truth. If there is, you should try to make an adjustment.

Martin Luther King's birthday yesterday coincides with Presidents' Day and the day of this inauguration.

The history of all countries is recorded with Allah and is still being recorded. Just as Allah is the best knower of what you and I do, He is the knower of all countries.

Prophet Muhammad (PBUH) said to help your brother whether he is an oppressor or if he is being oppressed. His companions said, "We understand that we are to help him when he is oppressed, but how do we help him when he is an oppressor." The Prophet responded by saying, "By holding him back from his oppression."

Allah says in the Qur'an that taking a life unjustifiably is like taking the life of all humanity, and to save a life is like saving all humanity.

The Holy Qur'an chapter 3:8 provides a closing prayer:

"Our Lord! Let not our hearts deviate now after you have guided us on the right path, but grant us mercy from your own presence, for you are the grantor of bounties without measure." Ameen.

بِسْمِ اللهِ الرَّحْمَٰنِ الرَّحِيمِ

With Allah's name, the merciful Benefactor, the merciful redeemer

Eid-ul-Adha 2005

The Value of Sacrifice

Imam Omar Hazim

As-salaam alaikum. That is peace be unto you. I seek refuge with Allah (SWT), the Merciful Benefactor, the Merciful Redeemer.

I am going to say a few words on the value of sacrifice, and I promise you that I will keep it as short as possible.

We are here tonight to celebrate the Muslim Eid-ul-Adha of peace and sacrifice.

This tradition came from the father Abraham, the prophet who spawned monotheism and the Prophet Abraham (AS) who was mentioned by the governor.

Abraham is acknowledged by Jews, Christians, and Muslims, and others around the world have a great respect for him.

Prophet Abraham (AS) is mentioned in the Holy Qur'an and the Bible, that he loved Allah (SWT) and a very pious individual and community life. He was becoming an old man, and he wanted to have a son who would represent him in righteousness and piety; therefore, he wanted to have a son when he became an old man to be a servant of Allah (SWT) and have dignity and respect for life and respect for Allah (SWT). But he began to wonder if he would have a child to carry on his legacy. He became old and wondered if he would have a son.

In the Bible, Genesis 16:16 states that he was eighty-six years old according to scripture when Ishmael was born. Then the same scripture tells us in Genesis 21:5 states that he was one hundred years old when Isaac was born.

He had prayed for a son for so long, then he received in a dream that he was to sacrifice his son. He understood that he was to sacrifice him for the sake of Allah (SWT). He asked his son Ishmael, "What do you think should we do?" This may sound strange and unusual because it is strange and unusual. He said, "If Allah (SWT) wills, you will find me patient." This story is told to Jews, Muslims, and Christians and all humanity.

When they were actually in the act, Allah (SWT) stopped him. Then Allah (SWT) stopped Abraham and said, "You have already fulfilled the vision." Because the vision had to do with the intention of the heart was already fulfilled because the vision has to do with the intention of the heart.

That is why when we slaughter an animal, we say, "Allah is the greatest. In the name of Allah [SWT], the Merciful Benefactor, the Merciful Redeemer. Truly my prayers, my service, my sacrifice, my life, my death are all for Allah [SWT], the Lord of the Worlds."

For the Creator knows the depth of the intention in our heart before the vision even began. So Allah (SWT) stopped him before the act was completed, and this tells us that we should place strong emphasis on life. When Muslims sacrifice, they sacrifice animals to provide food to others.

If we read the Holy Qur'an carefully, we never see that in his vision he sacrificed, killed, or saw his son dead.

Allah told Prophet Abraham, "Stop, you have already fulfilled the vision." The Creator knows our very dreams and visions and what is in our hearts and when the vision stops.

The story placed great emphasis on the value of human life. Many people see Muslims sacrifice our animals and think it strange. But we eat meat, fruit, and vegetables every day. The substance that Allah (SWT) provides in the earth has always been there. The call to sacrifice by the Creator is a call to increase the human excellence.

The story also mentions Cain and Abel and talks about a sacrifice. So the Christians and Jews also identify with that. From the very beginning of time, Allah (SWT) has ordered men and women to practice sacrifices. This is to remove greed, selfishness, and pride that creep up in our souls. It is designed for us to look at the diamond, to look at ourselves as diamonds made from black coal produced under pressure in the earth.

Allah causes a beautiful child to come from the love of Mom and Dad. Life is borne from the hardship, labor, and pain by the women, but a life emerges from that pressure.

We are living in a Stone Age of tall buildings, where the brick and steel are produced from the fires of pressure.

When Allah tells us to sacrifice, the greater sacrifice is defined as the sacrifice of human effort. And this celebration represents the sacrifice of Abraham and Ishmael.

And this sacrifice is acknowledged and commemorated until the Day of Judgment because it is so valuable. Most of us are not willing to sacrifice life for greater causes, or die for greater causes. And God is not asking us to do so. But many of us have to sacrifice for family and our children.

When we make a sacrifice for the greater good of society and the greater good of humanity, it does not belittle the work or value of our character but increases it. So when Allah (SWT) calls to the human being to sacrifice, it is a call that helps Him to work out our evolution and bring about our best ability, the best potential of our mind that Allah (SWT) has placed within us. The sacrifice of us and others helps complete the best evolution of humanity and increases our character and helps us work out our development.

Allah (SWT) has placed those great potentials in us to sacrifice for others and community life.

The test of the sacrifice increases moral excellence, goodness, faith, hope, love, and patience.

He knew that Abraham would be willing, then why have him do it? Then why would Allah (SWT) ask? The reality is that we are not rewarded for our capabilities and potentials until they are manifested. That is the test.

We cannot charge a person of being a criminal because someone has the potential for being a criminal. Likewise, you cannot reward a person for their potential. Good has to be manifested before the reward can be given. Thus does Allah (SWT) give us this great opportunity to do good and sacrifice for others. Any who does good will receive his reward with his Lord regardless of their belief.

Let our faith be translated into good actions.

Our Lord! Give us good in this world and good in the next world, and save us from the torment of the fire. Ameen.

بِسْمِ ٱللَّهِ ٱلرَّحْمَٰنِ ٱلرَّحِيمِ

With Allah's name, the merciful Benefactor, the merciful redeemer

Eid Prayer 2001

Power of Faith

Imam Omar Hazim

Praise be to Allah, praise be to Allah, praise be to Allah, praise be to Allah.

Praise be to Allah, Lord of the Worlds.

Praise be to Allah, the Lord and Cherisher of all the worlds, Lord of all the systems of knowledge. Eid Mubarak (Blessed Eid)

Dear brothers and sisters,

During this khutbah today, I ask Allah to guide me, to guide my thoughts, my heart, to put the correct words into my mouth.

Praise be to Allah, praise be to Allah, praise be to Allah.

We praise Allah (SWT). There is no deity but Allah, and Muhammad is the Messenger of Allah. Allah is one God, the one and only God, Creator of the heavens of the earth.

There is nothing worthy of worship but Allah (SWT). He created everything contained in the earth and is the same who made every living thing.

The same Allah, the one Allah who made Adam from dust without mother or father.

The same Allah, the one Allah who told Noah to build the ark.

The same Allah, the one Allah who gave revelation to Musa.

The same Allah, the one Allah who when they cast Abraham into the fire, He said, "O Fire be cool and a means of safety for Abraham."

This is the Allah we praise, the Allah we Worship, praise be to Allah (SWT).

The same Allah, the one Allah who guided Musa and his followers through the Red Sea.

The same Allah, the one Allah who guided and gave Jesus revelation.

The same Allah, the one Allah who made Jesus come into being through Mary without a father. Peace be upon all of them.

The same Allah, the one Allah who gave Jesus many miracles.

The same Allah, the one Allah whom we worship.

Allah (SWT) is the same Allah that taught Muhammad and created many miracles in his life.

This one Allah (SWT) who created everything in the heavens and the earth; by His guidance, Prophet Muhammad has become the number one influential person in history of the world. There is not one man who has had as much influence on society as Prophet Muhammad (PBUH).

This rating of number one of the most influential people was given by Michael Hart in his book titled *100 Most Influential People in the World*. We as Muslims know this to be true without a doubt.

Allah (SWT), whom we serve and worship, states in the Holy Qur'an, chapter (surah) 61, verses 10-12, "O ye who believe! Shall I lead you to a bargain that will save you from a grievous Penalty? That ye believe in Allah and His Apostle, and that Ye strive (your utmost) in the cause of Allah with your property and your persons that would be best for you, if ye but knew! Allah will forgive you Your sins and admit you to gardens which rivers flow and to beautiful mansions in gardens of eternity that is indeed the supreme achievement."

Faith, dear Muslims, is the same as belief; it is called *iman* in Arabic, being trustworthy and reliable. Such a small asking for such a great reward for us to have faith and act accordingly with goodness. These are some of the components of faith:

The first component of faith is belief in the heart, the second is by bearing witness openly that there is no Allah but one Allah, and the third is good deeds and works. There are over seventy-two components of faith according to the Prophet (PBUH).

This transaction is a transaction that is common in the sense that Allah (SWT) had created man to be one who makes transactions.

One transaction that Allah has made is the transaction with nature. The man makes seeds that he puts in the earth. This is a transaction that he makes with the earth. Then the earth will reap for the man what he puts in the earth.

It is natural for man to have a transaction within the earth where he lives.

Examples:

The trees and humanity have transactions with each another. The trees give off oxygen, and we humans will inhale the oxygen and exhale carbon dioxide, which they receive and benefit from.

We plant seeds in the earth for crops, and the earth gives us back much more in harvest than we plant. This is a beneficial transaction.

Prophet Muhammad (PBUH) had transactions with people before he became the Messenger; he worked for his wife and they had transactions.

Muslims come out on the Eid and are forgiven by Allah (SWT). They come out with their hands raised in supplication, asking for forgiveness, and Allah (SWT) said to the angels "to tell my male and female servants that I will tell them I have forgiven them their sins."

This is a transaction that Allah (SWT) has made with you and I. Prophet Muhammad (PBUH) said that Allah told him in Hadith Al-Qudsi that after the fast and after the physical life of the human being on earth and at judgment day, that the Holy Qur'an will speak and say to Allah that "your servants who have fasted through the month of Ramadan. I have denied them sleep because they were reading me so let me intercede on their behalf." And the fast said, "Oh Allah I have denied your servant pleasure of water and food so let me intercede on their behalf and Allah granted the request."

The Prophet said, "At times of discord and corruption, that one action, that is in accord with his example, will earn you the reward of a hundred martyrs." In this time in which we live, life makes it easy for a person to stray to do wickedness instead of doing good.

In the aspect of faith, another element is justice. Allah said that we should do justice regardless to who or what, even if it means doing justice to ourselves if we are wrong; then we point out the wrong to ourselves, that we should point out the wrong within ourselves and try to correct it.

Prophet Muhammad (PBUH) said if you see a wrongdoing, try to stop it with your mouth. If you can't stop it with your mouth, try to stop it with your hands, then at least hate it in your heart.

Wherever we see oppression and corruption in the earth, we should speak out against it and stand up for what is right. If wrong and corruption are in our own homes, we should protest them.

This is what Allah (SWT) and the Prophet said.

Justice is an element of faith. Allah says in the Holy Qur'an, surah 55, verses 7-9,

وَٱلسَّمَاءَ رَفَعَهَا وَوَضَعَ ٱلْمِيزَانَ (٧) أَلَّا تَطْغَوْا فِى ٱلْمِيزَانِ (٨) وَأَقِيمُوا ٱلْوَزْنَ بِٱلْقِسْطِ وَلَا تُخْسِرُوا ٱلْمِيزَانَ (٩)

"And the firmament has he raised high and he sat up the balance (of justice) in order that you may not transgress due balance so establish weight with justice and fall not short in the balance."

Allah is telling us here that justice is a heavenly mercy. Allah points out that the heavens are ordered and He has established that order so that we can see that order and recognize the balance of that order.

If there is ever to be peace in the earth, justice must be established. Justice is the essential ingredient to having that peace. There will never be peace in the earth as long as there is a double standard in the society in which we live. Justice is a component of faith.

Imam Omar Hazim

The value of human life was established by Allah. Allah says in the Holy Qur'an that destroying one life is like destroying all life. The life of the human is established by Allah.

In the story of the two sons of Adam, life is so precious, so valuable that even the raven, which will eat anything, came to Cain and scratched the ground and showed him how to bury his brother. We do not take the life of another person that is innocent. Charity is the center of faith.

For those who have abundance will they give in charity. Thus, this is a test for the rich.

Allah told the Prophet in Hadith Al Qudsi, an angel saw the magnificent structure Allah (SWT) created. The mountains made to stabilize the earth. The angel asked, "Is there anything stronger than mountains?"

Allah said, "Yes, I made iron, which is stronger than the mountains."

The angel asked, "Is there anything stronger than the iron?"

Allah replied, "I made fire, which is stronger than iron. I made water, which is stronger than the fire and wind, which the wind is stronger than water. But when humanity gives in charity from his right hand and the left hand does not know of it, then the charity is stronger than all of this."

America has the three largest Islamic charities in the world. This is the time when Muslims give the most; they open their pockets as we celebrate this Eid, and our minds have to reflect to the sick, needy, and the hungry.

In my conclusion, hope is another distinction of faith, which we must not give up.

In surah (chapter) 2:30 of the Holy Qur'an, the angels were looking at the dark side of man: hatred, disunity, and jealousy.

But Allah knows the potential in each human being. That humanity will create much mischief and shed much blood on the earth. But Allah's plan is moving the world, community, and society according to his plan, toward the betterment of mankind.

"Our Lord! Let not our hearts deviate now after You have guided us on the right path, but grant us mercy from Your own presence, for You are the grantor of bounties without measure." Ameen.

بِسْمِ ٱللَّهِ ٱلرَّحْمَٰنِ ٱلرَّحِيمِ

With Allah's name, the merciful Benefactor, the merciful redeemer

Historical Events of Ramadan

Imam Omar Hazim

Praise be to Allah, He is one without partner or peer. He is the creator of space and time; neither space nor time can exist without Him, Allah. Everything in the universe, every single thing is a witness to the existence of Allah (SWT). The sun rises and sets, the moon comes out and then disappears from view. Day gives way to night, the night turns into day. The months and the seasons change. They have done this throughout the centuries in complete and absolute order, never deviating from the command of their Lord and Creator (SWT). Praise be to Allah.

Fasting in Ramadan

When Islam introduced this matchless institution to the world, it planted an ever-growing tree of infinite virtues and invaluable products. It strengthens our faith and our piety, it strengthens our taqwa.

In chapter (surah) 14:24-25, Allah (SWT) says in the Holy Qur'an that

أَلَمْ تَرَ كَيْفَ ضَرَبَ ٱللَّهُ مَثَلًا كَلِمَةً طَيِّبَةً كَشَجَرَةٍ طَيِّبَةٍ أَصْلُهَا ثَابِتٌ وَفَرْعُهَا فِى ٱلسَّمَاءِ (٢٤) تُؤْتِى أُكُلَهَا كُلَّ حِينٍ بِإِذْنِ رَبِّهَا وَيَضْرِبُ ٱللَّهُ ٱلْأَمْثَالَ لِلنَّاسِ لَعَلَّهُمْ يَتَذَكَّرُونَ (٢٥)

"Seest thou not how Allah sets forth a parable? A goodly word is like a goodly tree whose root is firmly fixed and its branches (reach) to the heavens. It brings forth its fruit at all times by the leave of its Lord. So Allah sets forth parables for men, in order that they may receive admonition. An evil word is like that of an evil tree, it is torn up by the root from the surface of the earth, and it has no stability."

In all seasons, Ramadan produces good virtues—summer, spring, fall, and winter.

Revelation of the Holy Qur'an in Ramadan:

Surah 2:185:

> Ramadan is the month in which was sent down the Holy Qur'an, as a guide to mankind, also clear (signs) for guidance and judgment (between right and wrong).

In chapter 17, verse 82, the Holy Qur'an states,

وَنُنَزِّلُ مِنَ ٱلْقُرْءَانِ مَا هُوَ شِفَاءٌ وَرَحْمَةٌ لِّلْمُؤْمِنِينَ وَلَا يَزِيدُ ٱلظَّٰلِمِينَ إِلَّا خَسَارًا (٨٢)

"We send down in the Holy Qur'an that which is a healing and a mercy to those who believe."

The Battle of Badr occurred in the month of Ramadan.

In chapter 2:190, the Holy Qur'an states,

وَقَٰتِلُوا۟ فِى سَبِيلِ ٱللَّهِ ٱلَّذِينَ يُقَٰتِلُونَكُمْ وَلَا تَعْتَدُوٓا۟ إِنَّ ٱللَّهَ لَا يُحِبُّ ٱلْمُعْتَدِينَ (١٩٠)

"Fight in the cause of Allah those who fight you; but do not transgress limits for Allah loves not transgressors."

Three hundred Muslims had to fight one thousand battle-hardened soldiers. The Muslim army was victorious. They had to have faith in Allah and faith in self. Faith is the only known antidote to failure; try and try again. Faith is the mystical power that gives men and women the ability to master powerful difficulties. Faith in Allah (SWT) and one's self gives life, power, and action to the impulses of thoughts. Faith is a state of mind, which can be greatly developed as to make a person achieve what they thought could only be accomplished in dreams.

In the month of Ramadan, *Zakat* was instituted.

Zakat is obligatory charity and is derived from *zaka*, which means it grew (a plant); another meaning of this word is purification from sin. Therefore, we receive both growth and purification from giving zakat.

The Conquest of Mecca

Took place during the month of Ramadan; all the idols in the Kaaba were destroyed.

In chapter 17:81, the Holy Qur'an states,

$$وَقُلْ جَاءَ الْحَقُّ وَزَهَقَ الْبَاطِلُ إِنَّ الْبَاطِلَ كَانَ زَهُوقًا (٨١)$$

"And say truth has now arrived and falsehood will perish, for falsehood is bound to perish."

This statement was made with the destruction of each idol, but not a single life of the people was destroyed. The Prophet did not take, but he gave so much—forgiveness, love, tolerance, mercy, and understanding.

Prophet's Speech at Tabuk in Ramadan

Thirty thousand marched to Tabuk because of the threat of the Byzantine to invade the northern approaches of Arabia.

In chapter 9:41, the Holy Qur'an states,

$$انفِرُوا خِفَافًا وَثِقَالًا وَجَاهِدُوا بِأَمْوَالِكُمْ وَأَنفُسِكُمْ فِى سَبِيلِ اللَّهِ ذَٰلِكُمْ خَيْرٌ لَّكُمْ إِن كُنتُمْ تَعْلَمُونَ (٤١)$$

"Go ye forth whether equipped lightly or heavily, and strive and struggle with your goods and your persons in the cause of Allah. That is best for you if ye but knew."

There was no war at Tabuk, the Byzantine Empire backed down, and out of the Prophet's wisdom and mercy, he did not attack them. Instead, he taught and gave wisdom. The Prophet gave this speech in part:

Well, verily the most truthful discourse is the Book of Allah. The best of the religions is the religion of Ibrahim. The noblest speech is the vocation of Allah. The finest of the narratives is the Holy Qur'an. The best of the ways is the one trodden by the Prophets. The noblest death is the death of a martyr. The most miserable blindness is waywardness after guidance. The best actions are that which is beneficent. The best guidance is that which is put into practice. The worst blindness is the blindness of the heart.

The upper hand is better than the lower hand. The hand which gives charity is better than the one that receives it. The worst remorse is that which is felt on the day of resurrection. The worst apology is that which is tendered at death. Some men do not come to Friday prayer, but with hesitance and delay. And some of them do not remember Allah but with reluctance. The highest wisdom is fear of Allah, the mighty and the great. The best things to be cherished in the hearts are faith and conviction.

He or she who pardons others is himself granted pardon. He or she who shows patience and forbearance, Allah will give him or her double reward.

In the month of Ramadan, Salahuddin defeated the crusaders who occupied Palestine.

Fear Allah wherever you are, private or public. If you commit sin, follow it up with a good deed, and it will wipe it out. Behave well toward people, so says Prophet Muhammad (PBUH).

O, Allah, grant us good in this world and good in the next world, and save us from the hellfire. Ameen.

Chapter 7

Public Relations

(L-R) Kansas Governor Kathleen and Mr. Sebelius are greeted by Imam Omar and Mrs. Hazim.

يَٰٓأَيُّهَا ٱلنَّاسُ إِنَّا خَلَقْنَٰكُم مِّن ذَكَرٍ وَأُنثَىٰ وَجَعَلْنَٰكُمْ شُعُوبًا وَقَبَآئِلَ لِتَعَارَفُوٓا۟ إِنَّ أَكْرَمَكُمْ عِندَ ٱللَّهِ أَتْقَىٰكُمْ إِنَّ ٱللَّهَ عَلِيمٌ خَبِيرٌ (١٣)

O mankind! We created you from a single (pair) of a male and a female, and made you into nations and tribes, that ye may know each other (not that ye may despise each other). Verily the most honored of you in the sight of Allah is (he who is) the most righteous of you. And Allah has full knowledge and is well acquainted (with all things). (Holy Qur'an 49:13)

"A Day with Dr. Ingrid Mattson"
Topeka, Kansas, Conference Was a Success

Zulfigar Malik

It was a beautiful spring afternoon on Sunday, April 20, 2008. The temperature was pleasant at around seventy-five degrees at the campus of Washburn University, Topeka, Kansas. Over four huundred people across Kansas and Western Missouri gathered to attend "A Day with Dr. Ingrid Mattson."

The conference was sponsored by the Islamic Center of Topeka, the Islamic Society of North America (ISNA), Interfaith of Topeka, and Washburn University.

The welcoming remarks were made by Imam Omar Hazim of the Islamic Center of Topeka; governor of Kansas Kathleen Sebelius, with a video message; Dr. Jerry Farley, president, Washburn University; and Dr. William Gitchell, president, Interfaith of Topeka.

ISNA president Dr. Ingrid Mattson delivered the keynote address on the question of "Is Islam Compatible with Modernity?" Dr. Muneer Fareed, secretary general of ISNA, spoke about "The Responsibility of Muslim Leaders in Combating Terrorism." Rodwan Saleh, affiliates coordinator of ISNA, made a video presentation about various ISNA projects and sought the involvement and support of the local community.

U.S. congresswoman Nancy Boyda welcomed the diversity in American society and encouraged American Muslims to participate in the political process.

Conference presented the Community Service Awards to Phil Anderson, a staff writer of the *Topeka Capital-Journal* and to Zulfiqar Ali Malik, editor of the e-newsletter *Muslim News Digest*.

بِسْمِ اللهِ الرَّحْمَٰنِ الرَّحِيمِ

With Allah's name, the merciful Benefactor, the merciful redeemer

Ramadan: Time of Repentance, Gratitude

Imam Omar Hazim

The holy month of Ramadan starts Wednesday and ends March 2, depending on the sighting of the new moon. We would like to share with readers some information about the fourth pillar of the Islamic faith, fasting.

The month of Ramadan is the most sacred month in the Islamic calendar. It is the ninth month of the Islamic lunar calendar; it begins eleven to twelve days earlier each year. The revelations of the Holy Qur'an (scripture of Islam) began during this month, and the Holy Qur'an is considered to be a guide to mankind.

Muslims fast to fulfill a religious obligation. Fasting is a religious institution almost as universal as prayer. In Islam, we believe it is a means of improvement for the moral and spiritual condition of the human being.

The Holy Qur'an says, "O ye who believe! Fasting is prescribed for you as it was prescribed for those before you, so that you may learn self restraint."

This fasting is considered to be a controlled or partial type of fasting. Muslims abstain from food, smoking, water or drinks, and sexual relations from dawn to sunset. We resume our normal life thereafter until dawn.

These are the physical aspects of the fast. The moral and spiritual aspects are that your heart, mind, soul, thoughts, and emotions all work together to abstain from any type of wrongdoing for the duration of the fast. This helps promote discipline and self-control during and after the fast and brings about an increased Allah (SWT)-consciousness.

In the month of Ramadan, Muslims should make repentance and ask for forgiveness of our sins, observe Allah's (SWT) beautiful creations, and show gratitude. Charity and good deeds are very important during this holy month. As we fast, we are to take a closer look at the problems of hunger and homelessness in the world and be encouraged to help the poor and needy.

It is also customary to increase the number of invitations to Muslims to come together in the evenings to break the fast, offer prayers, and socialize. This is done at the masjid and in people's homes.

Muslims all over the world follow the same procedure of the fast. In the regions where there is daylight eighteen to twenty hours a day, the people are recommended to observe the fast times of Mecca or Medina, the places of revelation, as a standard for fasting times, or the nearest temperate zone.

Fasting is meant for spiritual uplifting, self-discipline, self-restraint, and self-control.

Those who are exempt from fasting because of illness or traveling can make up the missed days at a later time. If they are physically unable to fast, they are to give a needy person food for a full day or its value for each day missed, if he or she can afford it.

When the fast is over, Muslims give charity and gifts, and then celebrate the holiday of Eid ul Fitr (feast of fast-breaking).

Our Lord! Give us good in this world and good in the next world, and save us from the torment of the fire. Ameen.

بِسْمِ اللهِ الرَّحْمَٰنِ الرَّحِيمِ

With Allah's name, the merciful Benefactor, the merciful redeemer

Condemnation of the Bombing in London

Imam Omar Hazim

The Islamic Center of Topeka joins Muslims worldwide in condemning the recent barbaric bombings in London. Our prayers have been offered along with Jews, Christians, and other fair-minded people for world peace and condolences to the families of the victims. This was a calculated, premeditated, cold-blooded atrocity, and the wrongdoers will be brought to justice, if not in this world, surely the next. The Holy Qur'an says,

مِنْ أَجْلِ ذَٰلِكَ كَتَبْنَا عَلَىٰ بَنِي إِسْرَائِيلَ أَنَّهُ مَن قَتَلَ نَفْسًا بِغَيْرِ نَفْسٍ أَوْ فَسَادٍ فِي الْأَرْضِ فَكَأَنَّمَا قَتَلَ النَّاسَ جَمِيعًا وَمَنْ أَحْيَاهَا فَكَأَنَّمَا أَحْيَا النَّاسَ جَمِيعًا وَلَقَدْ جَاءَتْهُمْ رُسُلُنَا بِالْبَيِّنَاتِ ثُمَّ إِنَّ كَثِيرًا مِّنْهُم بَعْدَ ذَٰلِكَ فِي الْأَرْضِ لَمُسْرِفُونَ (٣٢)

"If anyone kills the innocent people it is as if he killed all of humanity." (Chapter 5, verse 32)

The Holy Qur'an also condemns the act of taking one's own life (suicide), chapter 4, verse 29. Prophet Muhammad (PBUH) said, "The one who takes his life with a piece of steel will wake up in Hell repeating the same act."

The Islamic Center of Topeka asks the media to stop using misleading terms like Islamic terrorist, Muslim terrorist, and Islamic extremist. The words *Islam* and *Muslim* do not go with the words *terrorist* or *extremist*. Islam condemns terrorism and negates extremism. The words *Islam* and *terrorist* together create an oxymoron; they simply do not go together.

A criminal is a criminal, period. It is okay to identify a suspect by his or her physical attributes, but to identify a suspect by the religion that he or she proclaims is biased, unfair, and negative stereotyping.

The Irish Republican Army is not referred to as Catholic terrorists, but many of them are Catholic. It is reported that Hitler was a devout Christian, but he was never referred to as a Christian terrorist after exterminating over six million Jews. After four hundred years of slavery in this country, history has never referred to white America as Christian slave masters. However, many of them were indeed Christians. The BTK killer is not referred to as a Christian serial killer, and he was an active member of his church.

The bottom line is this: we cannot commit crimes and blame it on religion. Prosecute the criminal to the full extent of the law, but please leave a person's sacred religion out of it!

بِسْمِ ٱللّٰهِ ٱلرَّحْمَٰنِ ٱلرَّحِيمِ

With Allah's name, the merciful Benefactor, the merciful redeemer

Topeka Capital-Journal, December 15, 2007

Observation: Islamic Center Is Open to Public

Phil Anderson

Special services and dinners are scheduled at mosques around the world for Eid al-Adha, including in Topeka.

"Here at the mosque, we'll have prayers on Thursday morning," Hazim said. "Friday afternoon is our Jumuah service, and a lot of people will take off work three or four days to celebrate."

A special dinner also is scheduled to commemorate Eid al-Adha at the Islamic Center of Topeka.

During the dinner, children at the mosque will receive gifts, as is tradition, Hazim said. Many non-Muslim guests from the community also are invited to the annual Eid dinner.

Hazim said he and dozens of other Muslim clerics recently signed a letter denouncing terrorism and violence.

He said he was hopeful Eid al-Adha would be a time when non-Muslims would check out Islam and its teaching for themselves, rather than relying on reports that may not accurately reflect the religion.

"I think the time is right for people to have a better understanding of Islam," Hazim said. "I think people have been seeking out the correct information, because there has been so much misinformation out there, so much Islamaphobia.

"We've opened the masjid up on Fridays and Sundays to the public, and mosques across the country have done so, as well.

"People say, 'Why haven't Muslim leaders condemned acts of violence?'" Hazim added. "We have always condemned acts of violence, way before 9/11, whether the perpetrators of the terroristic acts were Jews, Christians, Muslims, or others."

Hazim said the Holy Qur'an, Islam's holy book, teaches that "to save a life is like saving all of humanity, and to destroy a life is like destroying all of humanity."

بِسْمِ ٱللَّهِ ٱلرَّحْمَٰنِ ٱلرَّحِيمِ

With Allah's name, the merciful Benefactor, the merciful redeemer

Id Ul-Fitr: Feast after the Fast

Phil Anderson

Every day for the past month, Khalil Green has observed the Islamic month of Ramadan by fasting from sunup to sundown, saying prayers, and doing charitable acts in accordance with religious teachings.

With the sighting of the new moon, expected Tuesday, Ramadan will end and the three-day holiday of Id ul-Fitr will begin.

During Id ul-Fitr, Muslims will gather with family members for feasts and to exchange presents, while also attending mosques and paying special alms for the poor as required by Islamic Law.

While the thirty-one-year-old Green looks forward to celebrating Id ul-Fitr, he said the end of Ramadan brings with it certain sadness because it marks the end of a particular sacrifice to Allah.

"Id ul-Fitr is the culmination of a great sacrifice," said Green, a member of the Islamic Center of Topeka, "and that sacrifices is for Allah [SWT]."

Imam Omar Hazim of the Islamic Center of Topeka said Id ul-Fitr is commonly known as "the feast after the fast."

It marks the return to a natural course of life for Muslims, who share happiness in having fulfilled one of the five pillars of Islam.

"The day of Id ul-Fitr is a day of forgiveness," Hazim noted, "also of celebration, togetherness, the giving of gifts and visiting loved ones and friends."

The word *Id* means a recurring happiness or joy, Hazim said.

Before meeting with family and friends, approximately five thousand Muslims in this vicinity will mark the beginning of Id ul-Fitr by gathering for prayer Tuesday morning at the Market Center Square in Kansas City, Missouri.

During the month-long Ramadan observance, special programs have been held nightly at the Islamic Center of Topeka, 1115 SE Twenty-seventh.

A program on the night of January 9 at the Islamic Center of Topeka, during which the daily fast was broken, was attended by Joan Wagnon and members of Topeka's Interfaith Community. Besides Ramadan, other pillars of the Islam faith are (1) the belief that there is no Allah (SWT) but Allah (SWT) and Mohammed is the last prophet; (2) praying five times a day; (3) performing acts of charity; (4) and attending the hajj, or pilgrimage to Mecca, at least once during a lifetime if the person's health and finances allow it.

— Nik Wilets/The Capital-Journal
Imam Omar Hazim discussed Ramadan with Mayor Joan Wagnon during a program the night of Jan. 9 at the Islamic Center of Topeka.

Left to right: Mayor of Topeka Joan Wagnon and Imam Omar Hazim

بِسْمِ ٱللَّهِ ٱلرَّحْمَٰنِ ٱلرَّحِيمِ

With Allah's name, the merciful Benefactor, the merciful redeemer

January 20, 1995, *Muslim Journal*

Out of Topeka Masjid Comes One Calling to Faith: The Contribution of Islam to a Pluralistic Society

Imam Omar Jaleel Hazim

Historians agree that the brilliant achievements of the twentieth-century science and technology have been greatly enhanced and inspired by early philosophers, scientists, chemists, mathematicians, architects, and physicians of the Muslim world.

Islam has made great contributions to the cultivation of sciences. Chemistry, as a science, is unquestionably the invention of Muslims. Abu Musa Jabir is called the true father of modern chemistry (the Geber of Christian writers).

Every higher branch of modern mathematics bears traces of Islamic genius. Zero comes from *sifr* in Arabic and points to the fact that our numbering system, Arabic numerals, is an Islamic contribution to the world.

Muslims were especially strong in mathematics, algebra, trigonometry, geography, agriculture, and poetry. The word *algebra* comes from the Arabic word *Al-Jbar*, which is the Arabic name for that branch of mathematics.

Muslims were pioneers in research in astronomy. The first observatory in Europe was built by Muslims, the Tower of Seville (or the Giralda) in AD 1190.

The science of medicine and the art of surgery have attained a high degree of excellence from Muslims. Intellectual development and the freedom of thought among Muslims was the cause of great civilizations to be built during the centuries of moral, intellectual, and social decay in Europe called the Dark Ages.

It was the literary and scientific spirit of Islam that gave inspiration and contributed immensely to the reawakening of Europe, known as the Renaissance.

Reports indicate that there are more than six million Muslims in America today who are making positive contributions to the success of this country in every field: medicine, science, technology, education, and business. Muslims have established information centers, places of worship, academic institutions, elementary and high schools.

One of the most profound contributions of Islam in this era of American history was in 1975, when Imam Warith Deen Mohammed was elected unanimously leader of the Nation of Islam. He quickly influenced and led hundreds of thousands of its members and associates to mainstream Islam, which paved the way for a greater respect and tolerance for all creeds and religions. I believe through time and history the world will be able to perceive the greatness and real value of that contribution.

American Muslims have organized hoc committees against crime across the country and have been very successful in many cities. Confronting the many problems that affect us all, these committees also work closely with law enforcement agencies.

It was a Muslim chief architect who designed the Sears Tower and John Hancock buildings in Chicago. Locally, we have Muslim doctors and nurses in every hospital in our city, working to save lives and improve the quality of life of human beings. We have educators and businesspeople.

It was a Muslim masonry contractor (Imam Omar Hazim) who built the additions to the Young Men's Christian Association and the addition to Temple Beth Shalom.

Temple Beth Shalom in Topeka, Kansas

Muslims live in peace and harmony among themselves and in all cities in America with their neighbors.

بِسْمِ ٱللَّهِ ٱلرَّحْمَٰنِ ٱلرَّحِيمِ

With Allah's name, the merciful Benefactor, the merciful redeemer

Prayer for the United States of America

Governor's Inaugural Interfaith Service

January 8, 2007

Submitted by Imam Omar Hazim, Islamic Center of Topeka

With Allah's Name, the Merciful Benefactor, the Merciful Redeemer, the Sustainer, Cherisher, and Lord of all Worlds, Creator of the heavens, earth, and everything therein.

O, Allah, Highly Exalted and Glorified are You, we give praise and thanks to You for the many blessings You have bestowed upon humanity; so many of Your bounties have we received, all human beings, collectively, could never perceive them all. We believe as mentioned in the Holy Qur'an that "there is not a moving creature, small or large in the earth, nor a bird that flies in the air, nor any sea dwelling creature that can exist without the provisions you provide. With you are the keys of the unseen, the treasures that none knows but you. Not even a leaf falls off of a tree without Your knowledge. You know and understand what is in the hearts of humanity."

O, Allah, the Exalted and Most High, we come before You today with sincere prayer for our country, the United States of America. We want to show gratitude for the progress the United States has made in the last century in the fields of medical science, technology, education, scientific research, and human rights: the progress of opening the doors of opportunity and encouraging its citizens to strive for moral excellence, spiritual excellence, and the pursuit of happiness. We are thankful that you have predestined our lives to be here in the United States of America.

O, Merciful Allah, let the United States of America make continued progress in the direction of recognizing and respecting the inherent dignity, worth, and value that You, Our Creator, has given every human soul. O, Allah, Most Merciful, Most Gracious, make America an inspiration to the thoughts of humanities, unity, and equality. Let America continue to advance on the course of seeing and understanding that women have great capacities for leadership and that your judgment is not based upon gender, color, nor one's language. We pray that the United States will remain steadfast on the course of religious freedom, religious tolerance, and religious diversity. Please enhance our prestige and influence in the world. Let the prestige and influence of America be used to promote peace, love, brotherhood, and justice for humanity at large. Let it be used to acknowledge the mutual rights, cooperation, and obligations that we share with other countries.

America! America!

O, Allah, shed Your grace on America.

And crown America's good with brotherhood

From sea to shining sea. Ameen.

بِسْمِ ٱللَّهِ ٱلرَّحْمَٰنِ ٱلرَّحِيمِ

With Allah's name, the merciful Benefactor, the merciful redeemer

Unity through Diversity

Imam Omar Hazim

One of the beauties of Islam is that it emphasizes the concept of unity: oneness of God and the oneness of mankind.

Muslims are united under the banner of al-Islam although most of us have come from different countries, are of different races and cultures, and speak different languages. These differences are insignificant in the sight of Allah. What is most important is the ideology of Islam and the faith itself.

Allah says in the Holy Qur'an (chapter 49, verse 13),

يَٰٓأَيُّهَا ٱلنَّاسُ إِنَّا خَلَقْنَٰكُم مِّن ذَكَرٍ وَأُنثَىٰ وَجَعَلْنَٰكُمْ شُعُوبًا وَقَبَآئِلَ لِتَعَارَفُوٓا۟ إِنَّ أَكْرَمَكُمْ عِندَ ٱللَّهِ أَتْقَىٰكُمْ إِنَّ ٱللَّهَ عَلِيمٌ خَبِيرٌ (١٣)

"O Mankind, we have created you from a single male and female and made you into nations and tribes so that you may know one another. Verily, the most honored of you in the sight of Allah is the most righteous of you, and Allah has full knowledge and is well acquainted."

The Prophet (PBUH) said, "O Mankind, you are children of Adam and Adam is from the soil."

Diversity means the quality, state, fact, or instance of being diverse, different, various, dissimilar, or varied. We constitute a diversified group in Topeka, and in America. We are different in our ways of thinking, in our actions and reactions. We may differ in the way we handle the same problems or situations. We have different economic circumstances, different life experiences, and different educational backgrounds.

Unity means the state of being one—in spirit, sentiment, or purpose; harmony, agreement, and concord. As Muslims, our unity is based on our consciousness of the oneness of Allah, oneness of prophethood, oneness of religion, and oneness of humankind.

We have one basic Islamic ideology with respect of various schools of thought. We have one book, the Holy Qur'an; it is one text, one language, one dialect, and one standard for every Muslim (over one billion).

We have one prophet, Prophet Muhammad (PBUH). There is no disagreement on his character and his personality. He is our leader and the leader for mankind.

We have one qibla (direction) in which to pray—the Kaaba at Mecca. The Holy Qur'an says, "It is not righteousness to turn our faces towards the east or west." However, it is obedience to Allah's will.

We, as Muslims, should have one goal, one aim, one intention, and one purpose; and that is to be true and worthy Muslims. We should hope to please Allah and be of service to all humanity. This unity (oneness) is so much greater and significant than our diversities.

O, Allah, have Mercy on us and forgive us our sins. Ameen.

بِسْمِ ٱللَّهِ ٱلرَّحْمَٰنِ ٱلرَّحِيمِ

With Allah's name, the merciful Benefactor, the merciful redeemer

Kansas Governor Kathleen Sebelius and Mayor James McClinton of Topeka Attend Eid Celebration

Imam Omar Hazim

Left to right: Imam Omar Hazim, Mrs. McClinton, Mayor James McClinton

Looking upon the crowd of people this past Saturday night, it was evident that people from all races, religions, and walks of life had come together for one reason—to celebrate Id al-Adha. Known as the Feast of the Sacrifice, Id al-Adha is the annual Islamic festival that commemorates the willingness of the Prophet Abraham (AS) to sacrifice his son Ishmael and Ishmael's willingness to be sacrificed for the sake of God. Id al-Adha is the Islamic annual holiday and feast celebrated worldwide after the completion of the fifth pillar of the Islamic faith, the hajj or pilgrimage.

On January 29, the Islamic Center of Topeka was host of an Id al-Adha program at the Washburn University Memorial Union. The event attracted a crowd of about three hundred people. Special guests were Governor Kathleen Sebelius and Topeka mayor James McClinton. Both the governor and mayor expressed their appreciation for the Islamic community.

Left to right: Rehan Reza, Governor Kathleen Sebelius, Imam Omar Hazim

In appreciation for his leadership, Imam Omar Hazim of the Islamic Center of Topeka presented both with a plaque and a copy of the Holy Qur'an. Prophet Abraham (AS) is a figure revered by Muslims, Jews, and Christians alike. Governor Sebelius commented on the similarities between Islam, Judaism, and Christianity. She said that all people need to value and respect each other's faiths and traditions. Sebelius also said that she was grateful for the opportunity to join the Islamic Center for the Id celebration.

According to the Bible and the Holy Qur'an, while Prophet Abraham (AS) was in the act of sacrificing his son, God replaced his son with a ram or a goat. After sacrificing the ram or goat, Prophet Abraham (AS) was told to share the meat with family, neighbors, and the needy. Imam Hazim said that sharing the food with the community represents community consciousness and service. Prophet Abraham (AS), by not sacrificing his son, emphasizes the sanctity and value of human life, Hazim said, and sacrifices for the greater good of humanity advances the moral and spiritual excellence in those who make sacrifices. Hazim quoted chapter (surah) 22, verse 37 of the Holy Qur'an in stating that,

لَن يَنَالَ ٱللَّهَ لُحُومُهَا وَلَا دِمَاؤُهَا وَلَٰكِن يَنَالُهُ ٱلتَّقْوَىٰ مِنكُمْ كَذَٰلِكَ سَخَّرَهَا لَكُمْ لِتُكَبِّرُوا۟ ٱللَّهَ عَلَىٰ مَا هَدَىٰكُمْ وَبَشِّرِ ٱلْمُحْسِنِينَ (٣٧)

"It is not the meat nor the blood that reaches God, but it is your piety that reaches Him."

After the celebration, Hazim had this to say:

"Imam W. Deen Mohammed has led the way for interfaith dialogue and understanding," Hazim said. "We are grateful to be associated with his leadership."

بِسْمِ اللهِ الرَّحْمَٰنِ الرَّحِيمِ

With Allah's name, the merciful Benefactor, the merciful redeemer

Invocation to the Kansas House of Representatives (April 28, 2004)

Imam Omar Hazim

Merciful Benefactor, Creator of the heavens, earth, and everything contained therein. We come before you today in humble prayer and ask you to have mercy on and give guidance to this governing body of honorable minds: the Kansas House of Representatives. Please grant to them the wisdom and the courage to make the best decisions for the people and communities that they serve. Reward them for the noble work that they do.

Our Lord, help every individual of this house recognize and respect the inherent worth that You, our Creator, have given every human soul. Let the larger societies and governments of the world give due process and justice to its individual members and help the individual members of societies accept their responsibilities. Our Lord, let us, your servants, have increased dialogue, respect, cooperation, and brotherhood among each other.

Merciful Redeemer, with You are the keys of the unseen, the treasures that none knoweth but you. You knoweth whatever there is on the earth and in the sea. Not a leaf doth fall but with Your knowledge. There is not a grain in the darkness of the earth, nor anything fresh or dry (green or withered) but is known clearly by You (Holy Qur'an). Creator of all mankind, as we worship you in our diverse ways and traditions, help us not to forget or to neglect our duties and responsibilities in this life. Help us to serve humanity and foster goodwill and peace on earth.

Ameen.

بِسْمِ ٱللَّهِ ٱلرَّحْمَٰنِ ٱلرَّحِيمِ

With Allah's name, the merciful Benefactor, the merciful redeemer

Prayer for the Second-District Convention: Barack Obama for President

Imam Omar Hazim

O, Allah (SWT), highly exalted and glorified are You, all praise belongs to You. We bear witness that you are the Master of the Day of Judgment, Thee do we serve and Thine aid we seek.

Our Allah (SWT), we believe you have made humanity with limited free will and reasoning and have placed us as guardians and trustees in your precious earth.

We come before You today in humble prayer and ask You to have mercy on us and give us guidance as we strive for peace, justice, and hope in our country, through our support for Barack Obama for president.

O, Allah (SWT), help humanity recognize and embrace the reality that we, as human beings, belong to one family with the same set of parents, Adam and Eve. Help us to recognize and embrace the beauty in the plurality and diversities that You, Our Lord, have created in humanity. O, Allah (SWT), You have conferred dignity and honor on the children of Adam and Eve. It is You who have established the value of human life. Help us to recognize that we are all one human family in your earth.

O, Merciful Allah (SWT), help every individual in the world recognize and respect the inherent dignity, worth, and value that you, Our Lord, have given to every human soul, male and female. Inspire the societies and governments of the world to give due process and justice to its individual members, and help the individual members of societies accept their responsibilities.

O, Creator of all Mankind, you have given us the power of intelligence, the faculties of reasoning, will, judgment, understanding, and many other mental powers. Please help us to use them in positive ways of worshipping You and serving humanity. Help us to foster goodwill, peace, justice, and love on this earth. Help us to be successful in supporting Barack Obama for president.

Ameen.

بِسْمِ ٱللَّهِ ٱلرَّحْمَٰنِ ٱلرَّحِيمِ

With Allah's name, the merciful Benefactor, the merciful redeemer

Invocation for City Council

Topeka, Kansas, 2010

Imam Omar Hazim

With God's Name, the Merciful Benefactor, the Merciful Redeemer.

I wish to greet you with the greeting of Islam, and that greeting is the greeting of peace, *as-salaam alaikum.*

Merciful Redeemer, with You are the keys to the unseen, the treasures that none knoweth but you. You Knoweth whatever there is on the earth and in the sea, not a leaf doth fall without Your knowledge. There is not a grain in the darkness of the earth, nor anything fresh or dry, green or withered but is known clearly by You (Holy Qur'an).

Merciful Benefactor, Creator of the heavens, earth, and everything contained therein, we come before You today in humble prayer and ask You to have mercy on and give guidance to this governing body of honorable minds, the City Council of Topeka. Please grant to them the wisdom, the patience, and the courage to make the best decisions for the people and communities that they serve. Reward them for the noble work that they do.

Our Lord, help every individual of this council recognize and respect the inherent worth that You, our Creator, has given every human soul. We are here this evening to pray for the success of our leaders. We ask You, dear God, to grant success to our mayor, our city manager, and the members of the council of the city of Topeka. Our Lord, help us to understand each other without being biased or prejudiced. Help us and guide us to communicate and dialogue with each other for the benefits of our community.

We also ask You to guide the citizens of our city to help bring peace to our communities. Protect our neighborhoods from the crimes of gang fighting, drugs, shooting and killing, drunken drivers, etc., so that our city can live as one respectful community.

Creator of all mankind, as we worship You in our diverse ways and traditions, help us not to forget or to neglect our duties and responsibilities in this life. Help us, as one community, serve humanity and foster goodwill in our city. Ameen.

بِسْمِ ٱللَّهِ ٱلرَّحْمَٰنِ ٱلرَّحِيمِ

With Allah's name, the merciful Benefactor, the merciful redeemer

Appreciating Allah's (SWT) Generosity

Presentation by Imam Omar Hazim

To Interfaith of Topeka Thanksgiving Service in 2007

Islam teaches that Allah (SWT), nature, and humanity are not remote, alien, or opposed to each other. Allah (SWT) makes himself known through His creation, nature and humanity itself. Nature and humanity are two books that make Allah (SWT) known, meaning that knowledge comes to humanity by way of revelations to humanity and man's study of the creation of Allah (SWT) (nature).

When we reflect on the creation of the heavens and the earth as Allah's (SWT) creations, we will receive a greater benefit for our physical, moral, and spiritual life. When we look at the beautiful artistic design of Allah (SWT) and learn to appreciate and show gratitude for it, we will also be able to show appreciation for the work of humanity.

There is the vast, enormous sky with its sun, its moon and stars, the spacious earth with running rivers, trees, flowers, mountains, beautiful animals and humans. The months and the seasons change; they all run their courses with the same regularity throughout the centuries in complete and absolute order, never deviating.

Holy Qur'an states in chapter 43:11 that

وَٱلَّذِى نَزَّلَ مِنَ ٱلسَّمَآءِ مَآءً بِقَدَرٍ فَأَنشَرْنَا بِهِۦ بَلْدَةً مَّيْتًا كَذَٰلِكَ تُخْرَجُونَ (١١)

"It is Allah (SWT) who sends down water in due measure from the sky by which brings a dead land back to life."

In due measure, modern research estimates that in one second, approximately sixteen million tons of water evaporate from the earth. This figure amounts to 513 trillion tons of water in one year. It returns to the earth in the form of rain, snow, or hail. This means that water continuously circulates in a balanced cycle in due measure. All life on earth depends on this water cycle. Rain always falls on a community of people; it benefits many. Allah's (SWT) bounties are for all creations in the earth.

The Holy Qur'an states in chapter 57:25 that

لَقَدْ أَرْسَلْنَا رُسُلَنَا بِٱلْبَيِّنَٰتِ وَأَنزَلْنَا مَعَهُمُ ٱلْكِتَٰبَ وَٱلْمِيزَانَ لِيَقُومَ ٱلنَّاسُ بِٱلْقِسْطِ ۖ وَأَنزَلْنَا ٱلْحَدِيدَ فِيهِ بَأْسٌ شَدِيدٌ وَمَنَٰفِعُ لِلنَّاسِ وَلِيَعْلَمَ ٱللَّهُ مَن يَنصُرُهُۥ وَرُسُلَهُۥ بِٱلْغَيْبِ ۚ إِنَّ ٱللَّهَ قَوِىٌّ عَزِيزٌ (٢٥)

"Allah (SWT) sent down iron in which there lies great force and which has many uses for mankind."

Modern astronomical findings have disclosed that the iron found in our world has come from the giant stars in outer space; it is not produced in the earth. It is produced in stars larger than the sun, where the temperature reaches a few hundred million degrees. People who think see that it is Allah (SWT) who puts technology at the service of mankind.

Technology has advanced greatly from the uses of iron and steel that Allah (SWT) gave humanity as a gift. The foundation of every house, building, sidewalk, street, and bridge has steel for reinforcement. We have cars, trucks, trains, ships, airplanes, buses, helicopters, cookwares, and many household products from iron ore.

The Arabic word *inzal* means the sending down of a thing from above, but also means causing a thing to grow or bringing the means of it into existence. In the Holy Qur'an, this word is used for sending down rain, iron, the cattle, and also revelation.

All praise is due to Allah (SWT), and we render praise to Him for his generosity.

بِسْمِ ٱللَّهِ ٱلرَّحْمَٰنِ ٱلرَّحِيمِ

With Allah's name, the merciful Benefactor, the merciful redeemer

May the prayers and the peace be upon Allah's noble and kind messenger, Muhammad.

Zulfiqar Malik and Phil Anderson Receive the Community Service Award

Zulfiqa Malik receives award.

In April 20, 2008, at a conference held in Topeka, the capital city of Kansas, attended by over four hundred people, Zulfiqar Malik was presented with the distinguished Community Service Award.

Zulfiqar Malik is one of the pioneers of the Kansas City community. For the past thirty-eight (forty now) years, he has been active in the religious, cultural, social, and interfaith organizations. He and his wife, Shaista, are immigrants from Pakistan. They are residents of Overland Park, Kansas.

They have two sons Adnan, Farhan and daughter-in-law Azra (and a granddaughter Zayna).

Mr. Malik earned his master's degree from the University of Punjab in Lahore. He has been working for the U.S. Postal Service for the last thirty-one (thirty-three now) years. He is the editor of the online newsletter *Muslim News Digest* circulated nationally. In December 2003, he received the Special Recognition Award from the Crescent Peace Society.

Phil Anderson

Phil Anderson is a staff writer for the *Topeka Capital-Journal*, where he has worked since 1981. He has covered a variety of beats for the newspaper and has written about the local religion scene since 1995. He also covers law enforcement in Topeka and northeast Kansas.

A native of Topeka, Phil is a graduate of Topeka High School and Emporia State University. He also pursued graduate studies in journalism and education at the University of Kansas.

In addition to his work at the *Capital-Journal*, Phil worked for a year at the *San Diego Union-Tribune*.

Phil and his wife, Gloria, have four children and live in Topeka.

بِسْمِ ٱللَّهِ ٱلرَّحْمَٰنِ ٱلرَّحِيمِ

With Allah's name, the merciful Benefactor, the merciful redeemer

May the prayers and the peace be upon Allah's noble and kind messenger, Muhammad.

Islamic Faith Blamed Unfairly

Imam Omar Hazim

Guest Columnist, *Topeka Capital-Journal*

What happened in Oklahoma City to the federal building is a shameful and disgraceful act. We should feel compassion, sorrow, and sympathy for the innocent victims of this hideous crime and hope all the perpetrators are caught and punished to the full extent of the law.

We Muslims at the Islamic Center of Topeka express condolences to the families of those lost in the bombing.

Islam strongly and unquestionably condemns terrorism, and we are outraged by violence against innocent civilians wherever it occurs in the world—Oklahoma, New York, Bosnia, or Chechnya.

In April 20, a wire story appeared in the *Topeka Capital-Journal* entitled "Terrorism Experts Point to Islamic Extremists." At the time of that writing, it was unknown who was responsible for the bombing, and yet your paper and many others were quick to reach a false conclusion.

The justice system works best in its intended state; that is, when a person is innocent until proven guilty. Even some government officials, until the president spoke up, were quick to imply that this act was done by Muslims, despite an absence of proof.

Whoever commits such crimes against other human beings are criminals, whether they are Christian, Jew, Muslim, Sikh, Baha'i, or atheist. But criminals should not be identified by their religion or the religion they profess. If Muslim individuals or groups have any role in terroristic activity, they have acted on their own and against Islamic principles.

The Serbs, the Irish Republican Army, Jim Jones, David Koresh—none has been identified as Christian in news reports that have detailed their atrocities against human beings, and rightly so. The attorney general Janet Reno announced a $2 million reward for information on two white male suspects in the Oklahoma bombing; she said nothing about their suspected religion.

When it comes to Muslims, there's a double standard. To invoke the name of the religion of Islam with criminal activity is wrong, biased, unfair, and negative stereotyping.

Islam is one of the great religions of the world that teaches moderation and balance: spiritually, socially, culturally, educationally, morally, politically, and so on. In every aspect of life, Islamic teachings negate extreme activity.

We appeal to the media to stop using misleading terms like "Muslim fundamentalists" or "Islamic extremists." The implications of these terms can be harmful for innocent individuals or groups of God-fearing and God-worshipping people, good people that love and respect other human beings and value life. These terms are confusing to the public.

Islam means peace and submission to do the will of Allah (SWT). It encourages brotherhood, mercy, kindness, forgiveness, compassion, tolerance, and understanding. Those who would suggest otherwise should take another look at the intricacies of the religion and the life of Prophet Muhammad (PBUH).

The Islamic Center of Topeka: An Important Contributor to Interfaith of Topeka and Religious Understanding in the Community

Carol W. Christensen, former president of Interfaith of Topeka

It is a great honor and pleasure for me to have been asked by my friend Omar Hazim, the imam of the Islamic Center of Topeka, to write briefly about the Islamic Center's involvement with Interfaith of Topeka, an organization in which I have been very active for nearly two decades.

Interfaith of Topeka (sometimes referred to as "Interfaith") was established in 1979 to foster greater religious understanding and cooperation within the community. Prior to that year, Topeka had had an organization that was composed only of Christian churches. Many leaders of that group and other people in Topeka, though, recognized that our city had become more religiously diverse and wanted to bring all interested faith groups in the community together for ongoing dialogue, interaction, and service. To accomplish those purposes, Interfaith of Topeka was founded and welcomed the involvement of congregations and individuals of many different religious backgrounds.

In 1987, a small group of Muslims began meeting in Topeka and, shortly afterward, joined Interfaith of Topeka. Ever since then, the Islamic Center of Topeka has been an active member of that interreligious organization and has worked consistently to build bridges of religious understanding and friendship in Topeka.

Beginning in 1987, when Imam Omar Hazim began serving as an Interfaith board member, the Islamic Center has continuously provided a representative to that interreligious group. I served many years on the board with Imam Hazim, Dr. Syed Akhtar, and Dr. Ashraf Sufi and know firsthand of their dedication to the work of Interfaith of Topeka and of their generous contribution of ideas, time and, sometimes, money to it and its activities. All these representatives from the Islamic Center were team players when serving on the Interfaith board. All were genuinely friendly, warm, and respectful in their interactions with people of other faiths. Though I am not serving on the Interfaith board currently, I have visited several times with the Islamic Center's newest representative Khalil Green and find him also to be friendly, open, accepting, and anxious to promote interreligious understanding and cooperation.

Ever since joining Interfaith of Topeka, the Islamic Center of Topeka has been very involved in and supportive of Interfaith-sponsored activities. For many years, a member of the Islamic Center has taken part in the annual Community Thanksgiving Service sponsored by Interfaith: for example, by giving a prayer, sharing a scripture, or giving a message. In addition, numerous people from the Islamic community have attended that service and stayed afterward to mingle with people of other faiths during the reception that followed.

Members of the Islamic Center took part in the community service projects that Interfaith of Topeka organized in 1998 as a prelude to its twentieth anniversary celebration. Many of its members have also attended Interfaith's annual meetings and educational programs. The Islamic Center of Topeka has also hosted several events sponsored by Interfaith: for example, its annual meeting and an educational program. In addition, Imam Hazim has participated in Interfaith-sponsored remembrance services for the victims of the September 11 terrorist attacks.

Speakers from the Islamic Center have also often shared information about their Muslim faith at several Interfaith-sponsored forums, seminars, or other programs for the public. Their participation in such events has helped people of other religions learn more about Islam and has helped the Muslims who attended learn more about other faiths too. Attendees at these events have been able to see differences between various religions but also, very importantly, many similarities as well. I remember one particular educational program in the 1990s, when representatives of the Muslim, Baha'i and Sikh faiths and of my church (the Church of Jesus Christ of Latter-day Saints) spoke about their views about families and about some of the moral issues in the news then. I think that many people in the audience—and, probably, even the organizer of the event himself—were surprised to see how many similar views all those faiths shared!

Anxious to continue building bridges of understanding and friendship in the Topeka area, the Islamic Center has also been proactive in reaching out to the interfaith community. For example, several times it invited Interfaith of Topeka leaders to its Eid-ul-Fitr feast at the end of Ramadan. Twice it brought to Topeka the current president of the Islamic Society of North America and invited Interfaith to help cosponsor an event at which each leader could speak to an interreligious audience.

In a wonderful display of interfaith cooperation earlier this year (2010), the Islamic Center of Topeka joined Topeka's Grace Episcopal Cathedral and Temple Beth Sholom in sponsoring "A Walk through Jerusalem," an interactive, traveling exhibit about the city that Muslims, Christians, and Jews all consider holy.

Over the last twenty years, Imam Hazim has been invited by many different Christian churches and community organizations to make presentations about Islam. In 1994, I invited him to speak to a group at my church, and he graciously agreed to come. Unfortunately, when the evening of his presentation arrived, I was in the hospital, in danger of giving birth to a premature child. As I had hoped, the educational program went on without me. But I was told later that Omar (as I usually call my friend) asked at the beginning of his presentation if he could offer a prayer on behalf of my unborn child and me. I was very touched to learn afterward of his prayer, which not only showed his audience of Latter-day Saints what a spontaneous Muslim prayer is like, but also revealed the gentle, caring heart of a true follower of Islam. (And, for the record, because of prayers and fasting by my family members and friends at my church, petitions to God from Omar and other friends from Interfaith and, especially, the great grace of God, my baby and I were fine.)

I see much good that has resulted from the Islamic Center of Topeka's active participation in Interfaith of Topeka these past twenty-three years. I think that Interfaith of Topeka itself has been strengthened as an organization. Friendships between Muslims and people of other faiths have been forged. Since accurate information has corrected many false ideas and stereotypes about Islam and other faiths, mutual religious understanding has grown in our community. Through rubbing shoulders and working together in different interfaith activities, adherents of different faiths have come to trust each other more. I know that my life has been enriched through my association with members of the Islamic Center, and I know many other people in Topeka's faith community feel similarly. Truly, there are many blessings that come to individuals, congregations, and the larger community when people of different faiths communicate, work together, and learn about each other!

Baha'i Community

Duane Herrmann

Chairperson and Former President of Interfaith

Chairman, Bahá'í Community of Shawnee County, Kansas

Imam Omar has generously asked me to relate my relationship with Islam and the Islamic Center of Topeka, so I will try to do so here.

My first direct, personal contact with Islam occurred in the mid-1970s during the time of the Islamic Society of Shawnee County, when Omar was imam. He and I both attended an interreligious discussion at a local church. From the moment I saw him, I knew we were friends. He and I were the only ones present who were outside the familiar sphere of Christians and Jews. He was soon called to be imam in Kansas City, and I became friends with the new imam in Topeka, but I missed Omar. During this time, I attended my first Qur'an class and received my first Qur'an.

I had wanted a Qur'an for a decade. When I was in high school, in the mid-1960s, I had begun looking for a Qur'an. I wanted to study religious texts outside the orbit of the church of my childhood. I first looked in the local religious bookstore figuring that, since the Qur'an was the Word of God, it should be there with the other Word of God. It was not, and I eventually stopped looking. It did not make sense to me that a Bible bookstore would not have a Qur'an, but I later understood the store catered only to Christian subjects. When the imam offered me a copy, I was overjoyed.

Between the time I had first searched for a Qur'an and the time I discovered there were Muslims in Topeka, I had discovered and embraced the Bahá'í Faith. When I learned that Baha'u'llah taught that Muhammad was a Messenger of God and the Qur'an was the Word of God, I was relieved. I had decided years earlier that I could not endorse for myself a religion that rejected Muhammad or the Qur'an. Actually, to be a Bahá'í, one has a spiritual obligation to accept Muhammad as Prophet and the Qur'an. Millions of people around the world, who may have never thought about Islam, have accepted Muhammad and the Qur'an upon becoming Baha'is. In that way, the Bahá'í Faith is promoting Islam. Similarly they accept the founders of all divine religions as receiving their inspiration from the same eternal Creator. When I learned that Baha'is were encouraged to study the Qur'an and defend Islam, I searched and found a Qur'an that I could order by mail, so I did. I did not think it was as accurate a translation as could be, but it was better than nothing.

I left Topeka to attend a university in a small town to help the Bahá'í community there and, later, began my career and family and was out of touch with Muslims for a few years. But I continued my own Islamic education. The national Bahá'í office had produced a short study guide on Islam, which I obtained and studied on my own, and I obtained books on Islam: *Qur'ánic Laws*, *Muhammad: Prophet and Statesman*, *Arab Science*, *Shahanshah*, and others. And books by Baha'is on Islam: *Islamic Contributions to Civilization*, *Muhammad and the Course of Islam*, *Shi'i Islam*, *Proofs from the Holy Qur'an (Regarding the Advent of Bahá'u'lláh)*, and others.

In 1979, I was surprised to find myself, along with the local imam, to be elected to the first board of directors of Interfaith of Topeka. I welcomed his presence. Again, we were the only ones outside the Western Judeo-Christian culture. The rest of the board members could easily accommodate the Jewish member of the board, but the imam and myself were a different matter. Where did we fit into their Christian constellation? Islam could no longer be the enemy, but how to embrace it, and the Bahá'í?? That was a difficulty that took years to resolve.

In 1980, Omar returned to Topeka, took a place on the Interfaith board, and I was delighted to see him again. I regretted that he and I were both so busy (I was also at the time chairman of the Baha'is of Topeka) we were seldom able to attend meetings at the same time, but our friendship was as strong as ever. We both took courage from the knowledge of the other.

The constitution of Interfaith of Topeka is written to ensure that membership on the board of directors rotates, so Omar and I were not often on the board at the same time, but we would occasionally see each other at various Interfaith-sponsored meetings or other community events.

Some Interfaith events were hosted by the Islamic Community of Topeka, and I began attending Qur'an class from time to time.

Because of the rotation of membership of the board of Interfaith, I got to know other Muslims who were also elected to the board. The times when I was on the board, and especially those times when I shared responsibility for programs, I made sure that the orientation was not solely based on the assumptions of the Judeo-Christian majority. Passing a collection plate was one practice the board decided to eliminate from its programs when I pointed out that Baha'is don't do it, Muslims don't do it, Hindus don't do it, Buddhists don't do it—so why should Interfaith? The added presence over the years of Hindus and Buddhists helped to broaden the understanding of the board.

I also supported the faith-sharing component of Interfaith board meetings because it was the only way to really learn what it was like to be a member of another religion. I tried to incorporate more and more faith-sharing aspects into various Interfaith programs. In the 1990s, I was elected president of Interfaith and resolved to emphasize interreligious education as a major focus of Interfaith of Topeka. As a result, a series of faith-sharing conferences were held in Topeka. For the first time, people of all faiths were able to meet at a neutral location and learn about several other religions. Those who attended expressed great appreciation for the opportunity. Unfortunately, Interfaith had no staff by that time and a very small budget, so publicity and, therefore, attendance, were limited.

I continued my personal interreligious educational efforts in additional ways. Baha'is of Topeka and Shawnee County held joint devotional services (I was in the county and chairman again), and when I was responsible for preparing the program, I made sure to include selections from the Qur'an. I also, from time to time, invited Omar or another Muslim as a speaker. Omar invited me to speak at the center as well.

All this changed in September 2001.

Immediately, as president of Interfaith, I called for an Interfaith devotional service. Several were held instantly by individual congregations the day after the World Trade Center attacks. It took a few more days to organize a community-wide service. We came together in shock and grief. In many cities, this was the first interfaith gathering and people were unsure of each other. In Topeka, with our decades of history of interfaith events, we came together as long-standing and trusted friends, knowing deep in our hearts that we could trust each other and would find comfort from each other. We did come together. We did gain comfort and support from each other. It was wonderful. It was a moment I was very proud of Topeka.

I knew there would be an anti-Muslim reaction. The Muslims in Topeka were my friends, and I knew they were in the minority here. I wanted to show my support, but I didn't know what I could do other than be present and defend the faith of Islam as distinct from terrorists, so I began to attend more events at the Islamic Center. I could fairly easily add a Qur'an class to my Sunday schedule, and I welcomed the community dinners during Ramadan. I took my children and invited other Baha'is and Quakers, whom I also pray with, to attend with me. From time to time, some would join me.

One Sunday, when I arrived for Qur'an class, I noticed new people present and learned they were from the church attended by an aunt of mine. I was not surprised to see her walk in the door, but she was very surprised to see me. "Duane!" she exclaimed with a big grin. "I didn't know you were Muslim!"

"I didn't know you were either!" I responded as we hugged in joy and laughed. She and a few others from her class sat beside me and asked questions. Noticing my Qur'an, she pointed to it and asked, "Does it teach about love?"

"Certainly," I responded. She was very relieved to know that. One of the others asked if all Muslims were terrorists. I asked, in return, if all Christians were like a well-known local fanatic who delights in publicly condemning others to Hell. "Oh!" Her eyes opened wide in sudden understanding. No more questions about that!

Another thing I hoped to demonstrate by my presence at events at the Islamic Center is that, despite the unjust treatment of Baha'is in Iran and a few other countries, Baha'is do not hate Muslims. "Let there be no compulsion in religion" (2:256) is a verse that seems to be overlooked by people in certain locations. And the desire to punish those who believe differently seems a contradiction of the verse: "Not for thee (but for Allah) is the decision; whether He turn in mercy to them, or punish them" (3:128).

To affirm the regard in which Bahá'is hold Muhammad, I can only repeat what the Guardian of the Bahá'í Faith wrote: "As to Muhammad, the Apostle of God, let none among His followers who read these pages, think for a moment that either Islam, or its Prophet, or His Book, or His appointed Successors, or any of His authentic teachings, have been, or are to be in any way, or to however slight a degree, disparaged" (*The Promised Day Is Come*, p.108), and he emphasized, "The exalted position occupied by the Prophet Muhammad among the entire company of the Messengers of God" (*The Promised Day Is Come*, p.109).

And there are the words of Baha'u'llah Himself referring to "Muhammad, the Seal of the Prophets, and the most distinguished of God's chosen Ones" (*Kitab-i-Iqan*, p.40) and, later, describing Him as "the Sun of Prophethood" (*Kitab-i-Iqan*, p.49).

So it is important to me to attend Qur'an class and pray with my Muslim brothers and sisters.

Insha'allah (God willing).

بِسْمِ ٱللَّهِ ٱلرَّحْمَٰنِ ٱلرَّحِيمِ

With Allah's name, the Merciful Benefactor, the Merciful Redeemer

Welcome to the Muslim Journal

Ayesha Mustafaa

Imam W. Deen Mohammed

Malcolm X—Al-Hajj Malik Shabbazz

Frederick Douglas

Pictures and icons courtesy of the *Muslim Journal*, published consistently since October of 1975!

256　*Islam In The Heartland Of America*

Muslim Journal has been in print continuously and weekly as a newspaper publication that stands on the legacy of the struggle to disseminate unadulterated news to the reading public. Beginning with the first African American newspaper, *Freedom's Journal*, published by editors John B. Russwurm and Samuel E. Cornish in 1827 and the decisive newspaper *The North Star*, published by Frederick Douglass, the great ex-slave and abolitionist who became ambassador to Haiti, *Muslim Journal* picked up the mantle passed on by Malcolm X as he represented the Honorable Elijah Muhammad in the creation of *Muhammad Speaks* and carried on by the mentor to Malcolm and son of the Honorable Elijah Muhammad Imam W. Deen Mohammed to establish an independent voice not just for African Americans but also for Muslim Americans.

Now with the misinformation about Muslims, it is to serve all Americans with a clearer picture and understanding of Islam. *Muslim Journal*'s masthead reads "Bringing humanity together with truth and understanding." Its working mantra is to "Fill the Void" for our readers and, in doing so, allow them to "See the Full Picture!" *Muslim Journal* recognizes itself as an American institution that takes full advantage of its resources protected by the U.S. Constitution—to be a free press uninhibited by government, corporate, or individual biases.

The Muslim population in the U.S. is said to be between six million and twelve million Muslims, given the variance in that religion is not a census question to American citizens. About 25 percent of this Muslim population has been attributed to Muslim African Americans. Its marketing audience has buying power that has caught the eye of media giants like the *New York Times*. Muslims in the United States are predominantly highly professional, educated, and working in high-paying positions as politicians, doctors, lawyers, engineers, franchise owners, and local store owners. They are white-collar, blue-collar, skilled, and manual laborers.

The average age of the population is forty to fifty years of age, making up 60 percent of Muslim Americans. Twenty-five percent are college and higher-learning attendees with aspirations of entering the American workplace and performing intricate roles in American life. For example, the first Muslim to become a U.S. congressman, Keith Ellison, has demonstrated the quiet preparation and climb to be a part of the highest decision-making body of this country. The second Muslim to be elected to the U.S. Congress, Andre Carson, also is a member of this population and a subscriber to *Muslim Journal*. The Muslim American target-audience buying power averages $143 billion; 60 percent are males and 40 percent females.

Muslim Journal also is a member of the National Newspaper Publishers Association (NNPA), a network of over two hundred African American-owned newspapers here in the United States. The NNPA's target market audience has a buying power of $572.1 billion. The average reader's age is 43.9; gender—54 percent female and 46 percent male. Education level: 60 percent have attended college; 90 percent have a high school diploma.

Muslim Journal is circulated via vendors in two hundred cities/towns throughout the United States, with the largest circulation in New Jersey, Georgia, Washington DC, Michigan, Texas, California, Nevada, Arizona,

Washington (state), Mississippi, Tennessee, Missouri, North Carolina, South Carolina, Maryland, Virginia, Illinois, Florida, Alabama, Mississippi, Louisiana, Oklahoma, Arkansas, Colorado, and Wisconsin.

Muslim Journal's subscribers are individuals and institutions representative of practically every state as well as embassies, congressional offices, libraries, prison institutions, military institutions, and schools. Subscribers come from outside of the United States, from places like the Caribbean, South Africa, West Africa; countries like Nigeria, Ghana, and Senegal; from the Middle East, Saudi Arabia, Kuwait, and Malaysia.

بِسْمِ ٱللّٰهِ ٱلرَّحْمَٰنِ ٱلرَّحِيمِ

With Allah's name, the merciful Benefactor, the merciful redeemer

About the Editor of the *Muslim Journal*

Ayesha K. Mustafaa

Ayesha K. Mustafaa has been editor of the *Muslim Journal* weekly newspaper since January 1989. She is a graduate of Bucknell University in Lewisburg, Pennsylvania, with a BA degree and double major in psychology and political science. She has a master's degree in journalism from Columbia College of Chicago, Illinois.

Ayesha is a Muslim convert and comes from a family of civil rights activists of the Dr. Martin Luther King Jr. era. She joined the community of Muslims in affiliation with Imam W. Deen Mohammed, the son of Elijah Muhammad and mentor to Malcolm X, in late 1974 while living in Atlanta, Georgia.

She moved to Chicago, Illinois, in mid-1975 and has worked throughout the Muslim community offices in Chicago prior to becoming editor of the *Muslim Journal*, including the prison services office as an instructress, administrative offices of the Clara Muhammad School, Masjid Elijah Muhammad/Muhammad Mosque No. 2, and the Muslim women's development class.

Most significant among those years was her work with the Prison Dawah or Islamic teachings to the incarcerated populations, prison services being part of her concentration as an undergraduate.

Ayesha traveled extensively as part of delegations led by Imam W. Deen Mohammed, several times going to Saudi Arabia, to Jerusalem, and the West Bank. She was a presenter at the three-day International Media Conference, hosted by the Focolare Movement's NetOne Media Group held in Rome, Italy, in 2004.

She made hajj to Mecca with the first largest group of Muslim African Americans under the leadership of Imam W. Deen Mohammed in 1977 and made several *umrahs* (lesser hajj).

Ayesha hosts one of the seven daily one-hour talk radio shows—every Friday from 6:00 p.m. to 7:00 p.m.—for Radio Islam, produced by Sound Vision Foundation, on WCEV 1450 AM in the Chicago area, which is simultaneously broadcast via the Internet at RadioIslam.com.

She is a frequent speaker at interfaith settings and to school/college audiences and works with a local Chicago group of Muslims on "intrafaith" issues.

Ayesha was named the Muslim Woman of the Year by Imam W. Deen Mohammed in 1994. She is the mother of four, grandmother of four, and an advocate for foster parenting.

Contacting the muslim Journal

Muslim Journal's website is www.MuslimJournal.net.
For information on advertising and prices, e-mail ad4mj2@comcast.net.
For circulation information, e-mail muslimjrnl@comcast.net.
For editorial submissions and information, e-mail muslimjrnl@comcast.net.
Or write to any of these departments in care of *Muslim Journal,* 1141 W. 175 St., Homewood, IL, 60430.
Phone: 708-647-9600
Fax: 708-647-0754

CONCLUSION

Islamic Center of Topeka

بِسْمِ ٱللَّهِ ٱلرَّحْمَٰنِ ٱلرَّحِيمِ
وَٱلْعَصْرِ (١) إِنَّ ٱلْإِنسَٰنَ لَفِى خُسْرٍ (٢) إِلَّا ٱلَّذِينَ ءَامَنُوا۟ وَعَمِلُوا۟ ٱلصَّٰلِحَٰتِ وَتَوَاصَوْا۟ بِٱلْحَقِّ وَتَوَاصَوْا۟ بِٱلصَّبْرِ (٣)

By (the Token of) Time (through the ages), Verily Man is in loss, Except such as have Faith, and do righteous deeds, and (join together) in the mutual teaching of Truth, and of Patience and Constancy

بِسْمِ ٱللَّهِ ٱلرَّحْمَٰنِ ٱلرَّحِيمِ

With Allah's name, the merciful Benefactor, the merciful redeemer

A Walk through Jerusalem: A Trifaith Historical Event

By
Khalil Green

Left to right: Michael Massey, Kathy Slawson, Robin Kempf, Lou Saadi, Imam Omar Hazim, Rabbi Debbie Steil

On June 21, 2010, Muslims, Jews, and Christians met at the Islamic Center in Topeka to celebrate the success of the Walk through Jerusalem exhibit. This was a banquet-style meeting complete with a panel discussion comprised of Imam Omar Hazim, Rabbi Debbie Steil, Michael Massey, Lou Saadi, Robin Kempf, and Kathy Slawson.

The exhibit is the product of Striar Jewish Community Center and the Bureau of Jewish Education of Greater Boston. They state that this event is a "free Interactive Exhibit for the Community." It is also the first time that Islam, Christianity, and Judaism have come together to host this event.

Michael Massey, of Grace Cathedral, whose church provided the location for the event, stated that the project was a great success and that he really enjoyed working with the other two monotheistic faith groups.

The tour began with a film titled *Jerusalem Is One*. This film provided a brief historical account of the establishment of modern Jerusalem.

The exhibit itself focuses on the eight gates of the Temple Mount through which a person can enter Jerusalem. In the case of this exhibit, each gate or room possessed certain aspects of the geography, archeology, customs, and traditions of Jerusalem.

Each gate is an interactive recreation of the actual gate in Jerusalem of which they represent. The gates are the Dung, Jaffa, New Gate, Lion's Gate, Damascus, Golden Gate, Zion Gate, and Herod's Gate. Each room provided artifacts and projects that a person or group could participate and interact with. One gate or room contained a bowl where prayers could be left and the exhibit producers would send to the Western Wall at a later date.

The exhibit also included a Power Point presentation, complete with Holy Qur'an recitation, provided by the Islamic Center of Topeka. This presentation, created by Khalil Green, also contained information about Imam W. Deen Mohammed (may Allah accept him into the highest parts of paradise) as the pioneering leader of Islam in America. Michael Massey stated that "people just kept watching it over and over again."

Michael Massey states that this is the first time that this particular exhibit has been presented and hosted by the three major monotheistic faith groups. He affirms that the Islamic Center of Topeka provided a very important addition to the originally Jewish presentation.

As such, groups, such as the Boys and Girls Scout, here in Topeka visited the exhibit as well as various religious and civil groups.

In conjunction with this exhibit, three women from the Jewish (Robin Kempf), Muslim (Lou Saadi), and Christian (Kathy Slawson) traditions met at Temple Beth Shalom on June 2 at 7:00 p.m. for a moderated panel discussion.

Left to right: Moderator, Robin Kempf, Kathy Slawson, Lou Saadi

Robin, Lou, and Kathy met again at the banquet hosted by the Islamic Center of Topeka. The banquet progressed well as each lady affirmed that their understanding of each other's belief system was heightened in a positive way during regular meetings with each other prior to the panel discussion. All three women stated that they would like to continue to meet.

During the banquet, Rabbi Steil, of Temple Beth Shalom, indicated that she appreciated the work of the various faith traditions in making the event successful. She further indicated that Jerusalem is important to the Jewish people because of the long history that the Hebrews have with this land. For the Jewish people, the land itself is what is important. The land is in the blood of the Jewish people and Jerusalem is its capital.

Michael Massey stated that Jerusalem is important for Christians because Jesus was a Jew. Furthermore, most of the important activities in the life of Jesus happened in Jerusalem. The life of Jesus, His death, and resurrection centered on the Temple Mount.

Imam Omar Hazim indicated that one of the reasons that the land of Jerusalem is important to Muslims is because the Holy Qur'an refers to it as the place where Prophet Muhammad (PBUH) visited during his night journey, from where, according to hadith, he ascended into heaven. The Holy Qur'an in chapter 17:1 states,

$$\text{سُبْحَٰنَ ٱلَّذِىٓ أَسْرَىٰ بِعَبْدِهِۦ لَيْلًا مِّنَ ٱلْمَسْجِدِ ٱلْحَرَامِ إِلَى ٱلْمَسْجِدِ ٱلْأَقْصَا ٱلَّذِى بَٰرَكْنَا حَوْلَهُۥ لِنُرِيَهُۥ مِنْ ءَايَٰتِنَآ إِنَّهُۥ هُوَ ٱلسَّمِيعُ ٱلْبَصِيرُ (١)}$$

"Glory to (Allah) Who did take His servant for a Journey by night from the Sacred Mosque to the farthest Mosque, whose precincts We did bless, in order that We might show him some of Our Signs: for Allah is the One Who heareth and seeth (all things)."

Imam Omar Hazim indicates that both the Dome of the Rock and the Al-Aqsa mosque sit on the Temple Mount in Jerusalem; as such, they are both a part of this tradition. Hence, these two structures are very important to the Islamic faith as they both sit on the same complex to which Prophet Muhammad (PBUH) ascended to paradise.

This trifaith exhibit is a historical event as Jews, Muslims, and Christians have come together and answered the call of Allah who states in the Holy Qur'an, chapter 49, verse 13,

$$\text{يَٰٓأَيُّهَا ٱلنَّاسُ إِنَّا خَلَقْنَٰكُم مِّن ذَكَرٍ وَأُنثَىٰ وَجَعَلْنَٰكُمْ شُعُوبًا وَقَبَآئِلَ لِتَعَارَفُوٓا۟ إِنَّ أَكْرَمَكُمْ عِندَ ٱللَّهِ أَتْقَىٰكُمْ إِنَّ ٱللَّهَ عَلِيمٌ خَبِيرٌ (١٣)}$$

"O mankind! We created you from a single (pair) of a male and a female, and made you into nations and tribes, that ye may know each other not that ye may despise each other."

Those in attendance were asked to raise their hands and acknowledge what faith tradition they represented. It was interesting to note that there was *mizan* (balance) in the evening as Imam Omar asked the attendees to raise their hand when their faith was called. A third raised their hands for Judaism, a third raised their hands for Christianity, and a third raised their hands for Islam.

Although these three faith traditions have different modes of worshipping Allah, this coming together represents the faithfulness of those who stand for the unity of humanity strictly for the pleasure of Allah.

All the people in attendance at the banquet agreed to pray to Allah for future endeavors and opportunities of working together.

بِسْمِ ٱللّٰهِ ٱلرَّحْمٰنِ ٱلرَّحِيمِ

With Allah's name, the merciful Benefactor, the merciful redeemer

Concluding Prayer

Chapter (surah) 3:193,

رَبَّنَا إِنَّنَا سَمِعْنَا مُنَادِيًا يُنَادِي لِلْإِيمَانِ أَنْ ءَامِنُوا بِرَبِّكُمْ فَـَٔامَنَّا رَبَّنَا فَٱغْفِرْ لَنَا ذُنُوبَنَا وَكَفِّرْ عَنَّا سَيِّـَٔاتِنَا وَتَوَفَّنَا مَعَ ٱلْأَبْرَارِ (١٩٣)

"Our Lord! we have heard the call of one calling (Us) to Faith, 'Believe ye in the Lord,' and we have believed. Our Lord! Forgive us our sins, blot out from us our iniquities, and take to Thyself our souls in the company of the righteous."

Our Lord, please open the hearts and the minds of the people of the world so that they may see the beauty, feel the peace, and understand the tolerance in the religion of al-Islam. Ameen.

GLOSSARY

A

- Adhan—Call to prayer
- Al Aqsa—Mosque that stands on the Temple Mount in Jerusalem. Prophet Muhammad visited during his night journey to Jerusalem before ascending into heaven.
- Alhumdulillah—Praise be to Allah
- Arhams—Womb; comes from the root word *rahima*, which means to love, have tenderness, forgiveness, have all that is required for exercising beneficence.
- Ayat—Qur'anic verse, sign, or proof

B

- Bashir—Mortal, good news.
- Battle of Badr—Significant battle in history
- Bilal—Freed slave, and close companion to Prophet Muhammad (PBUH) and the first caller to prayer.
- Bismillah—In the name of Allah

D

- Dawah—Sharing the religion of Islam with non-Muslims
- Dua—Short prayer
- Dunya—Material world

E

- Eid—Two celebrations; one at the end of Ramadan and the other ends when Hajj concludes.

F

- Fard—Obligatory
- Fatiha—Opening chapter of the Holy Qur'an and prayer
- Fitna—Test, trial, persecution, mischief
- Fuad—Heart, metaphorically; the emotions or desirous nature of the human
- Furqan—Criteria

H

- Hadith—Secondary source of Islamic law and sayings and actions of the Prophet (PBUH)
- Hajj—Pilgrimage to Mecca
- Hamd—Praised
- Hijrah—Beginning of the Islamic calendar, after the migration of the Prophet from Mecca to Medina
- Hikma—Knowledge
- Hubb—Love/grain

I

- Ibrahim—Father of the three great monotheistic faiths (Christianity, Islam, and Judaism)
- Iftar—Dinner after a day of fasting
- Ihdinas—Guide us
- Imam—Prayer leader
- Iman—Faith
- Injil—The New Testament
- Inzal—Sending down of a thing from above
- Isa (Essau) ibn Mariam—Jesus, the son of Mary
- Islam—Submission to do the will of Allah; peace
- Ismail—Firstborn son of Abraham
- Jannah—Heaven
- Jibreel—Angel Gabriel
- Jihad—Struggle; striving for excellence
- Jumah—Friday; the day Islamic services are held

K

- Khidr—Companion of Moses
- Kaaba—The first house of worship originally built by Adam and Eve and rebuilt later by Abraham and his son Ishmael
- Khutbah—Sermon
- Kitab—Book
- Kursi—Throne

L

- Lut—Prophet Lot

M

- Adhan—Call to prayer
- Marad—Sickness
- Marwa—One of the two hills in Mecca, close to the Kaaba, that Haggar ran between while looking for water for her son, Ishmael; wife of Prophet Ibrahim
- Masala—Room inside Masjid where prayers are conducted
- Masjid—Muslim place of worship
- Mecca—City in Saudi Arabia where the Prophet was born and where the first house of worship (Kaaba) is located
- Minhaj—Cultural belief
- Mizan—Balance, justice
- Mosque—French name for the Muslim place of worship
- Muhaiman—One that safeguards and protects
- Muhammad—Last Prophet and Universal Prophet to humanity
- Musa—Prophet Moses
- Muslim—One who submits to the will of Allah

N

- Nafs—Soul, self
- Niyyah—Intention

P

- PBUH—Peace be upon Him

Q

- Qulub—Heart
- Holy Qur'an—Holy Book of Islam revealed to Prophet Muhammad (PBUH) by Allah

R

- Rabb—Lord
- Rahim—Merciful
- Rahman—Beneficient
- Ramadan—Ninth month of the Islamic calendar

S

- Safa—One of the two hills located in Mecca near the Kaaba that Haggar ran between while looking for water for her son, Ishmael; wife of Prophet Ibrahim.
- Salahuddin—Muslim conqueror of Jerusalem; defeated the crusaders
- Salat—Prayer
- Sawm—Fasting
- Shia—Sect in Islam; party of Ali
- Sunna—The way of Prophet Muhammad
- Sunni—Sect in Islam; the way of the Prophet
- Surah—Chapter

T

- Tabuk—When thirty thousand Muslims marched to Tabuk because of the threat of the Byzantine Empire to invade the northern approaches of Arabia.
- Tafsir—Commentary
- Taharah—Purity
- Tauheed—Oneness of Allah
- Tawaf—One of the rituals in which pilgrims march counterclockwise around the Kaaba

- Tawrah—Torah; five books of Moses
- Tayra—A bird; metaphorically to mean fate in the Qur'an

U

- Umma—Community

W

- Wallahi—Mentioned in the Qur'an and pertains to Allah's (SWT) ownership

Y

- Yacob—Prophet Jacob
- Yusef—Prophet Joseph

Z

- Zam zam—A well in Mecca that saved the life of Haggar and her son Ishmael; still functioning today.

REFERENCES

Ali, Yusuf. *Holy Qur'an English Translation of the Meanings and Commentary.* Medina, Saudi Arabia: King Fahd Holy Qur'an Printing Complex, 1990.

Omar, Abdul Mannan. *Dictionary of the Holy Qur'an.* Noor Foundation International, 2008.

S. Abul A'La Maududi. Holy Qur'an translation.

Prophet Muhammad (Pbuh). Hadith.

Brief quotations from the following:

- Imam W. Deen Mohammed
- Sheikh Muzaffer Ozak Al-Jerrahi. *Irshad Wisdom of Sufi Master.*
- Ismail Buyukcelebi. *Living in the Shade of Islam.*
- Dr. Ahmad H. Sakr
- H. Jackson Brown
- Imam Mustafa El-Amin

Milton Keynes UK
Ingram Content Group UK Ltd.
UKHW041832131124
451149UK00001B/311